IN THE MOMENT

IN THE MOMENT

My Life as an Actor

BEN GAZZARA

CARROLL & GRAF PUBLISHERS
NEW YORK

In the Moment
My Life as an Actor

Carroll & Graf Publishers
An Imprint of Avalon Publishing Group Inc.
245 West 17th Street
New York, NY 10011

AVALON
publishing group incorporated

Copyright © 2004 by Ben Gazzara

First Carroll & Graf edition 2004

Library of Congress Cataloging-in-Publication Data is available.

ISBN: 0-7867-1399-2

Printed in the United States of America
Interior design by Maria Torres
Distributed by Publishers Group West

For Elke, forever

CONTENTS

CHAPTER 1

MAKING MY MOVIE

IN 1978 I MADE A MOVIE IN SINGAPORE. ON MY WAY BACK to Los Angeles I decided to visit Bali, an island in the Indonesian archipelago. I had intended to stop there for two days but stayed for two weeks. Its people had a dignity, a gentleness, a spirituality that touched me. The island's customs, its dances, its spectacle would remain with me for years.

In 1989 I returned to Bali, to star in and direct a movie I never thought would get made. I should've been on top of the world but instead I was down. I'd just lost my best friend. John Cassavetes died. My wife, Elke, was with me and she convinced me that once I put my head entirely in the work my juices would start flowing and things would be all right.

I persuaded some good actors to come to Bali: Jill Clayburgh would play my wife, Peter Riegert, my brother, Treat Williams, an American expatriate, and Rebecca Glenn, the woman my character meets there.

Anthony Foutz and I had written the screenplay together. Tony was a loner, a private person with deep-set eyes that told no story—which gave him an air of mystery. I liked him. He worked long and hard with me and we came to trust each other to the point where we'd not only share screenplay credit for *Beyond the Ocean*, but we also planned to codirect it.

We were trying to depict a man who has everything, and yet . . . John Tana, my character, has wealth: he's the CEO of a company that buys other companies, in order to buy more companies, in order to make him even wealthier. He has a beautiful wife, a devoted brother, and friends who love being around him. But he has trouble loving anything. He goes to the airport with a toothbrush, a razor, and a couple of books. It's there he decides on his destination—Bali. I, too, had experienced times in my life when things couldn't have been better, and yet I wasn't enjoying myself. *Beyond the Ocean* was probably my way of exploring that sense of being incomplete.

I chose Bali because if there ever was a place for a man in turmoil to find peace, it's certainly on that magical island. Tana is swept away by its beauty and the inner tranquillity of Bali's people. And, of course, he meets a girl, who he tries to keep at arm's length but, as we know, things have a way of happening.

Tana is tracked down by his wife and brother, who arrive in Bali to see what in hell is going on with him. He isn't quite in touch with himself, so he's unable to tell them. His wife is hurt, his brother is pissed off, and they leave. They figure they'll let this joker play out his scene and he'll return. Well, the involvement with Bali and the girl becomes more profound and complicated, so that by the end of the movie it's anybody's guess whether Tana will go home or remain in Bali.

After the first rehearsal, when I heard the dialogue coming out of the mouths of the players, I knew we were in trouble. The scenes screamed for more vivid dialogue. As a writer, Tony Foutz had a good sense of the visual, but seemed uninterested in the personal. I thought I'd succeeded in bending the screenplay toward my way of seeing things, but I was kidding myself.

Each of our rooms had a balcony that overlooked a row of palm trees that led to a beach and the ocean beyond. I was being caressed by a warm breeze while trying to come up with an answer to the problems I was seeing all too clearly. The man I would play was not well defined. He needed more revealing dialogue. The material didn't go deep enough. If I could have kicked myself in the ass, I would've. "Where were you, Ben? Why didn't you see it?" I'd thought the screenplay was ready but it wasn't, and now we were out of time. We were to start shooting the next day and

I was deeply worried. But I was determined to make the movie I'd envisioned. To do that, I was going to have to direct the picture myself.

The phone rang. It was my daughter, Liz.

– Dad, I'm getting married.

– That's great. When?

– Sometime in October. You have to be there.

– Who's the guy?

– His name is Tomàs. He's a doctor.

– A doctor. Every Jewish mother's dream.

I could tell there was something else on her mind, and I was going to see how long it would take her to get to the point. I didn't have to wait long.

– I guess there'll have to be a gathering of some kind.

– And the father of the bride has to pay. It's his duty.

– I guess so.

– How many guests?

– Seventy-five or so. But we don't have to serve champagne.

– Are you trying to make me look bad? There's gonna be champagne and plenty of it.

– Thanks, Dad.

– Where do you intend to have this wedding party?

– I have a few ideas. I'll let you know.

– Okay, keep me informed.

– I love you, Dad.

– I love you, too.

– Say hi to Elke.

– I will.

And that was that. I was pleased that Liz was happy, but why wasn't I happy? Instead of spending some time trying to answer that, I made myself a tall, straight scotch on the rocks.

It happened without confrontation. There was no apparent ill feeling. When I started to tell Tony how the movie could not be directed by the two of us, he didn't blink. He quickly agreed that I should take it on alone, adding that he'd give me all the support he could. "It's all yours now, Ben," I said to myself. "If it works you're a hero and if it doesn't . . ."

The first scene we were to shoot was between me and Jill Clayburgh. We walked around the beautiful suite my character has taken in an enchanting hotel. I wanted Jill to become comfortable, to find her own way. She's a brilliant actress and I knew she'd make choices that were surprising. But when we read the scene it felt spare. There was no real event. It seemed to be simply a bridge to another scene. But I fooled myself into thinking that the other actors and I were gifted enough to make the story points through our behavior, Franco Di Giacomo's photography and my direction.

While shooting, what my camera saw was often breathtaking—lush, green rice terraces, Hindu temples, colorful rituals, and thrilling dances. What I was putting in front of all this became the problem. It didn't take long to realize that the actors, including me, would not be able to excite or surprise anyone.

I thought of John Cassavetes a lot during those days. What would he have done in my shoes? It became clear why John financed his movies himself. He'd be able to shut the movie down and work on the screenplay with the whole cast present, rewriting and rehearsing the material. If he could do it in one week, so be it. If it needed more time, he'd take it. But I didn't even have *all* my actors in Bali. As is the case on most motion pictures, in order to save money, they would show up as dictated by the shooting schedule. I never had them all together in a room. The only rehearsal they'd get was on the set prior to filming a scene. I could've tried to improvise the scenes but then could I do that to Tony Foutz, who'd worked with me for so long on the screenplay? How could I tell him that his efforts were for naught, that it wouldn't work? If I couldn't be enthusiastic from the start, what would the end be like? And because the crew was hired, most of the actors were there, and the producer was there expecting results, I decided to make the picture the best it could be. So we continued shooting. I was hoping to make gold out of what we had.

I began having mood swings; I started drinking too much. I had a sense of foreboding, which I couldn't shake. Too often, after work, with a few drinks in me, I became irritable and short-tempered. I would even turn on Elke. When my comments were particularly cruel, I could have cut off my tongue, but it would happen again.

Elke was born in Germany and lived there, on and off, into her thirties. In our early days there were times when I'd throw what I thought was a pretty nifty, wry remark her way, and I'd get an unexpected reaction. Elke's clear blue eyes would darken and she'd turn away from me, showing only her soft blonde hair. She'd misunderstood. She thought I was attacking her. I wasn't but I apologized anyway.

This time was different. I could be downright cruel to her but somehow she remained patient and supportive. It was as though she understood before I did how painful things were becoming for me.

We shot for nine weeks on that beautiful island. I tried to put into *Beyond the Ocean* all the things I'd felt and imagined about Bali, but I was always swimming upstream. I was losing faith in myself, the story—the whole picture. I worked as hard as I could while still hoping that, in the end, the movie would interest and even touch people.

When the picture wrapped there were no tearful good-byes, no "let's stay in touch," no exchanging telephone numbers. I didn't wait around for any of that. Elke and I packed our bags and headed for the airport. Through the floor-to-ceiling windows of the waiting room, past the planes landing and taking off, I could see the ocean. I didn't take my eyes off of it for some time. I was saying good-bye. I knew I'd never return to Bali again.

On the long flight back to Rome, I turned to Elke.

– Funny thing. It was my dream to make this picture and now I'm sorry I did.

– Ben, people have told me that the work is good, that there are beautiful things in the movie.

– It doesn't go deep enough. It doesn't break your heart.

– You're going to break my heart if you don't cheer up.

* * *

Italy shuts down in August but there were still two weeks left of July. There I went to work in the cutting room in Rome to see what I could do with the footage I'd shot in Bali. During every one of those days, I became more and more despondent, withdrawn, lost, impotent. It was the movie I'd created, but I couldn't deal with it, I didn't like it. I thought it was hopeless. I saw only darkness.

All the other people involved were excited about the material. But I'd arrived at an almost zombie-like state. So the editor took matters into his own hands and went about making his own cuts, paying less and less attention to me and not asking my opinion. It was torture. All I wanted to do was hide in our apartment and try to sleep. I thought that perhaps, after sleep, I would wake up and the agony would be gone. But I couldn't sleep. And if I did for an hour or so, the nightmare was still present. People said things like, "Pull yourself together," or "What do you have to be depressed about?" To them, depression was not something tangible. It was not cancer, after all. But I think depression *is* cancer. A cancer of the soul.

For people who have never seen or lived with a person in depression, it's difficult to understand. Some weeks went by before Elke realized how serious it was and only then was she really able to comfort me.

August came and the cutting was suspended until September. I was pacing back and forth in the apartment. I would sit for a moment and then I would spring up and pace. I'd go up to the loft and lay in bed. I kept hoping that if I slept my despair about everything would go away. I would stretch out on the bed, settling first on my left side for a few minutes, then on the right. I could find no rest. I never slept. I was never hungry. I wore my gray checked robe morning, noon, and night. Elke couldn't get me out of the house. And when she had to go out, she would be so anxious and worried that she'd rush back as quickly as possible.

A specialist in depression came to our apartment. He gently and quietly asked questions, trying to get at a reason for my condition. I didn't have a clue. I could say very little. My voice, when I did speak, was weak and plaintive.

– You know, Mr. Gazzara, Dante Alighieri said that it does not get darker than midnight. We will get you out of this.

The trouble was that my midnight was the twenty-four-hour kind and I saw no light in the future. I knew what started it: John Cassavetes's death. He was gone. The work we'd done together called on some of the best parts of me and *that* was gone. I became convinced there was no time left for me, either. Superstardom had eluded me; that had not been easy to take. In the fifties, I'd sort of led the way for actors who were offbeat and hard to pigeonhole. A lot of guys who came after me went much further in notoriety and fame and in just plain getting more work. I defended my hurt feelings with humor, with drink, and with women, but I guess the hurt still took its toll.

Thank God for my pride. To keep going, that's what I called on. But mostly, I'd called upon the work—making sure that it was good, even special, maybe even unforgettable. But now I was convinced I'd failed. I was sure I was finished and there was no more time for other chances.

The doctor, who had a kind face and a concerned manner, said that he thought a few sessions of electroshock therapy would help me enormously.

– Mr. Gazzara, if you were my brother, that's what I would prescribe.

This guy's crazy, I thought. *He ain't gonna electrocute my brain.* I decided I'd better get home fast but we were invited to the 1989 Deauville Film Festival in France. I thought if I went there I might snap out of it. I would see a lot of old friends. A retrospective of my work was scheduled, and we would have a great time. There would be a lot of parties and, while I'm not a big fan of film festivals, I was looking forward to it.

The year before, the mayor of Deauville, Ann Onofrio, sort of adopted Elke and me for two days during a tribute to James Stewart held in Monterey, California. She, Ruda Dauphin (widow of the talented French actor Claude Dauphin), and we were inseparable. Because Ann thought I was the most entertaining man she had met in years, she and Ruda decided that we had to come to Deauville. I liked Ann and I liked Ruda. Elke and I had never been to Deauville. But when we arrived, Ann was dumbfounded. This was not the same man she had met only a year before. I seemed like an impostor.

They gave us the Bette Davis Suite at a hotel by the sea. It had a large photo of Bette on the wall, but not one taken when she was young and vibrant. Instead it was a picture taken just before she died. It really upset me, and I wanted to destroy it. She had been such a striking woman. How could they do that? Bette would never see herself as an old woman. I was sure she hadn't lost her desire to do good work. Her body may have aged but her brain was as lively as ever. Looking at Bette's photo, I would think, Isn't it a shame that at the moment the actor knows his craft best he's often no longer in demand? Aging is a bitch. I was beginning to feel its approach and it frightened me. But I would have welcomed old age then and there if only it brought the peace and serenity I longed for. I hated that suite. I never could rest there. Even the strongest sleeping pills didn't work. I would look up at Bette's sad wet eyes and pray that she'd help me fall asleep.

When the opening day of the retrospective arrived, I was sure no one would show up—that no one would be interested. But when Elke and I made our appearance at the theater, hundreds of journalists and photographers from most European countries were waiting outside. And I said, "We came to the wrong place." But it was for me. They were waiting for me. And when we entered the theater I was shocked. It was packed; people were sitting in the aisles. I think I made a speech. They were going to show *Husbands* and I talked about Cassavetes. When I finished, everyone stood and applauded, for what seemed like forever. Life is amazing.

Every time we'd go to the movie house, I'd say to Elke, "Stay close to me." "Don't leave me alone." "Nobody will be there." "There'll only be you and me." "Let's get out of here."

And at each of the screenings—*Saint Jack*, which I did with Peter Bogdanovich, *Tales of Ordinary Madness*, directed by Marco Ferreri, all of them—the reaction was always spectacular. I could not or would not believe it. That's how it goes with depression. You're so down on yourself, so devoid of self-esteem, it's impossible to believe that others see things differently. My insides were aching, but people saw none of that. To them I was a celebrity who was probably deep in serious thought. Instead, I was a sad sap. I couldn't look at *Husbands*. I knew it would hurt too much. I did sit through the first five minutes of *Saint Jack* but thinking about that creative experience with Bogdanovich made me sadder still. I was sure that work like that would never happen again for me. So that was it. I didn't attend another screening.

Then came the closing night gala. Ann, the mayor and hostess, wore a long, white, hand-beaded dress. She looked so stunning, so beautiful, and I was seated right next to her. Elke was supposed to sit at another table but I said, "Please let my wife sit next to me." I was desperate. Dinner was served and everything was very French, very chic, with a lot of courses and entertainment. The singer, a great soprano, came to me and said, "Oh Ben, you're here, I'm so glad." Lauren Bacall was opposite me, and to my left was the U.S. ambassador to France. Everybody was there, but I was somewhere else.

I knew I was being difficult. I was ashamed of that but, as I said, I was desperate. My neck, my ears, and my cheeks were on fire. I was starting to have trouble breathing. I felt that this thing that had taken over would never go away. There was a strong pressure in my temples. It was like my brain was trying to break through my skull. That morning I'd noticed a prominent vein running down my forehead that had never been there before. It was pulsating and I didn't know what to do. I'd been branded.

All of a sudden I got up and said to Ann, "I've got to go." She got up and there was a terrible noise. Ann stared at me.

– Ben, you're standing on my dress.

I had stepped on her white beaded dress, all made by hand. You could see it had cost a fortune. It seems my foot was tearing the dress apart.

Ann froze; she couldn't believe what had happened. Ben Gazzara, her guest of honor, had not only resigned from the evening, but butchered her beautiful evening gown. Elke and I rushed out of there and in the lobby we passed the singer who seemed surprised and disappointed that we were leaving. "Are you leaving, Ben?" she called out. I didn't answer. I knew I was being hurtful, even insulting, but I just had to get out of there.

Elke packed the luggage as I lay on the bed in the Bette Davis Suite. We were going to return to Rome because I wanted to get back to the Bali picture. I was anxious to get back into the cutting room to see what I could do with the material I had to work with. We wrote a lame letter of apology to the lovely lady mayor, Ann Onofrio, and we slipped out of town.

Back in Rome, the city was silent. It was a Sunday, and a very hot day. Nobody was on the streets, everybody had gone to the seaside, I guess. We pulled up in front of our building, and the taxi driver helped get the luggage to our top-floor apartment.

When the elevator opened, what did we see? The door of our apartment had been hacked apart by thieves who'd tried to break in. The door had been virtually demolished, but it hadn't collapsed. It was a big, old door and we could not open it wide enough to squeeze ourselves into the apartment. We had to call someone, a door specialist. And I said,

– This is a bad omen, this is a bad omen. Let's go to a hotel.

– How can we go to the hotel? We have all our things here and the door is wide open. We have to stay here, Ben.

The following morning, the door people came and talked us into buying a new door. We did, but enough was enough. I was through. I told Elke,

– Let's get out of here!

And without an argument, without a sideward glance, she went to work and found an apartment—overnight. It was in the same neighborhood, on Via Propaganda, just two streets away and I could still see the Piazza di Spagna. It was a nice, comfortable apartment. We could move in immediately. Elke packed all the clothes and placed them on a rack and rolled it through the quiet Roman streets. It was night and it took many trips. Finally, it was nearly dawn; Elke took me there and put me to bed. She was the only one I turned to; no one else was to know. Despite being so sick I refused to show weakness but my situation got worse and worse.

How often I wanted to cry, but there was something in the unreachable part of me that would have none of it. Tears might have brought relief; the monster would not let me have any. I had saved my sleeping pills, and counting them became a ritual. I would enter the bathroom, remove the vial of pills from the bottom of the leather bag that held my toiletries, lay them side by side on the glass shelf—blue, pink, purple, white, and green capsules. Very pretty. I stared at them. There had been twenty, then forty, and now sixty. Would that do the trick? Did I need more? My wife's face saved my life. I imagined her finding me, I saw her eyes asking why, the pain I would give her. I had to find another way out of it.

Elke had begged me to stop cutting the picture. "It must wait," she said. "We have to go home to New York because I'm sure we'll get help there." I was getting more and more agitated, still unable to rest, unable to sleep. Elke decided we would go. She had contacted a specialist there and he would be waiting to see me the moment I arrived. Before our departure, she consulted a doctor in Rome, explained the situation, and asked,

– How do I get my husband back to the United States?

– Put ten to fifteen of these drops into a glass of water and give it to him before you get on the plane, and while you're on the plane give him some more.

I was so out of my mind, she thought, why not put a little more in the water? To give the journey a good start, Elke put forty drops into my glass instead of the recommended fifteen.

So in the car, driving to the airport, I was already half asleep. As soon as the car stopped at the airport and the luggage came out, everybody was helpful. The director of security for the airport, Mario Esposito, who was a friend, took us to a side entrance so we wouldn't have to stand in line. I swore to him that everything Elke was carrying was legal and belonged to her. I was convinced they would jail her for carrying money and jewelry even though it was all hers. I was insane.

At that moment, a woman turned to me and said, *"Ben Gazzara, sono una sua ammiratrice."* She was an admirer. *But how could she be?* I thought. *I'm nobody, I'm nothing. If they take Elke away, if they put her in prison, I'll be even less.*

When we boarded, Elke asked immediately for another glass of water and put sixty drops in. That made me sleep all the way to New York. What a relief to finally arrive at Kennedy, where we were received by the TWA staff and our friend Helga with her people from Lufthansa. We went into the baggage claim with all the policemen walking around with their dogs, smelling the luggage for cocaine, and when we approached the customs inspector I said, "I swear to you, sir, everything we have is ours." I was at it again.

It seems that Helga had prepared the customs agents for these outbursts, and there was no problem. We made it to the car and we drove directly to the office of a Doctor Wolfe. After listening and probing for two hours or so, he prescribed lithium: 300 milligrams, four times a day.

After four weeks of medication and daily meetings with him, I felt a change. I was able to sleep for longer periods without interruption. Like air from a punctured balloon, my paranoia diminished slowly until it disappeared. I was able to sit still, to read for at least a half-hour without losing interest. It was a miracle. One afternoon I turned to Elke:

– Elke, you're gonna have dinner tonight. With a stranger.

– Who's that?

– *That* is I.

– It would be my pleasure.

I took her to a charming, candle-lit French restaurant in our neighborhood where I was sure we wouldn't run into people we knew. I was not ready to mingle, but I wanted Elke to start having some sort of life. I owed her at least that, and so much more. I hardly ate a thing but I was able to enjoy the wine—it had been a long time since I had and I was happy that Elke was happy. Finally, I was able to do something for her.

I wasn't in shape to celebrate yet but I was going to have to make an effort: it was time for Liz's wedding party. She'd insisted that Elke attend. This caused some anxiety, as Liz's mother, the actress Janice Rule, would be present. I hadn't seen Janice since we'd divorced each other and she had never met Elke. What would that be like?

Liz had chosen a spacious SoHo loft for the reception. The place was packed when we entered, music blaring and people dancing. I saw my brother Tony seated with friends Jay Julien and Ed Trzcinski. They had known Liz since she was a baby. She led us toward the table. Janice came up to greet me and then said to Elke in exactly the right tone,

– It's such a pleasure to meet you.

– Thank you.

– This shouldn't be the last time we see each other. We should all get together now and then.

I smiled, thinking, *Not on your life.* Janice and I had not matched up well throughout our long marriage; why would things be different now? I had no intention of bringing the past into my life with Elke. I hadn't enjoyed it very much the first time around. Why should I visit it again?

Then I turned and saw Kate, the daughter Janice had with her first husband, Robert Thom. I walked Elke to my brother's table and sat her there. I told him to take care of her, poured her a glass of champagne, and said I'd be right back.

I went up to Kate and said "Hello." There was an awkward pause and an attempt at conversation—small talk really. But I was thinking between the lines. So many years had passed since we'd seen each other and yet it seemed to me that only days had gone by. Separation didn't kill memory or my mixed feelings at having distanced myself from her. During the years she had lived with Janice and me, there was never what people would call intimacy between Kate and me. I'd thought about that often and knew it was my fault. I had no problem with affection, love, passion, but heart-to-heart talks, one-on-one conversations, were not my thing. Was this passed down by my parents? My father was affectionate but he never verbalized his feelings. Had I been the same with Liz? Is it the same with Elke? Had I found intimacy only when I played a character interacting with other fictitious characters?

As I returned to my wife, I felt myself sinking. I sat down, was given a glass of champagne, and I looked around at people talking, laughing, dancing, having a good time. Elke, too, seemed to be having fun with the group at our table. I tried to join in, but it was hard. I wanted to feel a part of my daughter's wedding but I couldn't. I wasn't out of the dark tunnel, not yet. It was then that I felt Elke's hand caressing my cheek just as my mother did when I was a child.

CHAPTER 2

STARTING OUT

MY MOTHER, ANGELA CUSUMANO, CAME TO AMERICA IN 1902; she was seventeen years old. I never had a young mother. By the time I was born in 1930, she was forty-five. Although her face was already lined, she wore no makeup. She had a high forehead surrounded by lush black hair speckled with gray, which she always wore in a bun. The first time I saw my mother let down her hair I thought it would never stop unraveling. It rolled slowly over her back until it came to rest below her knees. But what always got me were my mother's eyes. They changed color depending on how the light struck them. Sometimes they were brown, then gold, then green, and even blue. (I was lucky; I have my mother's eyes.)

In 1908, my father, Antonio Gazzara, arrived in the United States. He was twenty-eight years old. He always wanted to go back to his hometown in Sicily. Unlike my mother, he never grabbed hold of America. He didn't even learn English—America was only temporary, after all. He worked hard laying asphalt, brick, doing carpentry or any other job he could get. Whatever money he made he would take back with him to Italy. But he never made enough and he never went back. I knew there was a sadness in him so it pleased me when I made him smile. (I have my father's smile.)

* * *

My brother Tony and I were both born in the Italian Hospital, on Manhattan's East Side. My brother was born sixteen years after our parents got married and I was born five years after. My parents never told us what accounted for the delay in having children. They were, however, loving and devoted to each other, so I know it had nothing to do with a lack of affection.

They brought me home to East Thirty-ninth Street between First and Second Avenues. It was what was called a railroad flat, one room attached to the other like a line of railway carriages. The kitchen was the first room you entered, then you walked in a straight line into the living room, then from there into the bedroom. I don't remember there being a door in that apartment. The bathroom was in the hall. It served two families. There was only cold water, no steam heat. My father had rigged up a small boiler in the kitchen, so there was always hot water if we were careful not to use too much. I was given my bath in the washtub, which was attached to the kitchen sink; that's where a mother washed her children, near to where she washed the dishes. And when we kids were asleep, our parents took sponge baths there. For a complete soaking, they would visit the public baths, of which there were many around New York during the thirties and forties.

In 1934, when I was four years old, we moved to 316 East Twenty-ninth Street. My mother and father had bought that building in 1929 with every penny they'd saved. It was a five-story structure with six apartments on each floor. They took out a mortgage just three months before the famous stock market crash, and in the long and terrible Depression that followed, their dream of striking it rich in America was crushed. They could never break even. They had to take out a second mortgage, and even though my father did a great deal of the tenants' maintenance work himself, it was a struggle. Rents were very low; the most expensive apartment cost $25 a month. Tenants paid cash, because nobody had a checking account.

One evening, when I was about eleven years old, I came up the stairs and heard banging coming from my apartment. As I walked in, I saw my father slapping a small pile of paper burning on the kitchen table. They had accidentally burned the building's rent roll for the entire month. My mother had been preheating things for the evening meal, forgot she'd put the money in the oven for safekeeping, and it went up in flames. I'll never forget my mother sitting at the table, my father looking down at her, stunned. I didn't know whether she was laughing or crying. The money was gone. Up in smoke.

Later they put the ashes in a paper bag, thinking maybe they could take them to the bank in the hope that these ashes might mean something. But the next morning, my father must have decided it was a lost cause because he flushed the ashes down the toilet. He was a proud man who always had trouble asking for anything.

Our home at that time was a living room, a kitchen, and two bedrooms. Linoleum on the floor, no steam heat ever. I didn't care. We had a black, cast-iron potbelly stove. I liked when my father gave me the keys to the cellar and told me to bring up a bucketful of coal. When I got to be about ten years old he would also let me open the little iron door of the big, round stove and prepare the fire. I'd crinkle up a sheet of newspaper, then put little pieces of wood on top of it. He'd strike a match and hand it to me to light the paper, and when the wood began to burn he'd let me put some lumps of coal on top of it. When the fire started to make things warm and cozy, I was proud and happy. My father would often peel tangerines and put the skins on top of the stove. The sweet citrus smell wafted into all the rooms. I loved it. We'd sit together on wooden chairs and talk while enjoying the heat. That is, my mother, father, and brother talked. I always just listened. I liked that more than talking.

If winter in New York was murder, then summer was a bitch. It got so hot sometimes that I'd ask my parents if I could sleep out on the fire escape. My mother would find something soft for me to lie down on, and then I'd climb through their bedroom window, step out onto the iron grillwork and make myself a bed. My father would fasten a wooden board to two sides of the iron railing, to block the opening where the escape stairs were and make sure I wouldn't fall through it. My brother never wanted to sleep out there, but I liked being suspended over my dark and quiet block, staring straight up at all those stars and planets. And sometimes a cool breeze would come up from the East River and make it easier to go to sleep.

There were times I was scared awake by the sounds of screaming women. They were loud, pained, desperate, and angry, and they were coming from the Bellevue Hospital psychiatric ward, which was nearby on Thirtieth Street and First Avenue. So you can imagine how quiet the neighborhood was in those days, for those sounds to carry over to Twenty-ninth Street, make a right-hand turn, and travel halfway up the block to my fire escape.

I used to lie there and wonder about those women. Were they all alone in life? Did anyone love them? And if so, why didn't those people come and get these women out of there? I sure would've done so if it had been my mother or sister—if I'd had a sister (which I wished I had).

The screams never lasted very long, and that made me happy, because to me that meant those women weren't suffering anymore. I could relax and when the block became still again, I'd go to sleep.

The Sheffield Farms milk van would come up our block every day at about six in the morning. A milkman, dressed in white pants, white shirt, white hat, and white shoes, would unload his tin racks filled with bottles, and the noise they made when they hit the sidewalk would wake me up. I'd watch him as he walked into one building after another, putting a bottle in front of every apartment on the block. He never hurried.

There were no refrigerators back then. Instead we had a nice, wood-covered icebox to put our milk in. Ralph, the iceman, would deliver our ice. He was short and stout, with the ruddy complexion of a hard-working man who never stood still for long. He always wore the same dark baggy pants, held up by a thick black belt. When it was time to go to work, he'd slap a large brown leather pad over his back, and clamp big iron tongs around a block of ice. Ralph had arms that would have been the envy of all those guys who spend day after day in the gym, pumping up muscles they'd never otherwise have. He'd swing that heavy block of ice over his back as though it were only a ten-pound weight, and start his trek up the stairs of one of the many buildings on Twenty-ninth Street. On every landing he set down the block of ice, cut whatever size piece the customer wanted, and continue on up the stairs to the next tenant.

Living on Twenty-ninth Street in the 1930s was a lot like living in a little village. On that one block alone there was a brewery that made good beer, a factory that baked delicious doughnuts, a butcher, two grocery stores, a candy store, an ice cellar, a funeral parlor, and a Boys Club where I went after school. Between Second and Third Avenues were the outdoor produce markets. I used to enjoy walking the length of that block because the aroma of fresh fruits and vegetables and spices made me feel as though I were in the country somewhere, far away from the New York City asphalt.

We also had a grammar school on our street; in fact, the school was smack against the building I lived in. The place was run by the Carmelite church down the block and classes were taught by the Sisters of Mercy. The nuns and the priests indoctrinated us into being good boys and girls who adored Mary and Jesus and the saints, and convinced us that if you were really good, you would go to heaven.

I even served as an altar boy, and around the age of eleven, I volunteered to work the six A.M. Mass every day for one week straight. When I told my mother she had to wake me up at five-thirty every morning, she looked at me as though I were crazy. Now there were mothers, especially Irish mothers, who would have said, "Oh, my beautiful son. Oh, you love God, don't you, sonny? You want to be a priest, don't you? You want to make your mother happy." My mother had a concerned look of apprehension on her face when she said, "You're really going to get up in the morning to do this?" "Yes," I said. "All right, all right, I'll wake you up." And that's all. She didn't say congratulations or what a nice boy, I'm proud of you. I wasn't surprised. Although she considered herself Catholic, my mother rarely went to Mass.

In addition to all the Irish priests in the parish, there was one who came from Malta. At six in the morning he already smelled of alcohol.

He was always merry, always making jokes in broken English. I think his drinking gave me the idea of raiding the wine closet. Even though my father had given me a few drops of wine in a glass of water from time to time, it had never made me as happy as the Maltese father seemed to be. So I decided to try the real thing, straight—no water.

I soon found out where the priests kept the key to the wine closet. One morning, before the priest from Malta showed up to dress for Mass, a fellow altar boy named Freddy and I unlocked the closet door. There sat an almost full gallon of Gallo red wine. The jug was heavy so I helped Freddy hold it while he took a sip and then he did the same for me. But I didn't sip, I gulped—too much, in fact. By the time we put the wine back and returned the key to where we'd gotten it, I was already feeling dizzy.

As Freddy walked, his shoulders swayed from side to side, like he had to wind up before he took a step, and the fact that in our gang of friends he was the shortest guy and had the shortest legs slowed him down, so that he was always at least five paces behind the rest of us. We always yelled at him to hurry up.

About halfway through the Mass, right around the time for Communion, Freddy and I had to walk to the corner of the altar, he with a golden plate and me with a decanter full of water. We were to help the priest wash his hands before he touched the host, the holy wafer that signified the body of Jesus Christ.

Well, like always, Freddy was late and I wasn't in good shape at all. When he arrived and put the plate under the Maltese father's hands, I was having trouble holding the little decanter steady. I felt so sick I was afraid I would vomit all over his beautiful vestments. My hands were shaking so badly that most of the water spilled onto the marble floor. "Not on the floor, sonny," he said. "Over my fingers."

But the Mass wasn't over. We had to kneel and join the priest in a Latin prayer. I wasn't so good at Latin and that day I was even worse. We started the Confiteor Dei but I couldn't remember it so I mumbled the rest. The Maltese priest didn't speak the Latin, he sang it—and what a wonderful voice he had. Serving Mass with him was like working with a really talented actor.

Looking back on it, serving the Mass was not unlike acting in a play. We had our entrances, following the priest who was dressed in richly colored, ornate vestments. Altar boys wore black cassocks under loose-fitting white linen blouses, and as in the theater, we had specific duties. Everything was thoroughly rehearsed and took place in front of spectacular scenery—an altar, with its golden tabernacle and the giant painting of the sacred heart of Jesus behind it. When Mass ended, we followed the priest as he made his exit. The only thing missing was the curtain calls. I usually enjoyed Mass a lot, but on that day it was murder. I couldn't wait for it to end. When the service was finally over I got out to the street as fast as I could and I threw up. That was the beginning of the end of my career as an altar boy.

It was around this time that I saw my first play. One of my buddies, Jackie Passalacqua, was acting at the Madison Square Boys Club, which was across the street from my building. Jackie looked like he knew what he was doing on the stage. He got applause and I became jealous. *I could do that*, I thought, *maybe even better*. That I'd never before seen a play—much less acted in one—didn't stop me.

Jackie lived up the street from me and we played games together. He had the bluest eyes I'd ever seen and his cheeks were always red. Unlike most of the kids on my block, he was very quiet. In fact he was so serious that he seemed much older than the rest of us. I saw Jackie almost every day but I hadn't heard he had been rehearsing a play. The day after I saw his performance, I ran into him on the street.

– Hey Jackie, who's the man in charge of the theater?

– That's Mr. Sinclair.

– How long you bin doin' that acting stuff?

– I dunno. About three months.

– How come I never knew about it?

– I never told nobody. I didn't wanna hear any wisecracks like "There goes the actor. There goes John Barrymore." Crap like that.

– You were good.

– Thanks.

– Think you could get me into the group?

– Sure. I'll tell Mr. Sinclair that you wanna join.

One day, I was sitting in the lobby of the Boys Club and a very distinguished-looking man said to me,

– Come here, son. What's your name?

– Ben, sir, but they call me Benny, my name is Ben Gazzara.

He led me into the auditorium, and I saw Jackie and a couple of other kids with what looked like small books in their hands. They were walking around and reading and talking. Jackie winked at me. Mr. Sinclair said,

– Sit down, Ben.

I sat on a wooden chair. He pulled up another chair and sat facing me. He lit a cigarette and then placed a couple of sheets of paper in my hand. I read them as fast as I could, suddenly realizing that he was going to ask me to audition for the part of a seventy-five-year-old Arab in a play called *The Gods of the Mountain* by Lord Dunsany.

– I'd like you to read this aloud for me. Don't try to act. Just be yourself.

I stared at this man who was to me what I thought every actor should look like. Mr. Sinclair was tall and handsome, had a mane of silver hair, a pencil-thin mustache, and a smooth and pleasant speaking voice. I so badly wanted to impress this man who had taken an interest in me, and read as best I could. In all the time he watched and listened to me Mr. Sinclair never removed the cigarette from his mouth. The smoke always drifted toward his right eye, which he protected by keeping it half closed. When I finished he looked at me with a hard, thoughtful stare.

– Yes, Ben, I think you can do this.

He told me to join the other kids on stage, that we'd start rehearsals right away. My heart was beating so fast I thought it would come through my chest. I had never felt more alive—here for the first time was something that I enjoyed but that also was all my own. The others had been rehearsing for a week already so I had a lot of catching up to do. I asked Mr. Sinclair what he wanted me to do about being an old man. Should I hunch over, walk with a limp, deepen my voice? "We'll see," he said calmly. First I should concentrate on learning my lines, then he would help me get comfortable with the moves. That initial rehearsal was the most exciting time I'd ever had. When it was over and Mr. Sinclair said we'd meet the next day at three P.M., those heavy feelings of loneliness that seemed always to be hanging around, disappeared. Now I had something to look forward to. I was excited but I was also worried: my father might need my help in the wine cellar.

When Gallo wine was selling in liquor stores for a dollar-fifty a gallon, Italians from Corona, from Astoria—from Canarsie even—would pay four-and-a-half dollars for my father's homemade wine. Before my brother was drafted into the army, he used to give my father a hand. Now it was 1944, Tony was away, and it was my turn. Wooden crates full of grapes were delivered after dark. I would slide the boxes, one at a time, across the sidewalk and onto the chute where they would fly down into my father's arms. And so the winemaking began.

I was almost fourteen years old when he'd asked me to help out. Handing me a chisel, he said I was to pry open the lids that had been nailed down. Even though he looked pale and weak to me, not as strong as usual, he still lifted those heavy crates, and poured the batches of grapes into the crusher. I would rather have been out on the street with my friends, but helping my father made me feel closer to him, especially when he put his hand on my shoulder, a gesture that meant "thank you." As I got older I became good at reading meaning into the gestures my father used in place of words.

A week or so later, after the grapes had been put through the press, he worked entirely alone. He finessed and babied the liquid until it became as good as any homemade wine could ever be. That particular year he made forty barrels of the stuff single-handedly. But not everyone was pleased by his productivity. Someone, for some reason, ratted on my father.

I was running through the ground-floor hallway on my way to rehearsal when two men brushed by me. Right away I was worried. These guys wore suits, ties, fedoras, shiny shoes. They looked foreign to me, and in my neighborhood foreign meant only one thing—cops! They headed for the iron door leading to our courtyard. I was scared. My father was down there. What did they want? My mother caught sight of them, too, and was right on their heels. She stopped the two men on the wooden stairs outside the cellar.

– What are you doing here?

– Well, Missus, we're Treasury agents and got this report that your husband has been making a large quantity of an illegal substance here.

– That's right. When our son comes home from the army we are going to have a party to welcome him.

– Well, we'll have to take a look.

I watched my mother open the narrow door and lead them to the wine. One of the Treasury guys looked around the room and started counting barrels. He turned to my mother and, with a quizzical look, said,

– That's some party you're going to give, Missus. There's forty barrels here.

– We're a very big family.

It was as if I were watching a movie. These strong, handsome guys were cold, yet they were kind. Their mouths smiled but their eyes didn't. They scared me, and I was really worried that they'd arrest my father.

At that moment he stepped out from the dark storeroom nearby and walked toward us. He must have quickly sized up the situation, too, because he smiled and greeted the cops warmly. He then offered them a glass of wine. One of the agents, the top guy I think, accepted and my father rinsed a glass, opened the tap, and the wine flowed, ruby red, from the barrel. The guy sipped it and said to his partner,

– Jim, you gotta taste this.

So Jim did. When the glass was empty, he said,

– Mr. Gazzara, can I have another taste?

And his partner said,

– I'll tell you what, Mr. and Mrs. Gazzara. You see these stamps?

He had a large roll of small green stamps.

– Buy three dollars worth of stamps for each barrel, stick them on, and we'll call it a day.

My mother said, "You're good boys. Thank you."

My father smiled and I was relieved. It could've been a real mess.

Three or four days before we opened the play at the Boys Club, Mr. Sinclair gave me a battered old piece of wood to use as a support when I walked. That staff helped give the semblance of old age to a thirteen-year-old boy. My first character work.

I knew I belonged in the theater as soon as opening night arrived. As I sat in front of the set depicting an amber-colored mosque, warmed by the multicolored lights from above, smelling the greasepaint on my face and the glue around my mouth and chin where a beard and mustache were fastened, and saying my lines—"Alms for the love of Allah! Alms for the love of Allah!"—I was in heaven. During the curtain calls, when I stepped forward and all the people, mostly from the neighborhood, applauded, I was sold. I was going to be an actor. Just like that.

I finally had a goal, a dream. Maybe acting could get me off the corner, a very lonely place. Even if there were five guys hanging out with me, I always felt alone. Nobody talked about his feelings, about his dreams, and now that I had one I kept it to myself. I was sure I'd get no respect; I might even be laughed at. But I knew where I wanted to go. When the guys were ribbing and razzing each other, my mind discovered a place to wander to—acting.

It wasn't long before I was given all the lead roles in the plays put on at the Madison Square Boys Club. In one of them, *If I Were King*, I was fourteen and my leading lady, a professional actress, was thirty. I was surprised that this didn't make me nervous. Mr. Sinclair believed in me, and I began to believe in myself.

In *If I Were King* I played the French poet-brigand François Villon and Jackie played King Louis. I wasn't too shy to leap on tables and spout poetry. I was even able to make my speech sound aristocratic. I took my leading lady—who was shapely and very voluptuous—into my arms and kissed her on the mouth. I felt brave, like a great matinee idol. I could do anything. Hiding behind the character gave me the courage to do things I couldn't—or wouldn't—do in life.

CHAPTER 3

GOING TO THE MOVIES

THERE WAS ALWAYS PLENTY OF LOVE IN OUR HOME. STILL, I was often lonely. That's probably the reason I looked forward to holidays so much. Usually at least twenty-five people gathered at the dinner table to tell stories, shout, and cross-talk over each other. This, too, was family—aunts and uncles, first and second cousins, all in good spirits and full of affection, which made me proud to belong to them.

When dinner was over, it was time for fruits, nuts, wine, and smoking. My uncle Paul seemed like he had a cigarette in his mouth at all times. When he would tell a story the smoke never stopped coming out of his mouth and his nose. I wondered why it didn't also come out of his ears. When I started smoking, I would try to do that, I thought—exhale out of my ears. I was sure it would get a lot of attention.

I was always the youngest at these dinners but it didn't matter to me. I enjoyed the company of my elders, listening intently to their stories. My favorites were the ones about the old country. When they spoke of their youth in Sicily they made their past come alive.

My father's mother and father died by the time he was twelve. He had four brothers and four sisters. His older brother, Paul, was only seventeen but he assumed responsibility for the whole family. Everyone worked, my father in the sulfur pits in nearby Canicattì, his hometown. I pictured him, a twelve-year-old boy, covered with sulfur dust, toiling and sweating under a hot Sicilian sun. My mother's father was the overseer of a baronial estate near her birthplace, Castrofilippo. Sicily was still something of a feudal society when she was a girl. Her three brothers would work the fields, gathering the crops that the baron owned and would take for himself. She and her five sisters would look after his home.

In one story my mother told, she was standing under an olive tree one morning, combing and drying her long black hair, when a powerful black stallion approached. Its rider was a handsome young man wearing shiny tan boots and a beautifully tailored jacket. It was the baron's son, looking for my mother's father. He was polite but looked at her as no man had before. While she told the story, and I pictured it in my mind, I was sure I saw a trace of a blush come across her cheeks.

In those days my imagination got most of its exercise as I listened to my favorite radio shows. *Lux Radio Theatre* broadcast a different drama every week, with Hollywood stars performing them. Part of the fun of hearing those shows was imagining the costumes, the scenery, the weather—just like listening to my relatives. I tried to visualize how they used to dress, the countryside they walked in, even their faces when they were young, living and working in a paradise that couldn't sustain them.

I liked being with large groups of people because we were a small family, and with my brother drafted into the army, we were suddenly even smaller. I missed Tony a lot. Despite the fact that he was more than five years older than I was, and although we didn't really share our most personal thoughts very much, I liked having him around. He was tall and lanky and had a deep voice, much like mine—inherited from my mother, I'm sure. There were some pretty powerful voices in her family.

Tony was smart. Although we grew up in the same house, he seemed to live in another world. He read a lot of books, which he brought to life when he talked about them. When he was home, the radio was always tuned to the classical station. My mother and father liked that because when he wasn't around I'd always tune in to the popular stuff that to them was only noise.

I was thirteen when my courage was tested for the first time. Some kids and I were playing a game of box-ball in the street when my brother walked by. He never hung around with the kids on Twenty-ninth Street. True, he was older, but even when he was my age he seldom played with other boys. He spent most of his time at home or on the block where our cousins lived. My buddies all knew that he was my brother. As he walked by, Jimmy, an Irish kid, said, "There goes the fairy." I heard tittering, too, but Tony passed us by with his head held high. I was ashamed of my brother and I was ashamed of being ashamed. I loved him and felt like a Judas for not defending him.

Later I was sitting on the window ledge looking down from our third-floor apartment at some of the guys who were in the middle of one of the many games we used to play—Jimmy, the kid who had insulted my brother, among them. He was big, strong, and older than I was. As I watched him, an anger welled up in me. But what could I do with it? If I fought him I was sure to lose and get messed up to boot. But the longer I sat and stared, the angrier I got.

On a sudden impulse I ran down the stairs and out into the street. I rushed right up to him and shouted, "Say it again, Jimmy." He looked startled. I let go with the hardest punch I could throw. The blow pushed him back but didn't knock him down. Then he landed one on me and our fight continued until the guys from my gang broke it up. They felt I'd had enough. I lost the fight, but I got respect. I never heard those remarks again.

A few months later my brother turned nineteen and went into the army. My family was proud but worried. Would Tony get through it and come home in one piece? Almost the last thing Tony did before leaving was hand me a copy of *Gulliver's Travels* by Jonathan Swift. "Read this," he said, "I think you'll enjoy it." It was the first book I ever read from cover to cover. It was given to me by my brother who was off to fight for our country, and I would get through that book no matter how long it took. It was precious to me even though I didn't understand it all.

My mother and father wanted me to read and learn. They'd gone to school only briefly but they respected knowledge. They wanted my brother and me to be as well educated as possible, and their dream was to get us both into college. I remember my mother looking at maps; she loved geography. I knew she was visiting places in her mind. And my father was a sage politically. He read the newspaper every day and politics was his game. Whenever he was on the corner, all the men would listen to him because he seemed to be making the most sense of it all. At the beginning of World War II in 1939, my father admired Mussolini, but when the United States entered the war and once my brother was involved, he followed every battle, every skirmish, every advance, every retreat. That war made him a patriot.

My brother was more talkative than I was so that when he was at home there was a little more noise in the house, but now I felt alone. My parents spoke very little English. I tried communicating with them in the Sicilian dialect but that took us only so far.

On the streets and even at the Boys Club I always pretended to connect with the other kids more than I actually did. Even though I grew up with them, I never felt a part of them. I always had the feeling that I should be somewhere else, only I didn't know where that would be.

An answer came with the arrival of Aunt Ida, my father's favorite sister, who lived in the Bronx. She visited our family despite being ill and walking with the help of a cane. If she was suffering, you'd never know it. For three hours she regaled my parents with stories.

My love for my Aunt Ida grew by leaps and bounds that night: her bawdiness, her sweetness, her courage. When the evening ended, she told my parents that she was going to vacation in Maine that summer and, with a sly smile, she asked if I would like to spend a few weeks with her in August during my summer holidays. I was shocked and more excited than I had been in a long time. I told her I would love to join her. And my father said maybe it could be done if we started saving money right away.

So everyone kissed and said their good-byes and afterward my father got an empty gallon-sized can of olive oil, made a slash on the top large enough for quarters and half-dollars, and put in two of each to start me out. I got a part-time job working as a messenger for an advertising firm and each time I dropped a coin in the can my father would match it. By mid-April the oil can was full of money and I couldn't wait for summer to arrive. But late one night, a couple of weeks before the Easter holidays, the news came that Aunt Ida was dead. My mother and father had known for some time that she had cancer and would not survive, but they never told me. The word cancer was never spoken in those days. It was considered a curse, the worst kind of bad luck. So despite the fact that they'd known my summer with Aunt Ida would probably never happen they'd allowed me to dream. I was lost. Crushed. Getting to spend that time with her was all I had wanted and now there was nothing. I felt sadder than ever before.

Returning to school after Easter break was tough. I was a student at Stuyvesant High School, one of the most prestigious public high schools in the country. My brother Tony had made my parents proud by graduating from there, so I decided to gain admittance, too.

I'd been there almost a year when, because I'd done so well on the entrance exam, I was placed in the track that was to graduate in three years instead of four. At Stuyvesant there were two sessions for students, morning and afternoon. I was given the afternoon session, which was fine with me because I liked to sleep late.

I'd been at Stuyvesant for almost a year and had done pretty well but after the holidays I no longer looked forward to it. I walked from Twenty-ninth Street to Fifteenth Street, where school was located. Students used to hang out in front of the building, fooling around, laughing. One day, as I entered the gray, windowless lobby, I weaved through all those young people who oozed optimism and ambition. Some of them were fellow classmates, brilliant guys who were in love with science and math. They were highly motivated, but I wasn't. What was I doing there? Did I care about chemistry? Did I care about math? My dream was to be an actor, so what did I need this crap for? I turned around and headed home.

I got up the next day determined to return to school. Then from my window I saw Eddie Tucker on the street. He'd had infantile paralysis as a small kid, and walked with a very severe limp. His left leg was so thin I wondered how it didn't shatter when it touched the ground.

I liked him, so I yelled down to him,

– Hey, Eddie! You wanna go to the movies?

– Sure, but I don't have no money.

– Don't worry about it. I'll be right down.

My parents weren't home so I took out two quarters from the oil can they had hidden. Eddie had to go home for lunch first, so he asked me to come along. That's the first time I tasted a lettuce and tomato sandwich—at Eddie Tucker's house. We never used the word apartment in those days, we always said house, maybe because in the old country our parents never saw an apartment. They lived in houses, however humble.

Compared to my mother, Eddie's mother seemed like a young girl, too young to have had kids. She too had Irish red hair, freckled face, and spoke English without an accent. She made me a kind of sandwich I'd never seen before—two slices of thinly sliced Silvercup white bread, a slice of tomato, one leaf of lettuce, and a lot of mayonnaise. It was good, especially the mayonnaise, which I had never tasted. I thought, *I wish my life could be like this.* Having a young mother who speaks perfect English in a house where you eat only American food.

I began to feel ashamed of being Italian. I even started to prefer Silvercup bread, which had no taste at all, to the real thing—the big, round Italian loaves baked golden-brown in a wood-burning oven.

Eddie became my good friend and I started treating him to the movies. Fifteen cents apiece got us into the Superior Theatre on Thirty-first Street and Third Avenue. We called it the Soup. With the extra twenty cents we filled up on Baby Ruths, Tootsie Rolls, and potato chips. We watched the coming attractions and then the "chapter," which was a fifteen- or twenty-minute installment of a serial, *Hopalong Cassidy*, for example. We saw two movies. There was an A-movie and a B-movie. The B was often better than the A.

When it was time to go home, I stopped at Pizzuro's grocery store and bought a ten-cent loaf of Silvercup bread. When I placed it on the kitchen table, my mother said in the Sicilian dialect that I always spoke with my parents,

– What's that?

– That's bread.

– What do I do with it?

– You make sandwiches or even toast in the morning.

– This is not bread.

– Yes it is, Mama.

My mother opened the wrapper and removed one soft thin slice of very white bread. She then folded it, folded it again, and rolled it back and forth in her hands. When she opened them and showed me what looked like a ball of soft white putty,

– There's no wheat in this. You see, it doesn't open.

– How could it?

– If it was real bread it would.

Seeing that blob of stuff my mother held out to me didn't put a damper on my love affair with Silvercup bread. I looked forward to being invited to Eddie's house because I knew I would get some there.

But now I was hooked on the movies, with or without Eddie. I skipped class thirty days in a row. I even started going to the Broadway houses. On the late morning bus ride heading west on Forty-second Street to Times Square I'd often get nervous, asking myself, *"How long do you think you're going to be able to get away with this, Ben? What happens when Mama and Papa find out?"* I knew it would hurt them badly. Not to mention, if I was held back a year, they'd be furious.

But I was in heaven as soon as I stepped off that bus and walked under the colorful marquees of one big movie palace after another—the Paramount, the Strand, the Capital, the Roxy—where people were already lined up to see movies like *Mildred Pierce* starring Joan Crawford, *Spellbound* starring Ingrid Bergman and Gregory Peck, *The Lost Weekend* starring Ray Milland, and on and on. There were stage shows featuring the big bands—Tommy Dorsey's, Benny Goodman's, Artie Shaw's, with singers like Doris Day, Frank Sinatra, Jo Stafford, Bob Eberle, you name it.

Radio City Music Hall was my favorite theater, not only because of the long-legged, high-kicking Rockettes, but because the place was so big, so glamorous. I'd always arrive in time to see the first show of the day. There were not many customers at that hour, so I would go up to the mezzanine and sit in one of those big, soft, comfortable seats. When the lights were dimmed, I felt that I was all alone, that the movie was being shown just for me. Often I daydreamed my way into the story. I was a daredevil, I hung off thousand-foot cliffs. I was a test pilot, I flew in untried and dangerous aircraft. I was a war hero, I saved many a life as I fought and survived one war after another. I was a great lover as I kissed and seduced the most beautiful women in the world.

But it couldn't go on forever. I asked for it and I got it—boy, did I get it. When I came home one day, after seeing yet another movie, right away I knew. The truant officer had been there and my father and mother did not look too happy. There was no yelling, no finger pointing, there was simply a deep disappointment.

When I showed up at Stuyvesant I received the bad news: I'd have to go to summer school to make up all the classes I'd missed. If I worked hard I might be able to do it. So I spent half of June and all of July with my nose in my textbooks.

Not that I ever went far during summertime. Mainly I would hang around the neighborhood. All my pals were there, too, and we would take the elevated train to Coney Island or Rockaway. To be with the fancier folks we'd travel all the way to Jones Beach, where the water seemed to be bluer. That summer I could join my friends only on weekends. That was all right with me. I liked my private time and, besides, there was always the roof. From there I could see the entire city. There were no high-rise buildings and very few skyscrapers in those days. I could see all the way downtown to the Woolworth Building and uptown, almost directly in front of me, were the mighty Empire State Building and the Chrysler Building, the most elegant of them all.

Sometimes Margie Sheridan would join me on the roof. She'd been in my grammar school class from the first grade through the eighth. But it wasn't until we graduated that I noticed how pretty she was. Margie was a strawberry blond with green eyes, freckles on her nose and dimples in her cheeks. She lived next door. At first, she lay on *her* roof, reading magazines and taking the sun. Then one day, she climbed the very low wall separating our roofs and joined me on my blanket. I was excited.

We met often. She'd usually bring movie magazines with pictures of Errol Flynn and Tyrone Power, Betty Grable, Alice Faye, and lots of other actors. We'd stretch out next to each other and as she lay on her stomach reading and sharing a naughty joke, I'd try to distract her. I'd nuzzle her neck, stroke her hair, kiss her cheek. Finally she'd turn over on her back, and we'd kiss and we'd kiss.

She had big breasts and a very curvy body that kept me up nights thinking of her. Margie Sheridan became my girl that summer, which meant that no matter what went on with our lives during our day, we would wind up mushing it up at night. That could only happen in one of four places—down by the river, under the stairs of my building, in the vestibule of hers, and, of course, on the roof. In that neighborhood, you never saw a parent who went out at night and left the apartment free to the kids. We had another big disadvantage, too. There was no Pill, so a girl's fear of pregnancy was a big obstacle to sex. And of the zillion mortal sins having to do with pleasure, sexual intercourse was sure to have her roasting in hell for all eternity. That made it difficult for a kid like me to get laid.

Margie was Irish and to us Italian boys Irish was foreign, even exotic. She drove me crazy. She'd let me press against her, rub against her, feel her breasts, but that was it. We'd bring things to the edge but with no payoff. Often, I'd go home with a real bad pain around my kidneys. It was what we called "blue balls"—blue with longing and disappointment. But I liked her a lot, regardless.

By the end of July I'd worked so hard in summer school that I was able to make up the credits I lost. I thought I'd be seeing a lot of Margie for the rest of that summer but no dice. She told me she was leaving town with her folks to spend a few weeks with relatives in New Jersey. I felt very bad. What was I going to do?

Some of my friends were working at Clear Pool Camp. When I was younger, I had gone there almost every summer for two weeks. It was a pretty spot owned and run by the Madison Square Boys Club. You slept in windowless cabins without mosquito netting, and you ate pretty bad food, but you were happy. All of your friends were there. You swam, you rowed on the lake, played ball on dirt instead of asphalt, sat around the campfire listening to scary stories, you sang songs.

We were now too old to be campers. That's why the guys I knew were there as workers. I thought I'd join them so I volunteered to work in the kitchen for the rest of the summer, peeling potatoes, washing dishes, setting the tables. Mr. Reid was the cook. He was a kind person and I liked him. When somebody made a remark about the quality of the food, I took it personally. I found myself defending it and Mr. Reid. I was proud of the kitchen and the people I worked with.

One August day, after serving lunch, I was outside the administrative cabin talking to a few of my friends. Seated on an old stone wall nearby were a group of older guys. One of them was talking about a big bomb we'd dropped that had destroyed two entire cities in Japan. They were betting that the war would be over in a few days.

— CHAPTER 4 —

LOSS

THE BOYS STARTED COMING BACK HOME. RALPH, THE iceman, had a son who'd landed on Normandy Beach and a few days later was severely wounded in the Battle of St.-Lô. He was hospitalized for over a year. On a cold Saturday morning in early 1946 a patrol car came up Twenty-ninth Street followed by an ambulance. Both vehicles had their lights ablaze. They stopped in front of 310 East Twenty-ninth Street, where Ralph and his wife were waiting for their boy. At that moment, from almost every window on the block, someone was looking down and watching the reunion. A few of those windows held gold stars, intended to make a mother proud of losing her son in the war. The following day a front-page photo in the *Daily News* showed a young soldier on crutches being embraced by his parents. Soon that young man, like many others, would be standing on the corner wondering what to do with the rest of his life.

When the big day of Tony's return came for us, our apartment was crowded with relatives. Some of my aunts and cousins had been with my mother since the day before, preparing for the feast. I must have gone up and down the stairs a hundred times that day, either to the grocery store or to one of the markets across Second Avenue or to answer the phone in Mr. Sapienza's candy store, which was in our building. There were few telephones in my neighborhood. Whenever any of the tenants received a call, Mr. Sapienza would stick his head out of his backyard window and

shout the name of whoever the call was for. One of the children was usually sent to run down the stairs and bring back the message. With so
many of our relatives and friends calling to check on Tony's arrival, I did
an awful lot of running that day.

When my brother walked through the door, my father was the first
to greet him. Tears came to his eyes as he hugged his son tightly. There
was applause all around. My mother appeared from the living room,
calling Tony by the name she always used for him, Nino, as though
saying it for the first time. She walked very slowly toward him, as if she
were afraid he'd disappear. My mother took him in her arms and kissed
him again and again. She wouldn't let him go. My brother then turned
to me and we gave each other a quick and embarrassed big brother–little
brother hug. Although I was always able to kiss my parents hello and
good-bye, I didn't do that kind of stuff with my brother. Kissing him
somehow didn't seem American.

Tony looked really spiffy. His cap was worn at a dashing angle. His
uniform was starched and clean. His heavy, laced-up boots were polished
to a high gloss. When I had last seen him, my brother was a private with
only one stripe on his sleeve. Here he was, three years later, with three
stripes on top and one on the bottom. *Jesus*, I said to myself, *he went all
the way up to staff sergeant.* I was more proud of him than ever.

Tony had been a medic in Oran, North Africa, Sicily, then up the
Italian peninsula to Pisa, where near the war's end he provided medical
assistance to prisoners of war. One of these prisoners was the great American poet Ezra Pound, who had been interned for his outspoken fascist
sympathies. My brother tried to make conversation with this legendary
genius, but Pound's remarks raced from one subject to the next, seeming
to make no sense, as though he were free-associating. That was a true
shame for a book-lover like Tony. He had read many of the classics,
including the great French and Italian books. But Tony didn't give up. He
brought Pound paper to use in his old, battered typewriter. I like to think
that my brother helped Pound write his masterpiece, *The Pisan Cantos*. I
envied Tony's wartime experience, and I wondered whether becoming an
actor would one day put me in contact with great writers and artists.

When the homecoming feast started, there was a comfortable number of guests. But with the arrival of more and more people, the festivities spilled out of our apartment and into the hallway. My father had invited all the tenants in the building—mostly Italian, but also Greek, Maltese, and Armenian families. Everyone was welcome regardless of his or her background.

Music blared out from each apartment, with all doors wide open. Different music played from every floor in the building. You could hear Artie Shaw's mellow clarinet playing "Begin the Beguine," Tommy Dorsey's sweet trombone blowing "Getting Sentimental over You," or Harry James's muscular trumpet crooning out "Stardust Memories." But when that music came together it didn't sound like noise to me at all. Everyone was joyful, helped along by my father's wine. They polished off an awful lot of it, but they didn't make a dent in those forty barrels he'd made the year before. That wine would outlive my father.

Around this same time, I was performing in a play at the Boys Club. *Seventh Heaven* told a romantic story that in 1927 had been made into a successful movie under the same title. Two starry-eyed lovers create their own heaven in a seventh-floor garret in the old section of Paris. My character leaves home to fight in the First World War. However, he's been blinded and does not want to return to his loved one in that condition. He fears becoming a burden. Finally, the young man is tricked into meeting his girl. I remember my last line in that play: "Cherie, my eyes are filled with you." There wasn't a dry eye in the house. Handkerchiefs came out every time. I was surprised that people in the audience had been touched by my performance. Would I ever be able to make them feel that way again? Did I have the talent to move them whenever a play called for it? I knew I had my work cut out for me if I was going to be a serious actor.

One night Tony surprised me by showing up backstage. "I liked what I saw," he said, "keep it up." I was happy that he took pride in me. That meant a lot not only because he was my brother but because it was in that play that I'd begun to understand the amount of hard work it took to build a character, to make things lifelike and believable. Until then, I'd been operating purely on youthful instinct, finding my way as if it were a game. But I was now realizing that there was more to being onstage than "play-acting."

Some months before, Mr. Sinclair had taken a group of us to see *The Glass Menagerie*, a play by a young southern writer named Tennessee Williams. It was the first time I'd been to a Broadway show. When I walked into the crowded Playhouse Theatre I was trembling with excitement. I'd never seen so many people dressed in such rich, elegant attire. I had entered another world.

When the curtain went up, an actor appeared onstage and began saying things like nothing I'd ever heard before. The words sounded like the poetry I'd tried to read sometimes but had a hard time understanding. Yet here I understood every word the actors said. I was transfixed. Still there was an actress whose performance confused and bewildered me; Laurette Taylor in the part of the mother was unlike any actress I'd ever seen. In the movies it didn't really matter whether an actress appeared to be thinking or feeling much. There was always that lush background music to guide the audience into feeling emotions. But here was a woman who sat still for long moments, who moved slowly and undramatically, in total silence. I couldn't take my eyes off her. When we left the theater I asked,

– Mr. Sinclair, what kind of acting is that? She didn't do anything.

– Yes, Ben. She didn't do anything but she did everything.

He added that Laurette Taylor was a troubled woman offstage and drank too much. She'd virtually disappeared from the stage until, after an absence of ten years, Eddie Dowling, the producer of *The Glass Menagerie*, brought her back to Broadway. Lucky for me. That was an acting lesson I've never forgotten. Her interpretation of the mother, Amanda Wingfield, was pathetic and touching, annoying and funny, and ultimately heartbreaking. I wondered how much a person had to suffer before he could give the kind of star performance Laurette Taylor showed us that night. She didn't push to make her point but behaved simply. Nor did she frame or underscore moments in order to make it easier for us to understand what was going on inside Amanda. She just *was*. Here for the first time ever I was witnessing an actress who had taken a character from the written page and given it the flesh, blood, heart, and soul of a human being. My notions about acting were changed for good.

Often in rehearsals, Mr. Sinclair's voice had boomed out from the dark auditorium, "Don't act!" He wanted us to be natural. I'd seen "natural" done very well by big movie actors like Gary Cooper and James Stewart but I had never had the experience of seeing an actor or actress take such exquisite writing and make it seem as though the words were her own. That performance is recorded as one of the greatest in the history of American theater. Even though I was a kid, I knew I had seen something extraordinary.

I tried hard to apply my newfound knowledge about acting as a craft. The first thing I did was lower my vocal energy. I wanted to appear more relaxed and conversational. But what about the fact that my character in *Seventh Heaven* was a Frenchman living in Paris during the early 1900s? What could I do about that? I would have to use my imagination, relying on youthful knowledge about soldiers in World War I. On my own, I outlined a young man who, oddly enough, was not unlike me. I was determined not to ham things up by trying to be like Charles Boyer. The character would be stuck with *me*.

My biggest insight into the process came while working on the blindness. I tried many approaches: not looking at the other actors, staring into space, finding three or four spots on the stage to focus on, but I was always ill at ease. Nothing I tried seemed genuine. A few days before opening night Mr. Sinclair took me aside and suggested that rather than try to show the blindness by looking past people or moving my eyes from one fixed point to the next I should tell myself a story, any story.

– I don't want you to worry where your eyes go.

– But, Mr. Sinclair, what if I'm so busy concentrating on my story that I miss my cue?

– You won't.

I didn't. Everything became easier. Thinking my own thoughts released me and made it a pleasure to be onstage. That was my first understanding of the amount of dedication and work required to become an actor.

With acting taking up more and more of my energies, I decided to make things easier on myself and change high schools. Johnny Kechejian, my best friend, was attending a small school in the Bronx, St. Simon Stock, taught by the Sisters of Mercy, the same order that taught us on East Twenty-ninth Street. I knew that after Stuyvesant High School I'd be able to breeze through courses there.

Among the teachers at my new high school was Mrs. Russo, the history teacher. Far from being a nun, she wore tight clothes that accentuated her body. Her skirt had a way of sliding up her legs and her blouse was always provocatively open to the third button. It was tough to concentrate on the Crusades when Mrs. Russo's body had my full attention. But I passed history. As a matter of fact, I got terrific marks in just about everything. Mrs. Russo couldn't understand how I could seem so uninterested yet still get such good marks. Once she asked me why I was so blasé. I didn't know what the word meant so I couldn't answer.

All things considered, 1946 was a pretty good year. A couple of other memorable things happened that year. The most important to me and a lot of other kids was Joe DiMaggio's return from the army to play baseball again for the New York Yankees. During the years he wasn't playing I didn't even bother to listen to the games on the radio. Without Joe, I just wasn't interested.

I was also a fan of boxing. And, like almost everybody else in my neighborhood, I rooted for Rocky Graziano. He was a young fighter who made a big name for himself that year by knocking out a lot of tough opponents. But there was one boxer he'd have to beat before he would earn our real respect. Tony Zale was as tough as the steel they made in his hometown of Gary, Indiana. He was the middleweight champion who possessed a lot of savvy in the ring. He agreed to give Graziano a shot at his title.

In that battle Graziano was knocked down more than once, but each time he got up, his face battered and bloodied, he fought like hell. Even though Graziano lost that fight, he won a lot of respect from us for his admirable courage. It wasn't until 1947 that Rocky beat Zale in a rematch. He was now middleweight champion of the world.

From all the hooting and hollering that followed, it was safe to assume that every Italian-American in New York City had listened to that particular fight on the radio. The next day, motorcades drove Rocky through all the neighborhoods on the East Side. When he came up my block, sitting on top of the backseat of a convertible, you'd think he was a king or a president. We went crazy. Rocky made us proud. I hoped that someday I, too, would make people proud like that.

Not all news was good at this time. My father was in poor health. He'd been in the hospital for two weeks for what I thought was diabetes, but it was something far worse: leukemia.

On the morning he died, I'd taken him his newspaper, *Il Progresso Italo-Americano*, to Bellevue Hospital along the East River. I could never look at that river without thinking of Iggy. On a boiling July day several years earlier, he stripped down, dove into the river, but never came up. I was twelve years old when it happened, but being born to older parents I'd already been to an awful lot of funerals. My aunts, uncles, and cousins were much older than me and it seemed that, one by one, they were dying. Iggy's was the first funeral I attended for somebody my own age. That scared me. I heard people say things like "It was the little boy's time" or "God wanted him so he called him." Even then I didn't believe that stuff about "God's will" and those comments made me mad. I knew that it was only a matter of luck and Iggy's had run out that day at the river. I wondered what it felt like to die. Would my luck last?

Usually when I approached the hospital, my father would be standing on an enclosed wrought-iron balcony waiting for me. He would look down and wave. But that morning he wasn't there.

I was nervous when I entered Ward C. I was afraid of what I'd find. Was my father doing badly? Was he suffering? I walked down the center aisle of that long, narrow room with too many beds against either wall, glancing occasionally at these men of all ages, struggling against one sickness or another. I found my father lying in bed, looking so fragile. I kissed him and handed him his newspaper. He smiled and asked about my mother, my brother, about school. He seemed very tired. He looked at me for a long time and then he told me to be a good boy and to be honest. I knew why my father said those things but didn't want to face it. My father knew he wouldn't be coming home.

I didn't cry when I was told my father died. A lot of people came for what's called "the viewing." The coffin was surrounded by wreaths of red, white, and pink roses and carnations. Very pretty, but the scent to me was sad and heavy. Death seemed to have already gotten into them. As I walked toward my father's casket, I saw Ralph the iceman seated in the front row. He had tears in his eyes when he looked at me and I realized that this honest, hardworking man was crying for *me*, for my loss. It was at this moment that I understood my father's life was finally over, that I'd never see him again. All the tears I'd held back came pouring out.

I put all my energy into rehearsals for *A Bell for Adano*. Here I could take myself outside of my own life to somewhere else, to become *someone* else.

The play, adapted by Paul Osborn from a book by John Hersey, takes place in a small town in Sicily. Mussolini has confiscated the bell from the church tower in order to turn the metal into guns for his war machine. When the Allied forces drive the Germans off the island, a troop of Americans bivouacked in Adano. I played Major Joppolo, whose staff takes over the town only to find himself bombarded with requests from the townspeople to replace the bell that hasn't been sounded in years. Despite all the *real* problems at hand, this one slowly becomes Joppolo's main challenge. Of course, he finds a way to replace the bell.

A Bell for Adano was a smash hit. The whole neighborhood must have seen it. I felt I owed part of my success to Fredric March, who played the role on Broadway. I admired his acting so much that I wanted my performance to resemble his as much as possible. His acting style was loose and easy, simple and even casual. I tried to take command without being strident, to be sensitive without being sentimental and I was having a lot of fun doing it.

My pal Jackie Passalacqua costarred with me in that show. We got a lot of curtain calls but something was wrong. Jackie was suddenly distant with me. Was it because I was getting the parts he thought he should be playing? My first taste of show business rivalry! Nothing wrong with that, but the tension made me uncomfortable so I pretended not to notice.

Once our one-week run came to an end, Mr. Sinclair told us that he would not be returning to the Boys Club. He was retiring, he said, planning to take his wife on a trip across America. I was dumbstruck. How could this be happening so fast? When he said good-bye to me, he put his arm around my shoulder and said, "You have talent, Ben. Take care of it and there's no telling where it can take you." I watched him as he walked away. Within a month, I had lost two fathers. What would I do? I loved the man. Would I ever see him again? Would I ever become anything without him? It was through him that I'd found that a whole other world existed beyond Twenty-ninth Street. I felt lost.

My dream of becoming an actor was pushed to the back of my mind. *Forget about it*, I told myself. *It'll never happen.* I worked hard to finish high school first in my class.

I intended to go to college but I had to make money first. Nick De Federico, a friend of mine, suggested we go down to Miami to see if we could get jobs in one of the many new hotels that were opening. Florida sounded romantic to me (I'd never seen a real palm tree), so I went.

We had enough money to last us a week, and within two weeks we were so hungry we started looking in cars to see if people had valuables we might steal. Desperate people can do desperate things, even nice, honest, young guys like us. Finally, thank God, we got jobs as bellboys at a new hotel that was about to open—the Sans Souci, a big, ritzy-looking place.

I was the worst bellboy that ever existed. Mr. Metcalf, our boss, seemed like a nice man. We were to check people in and take up their bags. Only I was too proud sometimes to hang around to wait for a tip. I'd just turn and leave. At the end of the week, Nick would throw bills and handfuls of change on the bed and ask, "What about you?" I'd say embarrassedly, "I got ten dollars." He'd have almost a hundred.

I was one of six bellboys, each of whom had a particular position in the lobby, standing at attention in front of a pillar, waiting for people to check in or out, or pointing them in the right direction. We were all given cigarette lighters, too, as no guest was to light his or her own cigarette.

The lobby was always full of women—rich widows mostly. They sat in the sun all day long, and returned with tanned skin wrinkled as leather. And despite the heat outside they wore their furs in the air-conditioned lobby. They drank martinis and showed off their coats. I hardly noticed because I was busy daydreaming: I was on Broadway, my name was in lights, I was the toast of New York. That's more or less how my thoughts always went.

I was just taking my curtain call when I heard Nick call, "Ben." I turned around and I saw a woman in harlequin glasses and a very fluffy fur coat, removing a cigarette from a silver case. I didn't know where I was and must have panicked. I whipped out my cigarette lighter, thrust it in the direction of her mouth and set fire to the collar of her coat. It started to sizzle and stink. Of course she put in a complaint and I was fired. Mr. Metcalf broke the news.

– I gotta let you go, kid. I like you very much, but I don't think you're cut out for this work.

I was on a Greyhound bus heading back to New York when I realized what I had to do. Staring out the window and seeing very little of the dark landscape made me feel especially lonely. *You never feel that way onstage, Ben,* I said to myself. *Why don't you give it a try?* Could someone named Ben Gazzara find room in the world of the Clark Gables, the Cary Grants, the James Stewarts? But what was the alternative? A lousy job that called on nothing but my presence? I knew it was a long shot, but the closer that bus got to New York, the more I was sure that, against all odds, I had to give it a try.

--- CHAPTER 5 ---

ACTOR

I'D HEARD GOOD THINGS ABOUT A PLACE CALLED THE Dramatic Workshop. It was located in the West Forties in Manhattan and headed by a German refugee named Erwin Piscator, who was also a peer of Bertolt Brecht. I decided to try to enter on a scholarship.

For my audition I did a soliloquy from *Seventh Heaven*. This was my first big step toward my dream and I was nervous. Mr. Sinclair's advice came into my mind: Relax, everything would go well. I don't know how or why but I found myself enjoying that audition. I was accepted into the Dramatic Workshop to start what I hoped would be my life in the theater.

The Workshop provided lessons in diction, swordsmanship, and dance, along with acting classes. And, if a student were good enough, he might work on a production that Erwin Piscator himself staged. These twice-yearly shows were lessons unto themselves. He took a little stage, the President Theatre on West Forty-eighth, which was the size of a small living room, and turned it into Radio City Music Hall. I don't know how he did it. He required a week just to light a show. He called this Epic Theater and it *was* epic. It was fantastic. It was the first time I saw a director work creatively with light and space. Piscator tricked the audience into seeing what was not there. Suddenly, theater for me was not only what you see onstage but also what you don't see.

Although he was a gracious instructor, Piscator's anger flared when he thought his students gave too little effort, which for him meant not enough respect for the theater. "The theater is a cathedral," he would often say. And we believed him, too. Acting, I realized, was only a part of great theater. I read books about scenic design by people like Gordon Craig, theater criticism by Stark Young, and of course the work of the great Konstantin Stanislavsky.

I costarred in a student production of Molière's *The Misanthrope* with a fellow by the name of Anthony Franciosa who, in fact, played the lead. Tony was a tall, good-looking guy with fair skin and sandy-colored hair. He'd decided to attack his part with high verbal and physical energy. Alceste, the misanthrope, finds deceit and hypocrisy everywhere and rants and raves about it. Tony went to town.

Playing the role of Philinte, Alceste's friend, I decided to do the opposite. I didn't want to get into a cockfight, so I didn't attempt to match Tony's energy. I wouldn't fight for audience attention but instead simply try to convince him that all was not black, that life was worth living.

Piscator and my classmates were impressed. I got attention by doing less. Like that living room-sized theater that Piscator lit to appear as big as a Broadway stage, I learned to attract attention by sometimes doing almost nothing.

Piscator had a house in Lake Placid, New York, where plays were performed in July and August; summer stock, they called it. The following summer I was invited, with a group of older students, to come. "Bring the boy, bring the boy," Piscator said.

Although I spent the summer there, I didn't do much. I painted scenery and handled props. I was onstage only once briefly, in Philip Barry's *The Philadelphia Story*. I don't remember what I did the rest of that summer, but just being in the theater, watching rehearsals, helping in any capacity at all, thrilled me.

When we returned to New York, Piscator cast me as Malcolm in his production of *Macbeth*. I'd never before done Shakespeare. I struggled with the verse, hoping it would come "trippingly on the tongue," but it didn't. There wasn't time enough to make the language part of me. While I knew I had the equipment to do Shakespeare, I didn't put in the time required to master the work. In those days American actors thought that to succeed in Shakespeare you had to have an English accent, and that scared most of us off.

In 1950, while working on the production of *The Scapegoat*, adapted from Kafka's *The Trial*, I met a very attractive girl named Louise Erickson. She had Nordic looks: a straight, almost perfect nose, round pink freckled cheeks, full lips, and green eyes. She wore her hair in the same short bob that Ingrid Bergman had made famous in the movie *For Whom the Bell Tolls*, and like Bergman she was blonde—and blonde for me meant class. It also meant inaccessibility. I could never get a blonde to notice me because she seemed to be above me.

The blondes I'd seen in movies owned villas or rode horses. On their breakfast tables were pitchers of orange juice next to seventeen eggs and piles of sausages and toast and bacon, but people never ate anything. I used to get hungry just looking at all this food onscreen and I'd say under my breath, "Eat something, eat something!" These people would be talking while all that wonderful food sat in front of them. And I'd say, "Eat the fucking eggs, please!"

To me, a blonde was elusive, ungettable, a fantasy object. Louise didn't look like my mother or any of the other women I'd grown up with. That type of woman never aroused me. Probably too close to home. I was introduced to her and the first thing she said was,

– Oh, an Italian name. I've only recently returned from Italy.

– I've never been there.

– You must go. It'll take your breath away.

Louise looked at me the way Ingrid Bergman must have looked at Roberto Rossellini. Bergman had recently left her husband, with whom she'd had a daughter, in order to live with the famous Italian director. This was not done in those days. Ingrid was ostracized, scorned by powerful Hollywood columnists, and given no work from the major studios. But she stayed with Rossellini anyway. How flattered he must have been.

I was surprised that Louise took an interest in me. She'd been an important radio star in *A Date with Judy*, which was broadcast nationwide once a week from Los Angeles. She told me that she had grown up in a big house with large grounds, had gone to private schools, and had traveled to Europe. But most important of all, she was interested in me. I was bowled over.

Louise supported me in my dreams of a career. In fact, it was she who convinced me to look into the Actors Studio. Although I was unfamiliar with the place, I did some investigating and quickly found out that people like Marlon Brando, who had caused a sensation both in *Truckline Cafe* and *A Streetcar Named Desire*, and Julie Harris, who wowed everyone in *A Member of the Wedding*, were attending sessions there. I thought, *These people are terrific. What do* I *have to do to get into that place?* Everyone said it was almost impossible to be accepted there. As soon as I heard that, I had to try. The real magnet for me was Elia Kazan, whose production of *Death of a Salesman* and *A Streetcar Named Desire* had impressed me like nothing else I'd seen since Laurette Taylor in *The Glass Menagerie.*

I auditioned for the Actors Studio in 1951. I chose a scene from *Night Music*, which Clifford Odets wrote and Elia Kazan had starred in for the Group Theatre in the 1930s. I asked a classmate from the Dramatic Workshop, Loretta Leversee, to help me prepare the scene. We teamed up with Michael V. Gazzo, who later wrote *A Hatful of Rain* and would become my friend. Loretta and I worked with Mike and auditioned for Daniel Mann, a successful film director. He was the sole judge of my first audition for the Actors Studio. May Reiss, who was Elia Kazan's personal secretary and also worked for the Studio, was on hand as well. I'd never been so nervous. This was it. If I was rejected, how would I feel? What would I do, throw in the towel? In those days becoming a member of the Actors Studio meant you were among the best. For some it was even more important than getting a part in a Broadway play.

The Actors Studio was on the fourteenth floor of an office building at Broadway and Fifty-third Street, the building that now houses the Ed Sullivan Theatre, where David Letterman does his nightly show. It was a clean, well-ordered place with a large open front office for May Reiss and a closed back office for Kazan. And then there was a stage in a big room down the hall where actors showed their work. Loretta and I took our places, my heart racing. I heard Loretta speak the first line of the scene and I turned to look into her sweet eyes. My response was full of the tenderness and gratitude the line had never had. In fact the scene was softer and more tender than we'd ever performed it. My answer to her was colored by what I felt about her helping me in this important moment of my life.

After we finished, my nervousness vanished. In fact, I was almost giddy. I just *knew* we'd done well. May turned to us and smiled—a terrific sign!

I was soon notified that I'd passed and my final audition would be scheduled in a few weeks. I'd won the first round but I knew we still faced the big time. My excitement was mixed with fear and foreboding. What to do? I called Loretta, and we again got together with Mike Gazzo and went back to work.

In life Mike walked with a sort of a loping shuffle; he never hurried. That may be where his piece of direction came from: "Wear heavy shoes," he said. So I went to a theatrical rental place and bought myself a pair of those thigh-high leather boots worn by GIs during World War II. I laced them up and pulled my pants down over them so that only the toes and heels would show. I told Loretta to meet me at the Studio. I had to walk, to get used to the boots.

May ushered us into a dark room where only the stage was illuminated. She introduced us to the three people seated there. Kazan, who at the time was probably the most important director in America, had a head full of black hair that stood up on one side. He was wearing a shirt open at the neck with the sleeves rolled up, khaki pants, and a pair of scuffed-up white sneakers. He was not a big man, but his enormous energy filled the room. He was outgoing and friendly from the start, showing me a smile that made us feel welcome. Cheryl Crawford had the kind of short hairdo that you didn't see often in those days. That and the fact that she wore no makeup gave her a serious and severe look. She raised her eyes from her reading material in her lap and gave me a quick nod. Seated on the end was Lee Strasberg, who examined me through black-rimmed glasses. He didn't seem too impressed by what he saw. You had the feeling he was a man who couldn't be easily convinced of anything. A glance was all he gave me. He scared me the most.

These three, with Harold Clurman, had founded the famed Group Theater in the thirties. Kazan had won raves as the gangster, Fuselli, in Clifford Odets's *Golden Boy*. It was Odets's plays—*Awake and Sing!*, *Waiting for Lefty*, and others—that gave the Group its renown. And the Group gave birth to the Actors Studio.

No sooner had I started the scene than I realized that everything seemed to take more time. Not only did my walk slow down, so did my behavior—the way I sat or gestured. I found myself looking at Loretta and seeing her in a different light. Things found a deeper meaning. My lines came out in new and surprising ways. Kazan had played that part fifteen years before and I heard him laugh more than once. Every time he did I became more comfortable on that stage.

When the scene was over, I would've bet the farm that Loretta and I had pulled it off. Crawford kept looking at us as we prepared to leave and I felt that Strasberg eyed me carefully. Kazan was beaming when he said "Thank you."

Well, I was accepted into the Actors Studio and so was Loretta—who wasn't even there to audition! Our hard work paid off. "Wear heavy shoes." What a terrific piece of direction.

Louise and I had been seeing each other for a little more than a year when we started arguing, or rather she would flare up and have strange tantrums about things I considered unimportant. I chalked it up to frustration. She had come to New York to continue her acting career but had done absolutely nothing about it. Having been the star of a long-running weekly radio show didn't seem to give her the courage to go after anything in the theater. I thought she should busy herself, and talked her into taking acting classes. She said she would, but she never did.

I was twenty years old and still living with my parents. Italian boys never left home until they were married. It's still the same in Italy. No chance of having your own apartment, either; where's the money to pay the rent? I'm sure my proposal of marriage to Louise had a lot to do with my need to get out of the house, to be my own man.

When it came time to marry, I was content to go to City Hall for a civil ceremony, but Louise wanted a big church wedding with a white bridal gown, long veil, flower girls, and beautiful voices raised in song. There was a slight impediment to all this. Louise was a Protestant. That was remedied by her taking religious instruction from the priest who married us and then pledging to raise our children in the Catholic faith. I sat through those lessons with her and was often moved, especially when the priest read from the Bible. Occasionally he'd use a Latin phrase that carried me back to my childhood when the Catholic Church meant so much to me. But there we were: young lovers who didn't know very much about each other, trying to bridge customs and cultures.

Louise left New York and went back home to pave the way for my meeting her folks. But they lived in Los Angeles and I didn't have the money for airfare. So I landed a job at Walgreen's Drugstore, near Grand Central Station, where I jerked sodas and served sandwiches eight hours a day, six days a week, for about four weeks. It took that long to earn enough cash to buy a ticket on one of those propeller-driven, chartered airplanes that got people to California in eleven hours. It would be the first time I'd ever flown.

Once in Los Angeles it was clear from the first hellos that I was not the guy Louise's parents thought she should marry. Her father, who was in the restaurant business, was affable and cordial. Her brother, John, was around my age and made an attempt at camaraderie, but it was forced. Her mother, however, a schoolteacher with a tight-jawed severity, made no effort at all. In fact, she failed to show up for dinner on my first day with the family. It got to be eight o'clock, then nine, then ten. Phone calls were made to the police and to hospitals until she reappeared. Louise's mother smiled at me but her eyes remained dead and disdainful. Clearly, she wanted me to go away. I was an unwelcome stranger in a very white Anglo-Saxon world.

Disappearing must have been in the family blood. When Louise's feelings were hurt, for reasons I usually couldn't fathom, she would rise and make a dramatic exit from the room. This had also happened once on Twenty-ninth Street at my family's home. Louise took offense to an offhand remark I made to my brother, left the table, walked through the door, and vanished. I let her go. I was both too embarrassed and angry to move. Still, I was sure our love would ultimately prevail over any problems we might have.

I spent a week at their Spanish-style home. Everything was large to me—the kitchen, the dining room, and especially the living room with a ceiling so high it had a gallery encircling it that led to all the bedrooms. It seemed an awful lot of space for such a small family.

Things became so tense that I invented a phone call. I told Louise's family that my agent said I'd been asked to come back to New York to read once more for a Broadway play. I added that the director and producer had been so impressed by my work that my return would likely be only a formality. The part was certainly mine. That news brought everyone to life, beaming, almost joyful, including the mother. I knew it wasn't my good news that lifted their spirits. I was leaving and that alone was cause for rejoicing.

Louise was confused and asked,

– When did you read for that play?

I knew she'd understand and insist that I go. We had our problems but she always wanted me to succeed.

– About two weeks ago. I never thought anything would come of it.

– Should I go back with you?

– No, no. You enjoy yourself. It's so beautiful here with your family. Take your time.

Louise's father turned to her.

– Honey, would you go down and choose a good bottle of wine? I think we should celebrate.

– Good idea, Dad. Ben, would you like to see the wine cellar?

– I sure would.

We descended into a large and very orderly cantina where floor-to-ceiling racks of white and red wines were neatly labeled by country and province. I was impressed. Louise reached under her dress and while she shimmied out of her panties and placed them on top of a row of bottles from the Bordeaux region she said,

    – Would you prefer a French or an Italian wine?

    – You decide.

    – Have you ever tasted Dolcetto d'Alba?

    – No, but I like the name.

    – It comes from the north of Italy.

She bent over a rack labeled The Piedmont, flipped her skirt over her back and said,

    – It's a bit fruity, but very smooth.

    As I entered her I thought, *Ben, you're a very lucky man. You've got yourself a girl who's well-traveled, intelligent, cultivated, and even something of a wine expert.*

On a sunny day in June 1952, Louise and I were married in the Church of the Sacred Heart, the same church in which I'd been baptized. My family—in spite of their doubts about Louise and our marriage—never verbalized their misgivings. No one from Louise's family attended, not even her brother, who she'd claimed was close to her. To her credit, she didn't allow it to affect her good spirits.

    We moved into an apartment in the East Sixties. At first we had a lovely time. Louise went about decorating and I'd never seen her more relaxed and content. We laughed a lot and enjoyed each other's company during those few months. But when the work was finished and every-thing was nicely put together, we had less and less to say to each other. Our sex life went downhill in a hurry—there wasn't much fun in bed anymore. Louise always protected herself so there'd be no children and I never asked for any. I think we both figured that this arrangement was only temporary. We were playing house.

The Actors Studio was the perfect place to get your mind off your prob-lems; you thought only about getting ahead and perfecting your craft. To me that meant becoming the best actor I could be. Not just a school, the Actors Studio was indeed a studio where newcomers and seasoned professionals attended the same two-hour session twice a week. Our spare time was spent rounding up partners and preparing scenes to present at those sessions. Often someone who'd already appeared on Broadway would work with a totally unknown actor.

Strasberg took over all sessions at the Studio in 1952, the same year I entered as a member. Prior to then, he shared teaching responsibilities with Danny Mann. Lee's passion for the theater and for acting was inspiring. But it took courage to face his unsparing judgment. I was there for a couple of months before I had the guts to perform a scene in front of him.

One particular scene, from *Romeo and Juliet,* was not received badly by Strasberg or the class, but it was clear that none of my fellow members were bowled over either. *How could they be?* I thought. Loretta and I had been able to meet only three or four times for a total of maybe five hours. How could anyone do justice to a serious piece of drama, especially Shakespeare, in such short time? I decided I had to find another way to get their attention.

I began to search for a book that could be adapted easily to play form—something we could rehearse for weeks instead of hours, that would show me at my best. Somebody suggested a novel that had recently been published, Salinger's *The Catcher in the Rye*. I read it and thought all I'd have to do is lift the dialogue and I'd have a very interesting play. It would be a perfect project for the Actors Studio.

Holden Caulfield could be a tough part for anyone but I felt I could handle it. I brought the book to the attention of Freddy Sadoff, a fellow member who had already been at the Studio for a couple of years. He read it and said that he would organize everything. Freddy would adapt it, cast it, direct it, and play the lead, Holden Caulfield. I was flabbergasted. The guy was taking the whole thing for himself.

What the hell, I didn't know my way around the place nor did I know any of the other actors, so I told him to go ahead. He figured we could start rehearsals in a couple of weeks.

From time to time I made trips to my old neighborhood, where I'd often run into some kid I grew up with and we'd talk and laugh, recalling our childhood on the streets. I tried to visit every week. My brother was usually there, too, sitting at the small kitchen table waiting for my mother to prepare us delicious food we'd loved as children. Although in time I'd live in fancier and more spacious places, I still consider that modest little apartment on Twenty-ninth Street my only real home.

After one of these visits, I ran into Jackie Passalacqua coming out of his building. "Hi, Jackie," I said. When he turned to greet me, my eyes locked onto the yellow lettering on his workshirt. It read SANITATION DEPARTMENT.

– How long you been working for the City, Jackie?

– About a month. It's got a good future. I mean, if I stay there long enough I get a pension and a lot of benefits.

– I'm happy for you.

But I wasn't happy at all. Jackie had a lot of talent, and here he was riding a truck—maybe for years—picking up garbage, while I'd become part of a place where I could dream of changing my life.

A week before we were to start rehearsals for *Catcher in the Rye*, I got a phone call from a man named Charlie Russell, who produced a weekly half-hour live television show called *Danger*. He told me that Sidney Lumet, the show's director, would like me to star in one of the episodes. Somebody must have suggested me for the part because I wasn't even asked to read for the role. I was surprised and flattered.

My costar was Martin Ritt, an actor who later turned director and who, like Lumet, went on to have a very solid career directing motion pictures. Although we'd never met, Sidney made me feel right at home. Acting with Marty was a pleasure, too. He was generous and made some helpful suggestions. It was the first time I'd heard the expression "framing a moment," that is, slowing down the action so that the audience gets a good look.

We rehearsed three days before the play was broadcast live. There would be no stopping, correcting, or going back if mistakes were made.

You had only one chance to get it right. At certain points, I'd finish one scene and have to race across the studio to another set, changing my shirt and tie as I ran. I'd arrive out of breath but trying to seem cool and calm. It wasn't easy. The shirt wasn't always tucked in all the way, the tie might not hang as it should, but I went on as though nothing were wrong.

Those were the early days of television and I think the public, knowing it was live, forgave us our mistakes, or maybe viewers were simply grateful for free entertainment. People now stayed home, watching everything and anything from the box that was changing their lives. Television soon changed mine, too.

When I walked into my mother's house after the show, her eyes were welled with tears and Louise embraced me. There was pride in Tony's face. I saw that look on a lot of faces on Twenty-ninth Street. People looked at me as if I were a star. They were far more impressed than they'd been about my Boys Club acting, and they let me know that I'd scored in the big leagues. That approval gave me the courage to keep going.

On top of all the praise, I was paid for doing what I loved. I received $250 for that show, and it was the sweetest money I'd ever seen. Working as a paid TV actor gave me more faith in myself when I went into rehearsal for *Catcher in the Rye*. I was now a professional actor and I was on my way. I was making a living.

Freddy Sadoff and I decided that I'd play Ackley, the pimple-faced fellow student Holden considers an utter pain in the ass. A fun part. I had no pimples so I put some black pomade, which my mother once used for boils, on the back of a white handkerchief and wrapped it around my neck as though I had something festering there. I wore my heavy boots but this time over bare legs dressed only in a robe. I wanted a noisy walk that would get on Holden's nerves. These elements gave me an absurd appearance that enhanced the comedy of the scene. I got a lot of laughs.

After rehearsing for weeks we performed it twice for the studio. A lot of older members were in it; I was the youngest in the cast. Despite the fact that Freddy Sadoff was too old to play Holden Caulfield and would never have been cast in the part by anybody else, he wasn't bad. In fact, Kazan liked the show so much, he went to meet the writer, J. D. Salinger, to try to convince him to allow us to mount a professional production. Kazan knew that Salinger had once sold a short story to Hollywood called "Uncle Wiggily in Connecticut." The boys in La-La Land changed the title to *My Foolish Heart*, which starred Susan Hayward and Dana Andrews. It was so soppy and saccharine it could give a person diabetes.

Salinger hated what they did to his story. He never again wanted to deal with the movies, or for that matter, with the theater. But Kazan was the most respected theater director of his time, and he was sure he could convince Salinger to let us adapt his novel. I knew that if Kazan got hold of the project there would be some recasting, but we were still excited by the prospect of a big-time production. Besides, I somehow felt that Kazan would not recast my part. I was good as Ackley and could be even better.

Gadge, as Kazan was also known, returned with the news that Salinger had said that if ever his work were allowed to be staged it would be by the Actors Studio. Nevertheless he'd taken an oath never again to allow anything he wrote to be performed on film or onstage. Well, that was that. Kazan tried again. Still no luck. To this day, *Catcher in the Rye* has never been staged.

A director named Sherman Marx came to one of our performances and asked me to take on an important part in a play starring Claude Rains. The show was to tour the Straw Hat Circuit, that is, theaters along the Eastern Seaboard that put on plays prior to their Broadway opening. Rather than reveal how excited I was, I held on to my composure and said yes. I had seen Claude Rains in many movies: *The Invisible Man, The Phantom of the Opera, Mr. Skeffington, Casablanca*, among others. He was always good. Who wouldn't want to work with him?

This was my first job as a professional stage actor. And my first taste of the actor's high, which I was sure would always be mine for the asking. In time I developed an iron will that has enabled me to travel the peaks and valleys of my career—periods of exciting work alternating with others of no work at all, parts you loved to play and those you *had* to play simply to work or to support yourself and your family.

The Rains play I was to do was called *Jezebel's Husband*, written by Robert Nathan, author of *A Portrait of Jenny*. It was going to be produced by Roger L. Stevens. The cast included Ossie Davis, Eileen Heckert, Brian Keith, and Carmen Mathews. Claude Rains played the biblical Jonah and I played the Prophet Micah, who came out of the desert. Before every entrance I covered my hands, legs, feet, and face with baby oil and rubbed sand all over myself. Then the prop man doused my hair and my clothing with more sand. I looked like a mess but it helped establish the reality of my character. Unfortunately, all this costuming didn't help the play. Although the show was a comedy, there were not many laughs on opening night.

The cast members seemed to be acting in different plays. I was trying hard to bring some reality to my character. Eileen Heckart, with her strong voice and professional know-how, realized where she could get laughs and went after them. Ossie Davis played Jonah's manservant and didn't seem to be having a particularly good time of it. Claude Rains was simply himself. He made no attempt to change physically or vocally. It was the performance I had seen so many times in the movies. But none of this mattered to me. I was just happy to be there.

In order to save the show, new material was added constantly, only to be taken out and replaced by other material when the replacement didn't work either. Through it all, Rains maintained an elegant dignity. It was hard to believe that I was onstage with this big star.

Rains and his wife, Frances, sort of adopted me during the show's run. I took all my meals with them. Claude was the first star I had ever known, and I was sure he liked my work because, with his wife present, he once told me that I could become a very important actor. That almost took my breath away. I was amazed that someone of his stature would think that. He talked about the importance of hard work, of his struggles with a stutter when he was a young man and how he had to persevere to conquer it.

Louise came to see the show during the third week of the tour. The Rainses had always been relaxed and outgoing with me, but it now seemed that their behavior was altered. I saw they were making an effort to be friendly. Louise was a stranger in our midst who interrupted my theatrical honeymoon.

* * *

In 1947 Congressman J. Parnell Thomas and his House Un-American Activities Committee had started a witch hunt for alleged Communists, ex-Communists, and "fellow travelers" in the movie industry. By 1952 the Committee was headed by a merciless representative named John S. Wood. Hundreds of people lost their livelihoods because of their compassion for causes considered left-leaning by these self-appointed inquisitors. There was even a suicide. The blacklisted actor Philip Loeb threw himself from a window after he could get no work. A small group of defiant screenplay writers, dubbed the Hollywood Ten, went to jail for their refusal to answer questions posed by the Committee: "Are you now or have you ever been a member of the Communist Party?" Among them were Dalton Trumbo, Ring Lardner, Jr., Edward Dmytryk, and John Howard Lawson.

Soon Kazan, too, was called to testify before the Committee. In his day it was no surprise that many painters, writers, and theater people sympathized with the oppressed or less fortunate people of the world. Many thought communism was the answer to social inequity. One of these was Kazan. It's no secret that he attended a few Communist cell meetings with fellow members of the Group Theater.

Everyone at the Studio saw the pressure Kazan was under. I asked May Reiss how he was bearing up and she said Gadge was going through hell deciding what he should do. His friends in New York theater circles told him to resist, to answer questions only about himself. The witch hunt would blow over, they told him, there would always be work for him in the theater. But Kazan also wanted to keep his movie career. Darryl Zanuck and Spyros Skouras had told him to clear himself with the Committee or he was through in Hollywood. In other words, to continue working in film, he would have to answer all questions posed to him, including naming the names of friends. And that's just what he did. However, in a move that only made matters worse, Kazan took out a full-page ad in the *New York Times*, defending his position.

That ad sent shock waves through the Actors Studio. The following day there were tears of sorrow and of rage. I even saw a chair fly across the room and smash against a radiator. We loved Kazan but many members of the Studio felt utterly betrayed. And yet Lee Strasberg was silent. We looked to him for guidance but he said not one word about the situation. That morning he tried to begin the session as though nothing had occurred, despite the fact that one of the names Kazan had mentioned was that of his own wife, Paula Strasberg. Unlike other individuals named, the Strasbergs had given Kazan permission to do that. I don't think Lee was ever political, and Paula had no career to speak of, so she had nothing to lose. Besides, her name was already known to the Committee, as were many of the others that Kazan gave them. I had heard that he notified those people, too. But none of this made any difference to those people who saw Kazan as a collaborator. They hated him for what he'd done.

All anyone at the Studio wanted to talk about was Kazan. After a very short session most of the members went over to Joan Copeland's apartment. Everyone asked what should be done. There were many opinions put forth, some sad, some stupid, some angry, some tearful. Joan, the sister of playwright Arthur Miller, would leave the living room every ten minutes to phone her brother. Kazan had directed the brilliant first production of *Death of a Salesman*, and he and Miller were close friends. After one of Joan's many calls to her brother, she announced that Arthur Miller's advice was that we should all resign from the Actors Studio.

It would be fair to say that the political views of the membership were left of center. So were mine, for that matter. You couldn't find one person who approved of what Kazan had done. But upset with him as I was I was even more scared that they would shut down the Studio. What would I do then? Where would I go? Where would *all* us actors go?

After what seemed like an endless repetition of the same speech, people drifted out of the apartment in a daze. Our hero was a stool pigeon. May Reiss, who adored Kazan, left his employ and never spoke to him again. I couldn't take that position; I felt grateful to Kazan for all that he'd done for me. But from that point forward he distanced himself from the Studio. I missed having him around. He'd taken an interest in me and once in a while he'd throw his arm around my neck and ask how things were going. I don't think he realized how important that was to me.

* * *

Not one person ever resigned from the Actors Studio and that was good, because when I was looking for work and having no luck, at least I had a place to go to practice my craft. I used to make the rounds every day. One of my daily stops was the building in Rockefeller Center where NBC had its television studios. I went to all the casting offices in the building and then found my way to the NBC drugstore where I would run into other unlucky and struggling actors. One of them was James Dean. He had recently been made a member of the Actors Studio. We hit it off and soon were keeping each other company while we looked for work.

Jimmy was short but he had presence. He had movie actor good looks, blond hair and blue eyes. You didn't have to be an expert to know he'd photograph well, and his eventual success didn't surprise me.

One day while making the rounds with Jimmy, a casting director suggested that it might be easier for me to get work if I changed my name, made it less Italian, more American. This was said in front of Jimmy, who had an all-American name and an all-American face. I thought of names—Anthony Dane, John Allenby, James Farnsworth, Charles Butler, and so on—but then my father and my Uncle Jack, who was still alive, came to mind. How could I insult them by giving up their name? *Fuck 'em all*, I thought, *I'm keeping it.*

Louise and I invited Jimmy over for an Italian dinner. She called me into the kitchen to taste the sauce before he arrived. The taste was flat. "It needs salt," I said, "and a little peperoncino." Well, I may as well have said it tasted like horse manure. "Call your mother and have her come over and cook the dinner," she shouted as she stormed out of the kitchen and locked herself in the bedroom. It took a half-hour of coaxing and cajoling to get her to come out. During that time, I had added the salt and peperoncino and stirred the sauce. When she reappeared, I told her I was wrong. I had just tasted it again and her sauce was delicious. It had just needed more time to sit. She was pleased.

It amazed me that an intelligent young woman could be prone to a tantrum over a simple disagreement. In order to keep peace, I began to censor my comments, and of course resented having to do so.

When Jimmy arrived, Louise turned on the charm. She was the perfect picture of the happy housewife. Jimmy enjoyed her and so did I. He brought with him a book of pictures on birds and wild animals. He was learning their names. I liked that. As we perused the book, he talked about Strindberg's *The Ghost Sonata*. I didn't know the play but Jimmy was intrigued by it and asked if I would be interested in participating with him in a reading of it at the studio. I said yes, but somehow we never got around to it.

That evening I told Jimmy about a project I'd been asked to be part of. Jack Garfein, another member of the Actors Studio, told me that he had met a writer named Calder Willingham. Calder had adapted his novel *End as a Man* into a play, and asked Jack to see what could be done with it. Jack was a short man with a shock of red hair, fair skin, and bright blue, intelligent eyes. I had first seen him at the Dramatic Workshop in a play called *The Burning Bush*. In it, Jack had an emotional and passionate courtroom scene that I still remember. I was pleased to be asked to work with him because I was sure that he knew something about acting.

At first Jack offered me the part of Marquales, the good guy, but I was more captivated by Jocko De Paris, the so-called villain of the piece. Jocko's mind is swift and his verbal assaults are diabolically clever and witty. Looking through Jimmy's book that night I spotted a picture of a black panther. I decided then and there that I would try to make Jocko's attacks be as surprising and graceful as that panther.

Jack assembled some other actors and we rehearsed late into the night, the only time some of us were available. (I was on the phone all day, selling subscriptions for the *New York Times*.) Jack's work impressed me. He got us talking to each other softly, avoiding the impulse to make "drama." Young actors are always anxious to show pain, rage, to scream and holler, to cry. Sometimes it's more difficult to say "good morning" believably. Jack wanted to be sure that we talked and listened simply. The fourth wall was to be closed, he said, not only during rehearsal but during our performance. What always disturbed me about the small amount of professional theater I'd seen was what they call projection. Too often actors sounded as if they were raising their voices and talking over each other's heads. This wasn't going to happen here.

The members of the cast were strangers to each other so any rapport we built was based not on personal relationships but on those of our characters. There were some good actors involved, too—Arthur Storch, Paul Richards, Albert Salmi, William Smithers, and Pat Hingle, the only real southerner among us.

In no time, Jack had us feeling—really knowing—our characters so well that when it was time to turn on the heat and make dramatic points, our acting was natural and unforced. This approach got bigger laughs than if the funny moments were "framed" to signal comedy for the audience. No one raised his voice to be heard, yet we were all heard. Nobody pushed a moment for effect or to make a point and, because of that, things became intimate and more intriguing. Jack gave me faith that the power of my performance would lie in its quiet simplicity.

One of the primary lessons we learned at the Actors Studio was that acting was not only internal but also involved the way a person walked, talked, and dressed. I combined Jocko's military bearing with what I imagined was a panther's feline grace, striving to insinuate hidden danger. As I worked on the character, I found that Jocko unleashed anger, even rage, in me that I had never experienced in life but could safely express while being someone else. It came out surprisingly, often when least expected, even by me. This gave Jocko his unpredictable power.

The first time we played *End as a Man*, I sneaked a look at the audience. Seated in the first row were Tennessee Williams and his agent, Audrey Wood, who handled many other successful playwrights, among them William Inge (*Bus Stop*), and Robert Anderson (*Tea and Sympathy*). Cheryl Crawford was seated in the same row dressed in her signature pantsuit, with Lee Strasberg next to her in a dark shirt and tie. To Strasberg's left was Kazan, wearing a light blue workshirt rolled up at the sleeves. He was the only one in that lineup who gave the impression that he was ready to enjoy himself. Tennessee was smoking a cigarette through a much shorter version of the cigarette holder I would be using in my entrance as Jocko De Paris. I saw that he was talking to Gadge and sharing a laugh. That made me nervous. My stomach started doing somersaults. *You'd better be good, Ben.*

I was hoping my costume would make a splash. Jack Garfein and I had come up with an attention-getting wardrobe. I wore a white army hat with visor, a dark red silk shirt, black silk shorts, black silk socks held up by black garters, and shiny black shoes. The audience would get a good look at my legs, which weren't bad.

Once we started the first scene, where Hingle and I tormented a couple of freshman plebes, we had the audience on our side. I knew the play was funny but Calder Willingham's dialogue got more laughs than I'd expected. The audience was riveted. Loud and long applause erupted after the first act.

The character I played has created mayhem and gotten away with it. Finally, he overreaches himself and, despite the fact that his father is the school's leading donor, Jocko is kicked out. In the scene where the fellow cadets take me away, Jack threw in a surprise: two or three of those cadets were played by people who had not been in the scene before. One was James Dean. He had no lines but his look conveyed the severity of his character. Jimmy was really thinking, even in this tiny part. Some actors have eyes that tell a story all by themselves.

That night was a big success. However, we were to do *End as a Man* just once more; a two-night run was typical of the Actors Studio. I went to Jack and told him we were fools if we didn't try to take the show off-Broadway, where I was sure it would succeed. I kept the pressure on and eventually he came up with someone who could make that happen. Her name was Claire Heller, and Jack had met her at the Dramatic Workshop, where she was studying to be an actress. Her father was rich, he gave her the money to invest in our show.

We mounted the production for $6,000 and Claire became our producer. We opened downtown at the Theatre de Lys in Greenwich Village in October 1953. My brother escorted my mother, who sat next to the famous newspaper columnist Leonard Lyons. My mother had no idea who he was but she turned to him, at one of my particularly villainous moments in the play, and said: "Benny is not like that, Benny is a good boy." The following day, my mother's remark was the lead item in Lyons's *New York Post* column.

I was twenty-three years old and starring in a smash hit, receiving the best reviews any young actor could hope for. So, who comes backstage? Mr. Metcalf, my former boss from the hotel in Miami. "I'm proud of you, Ben. I'm glad I fired you. See, if I hadn't fired you, you might have still been down there."

End as a Man was the first Actors Studio production to be embraced by the major New York critics. Walter Kerr of the *New York Herald Tribune* especially applauded our work. He made it clear in his review that something new and exciting was happening among these young members of the Actors Studio. We had done something that even Kazan had failed to do. Just before my time at the Studio he'd mounted a production of a play called *Sundown Beach* starring Julie Harris, Steven Hill, and a lot of other good actors. It opened at the legendary Belasco Theatre in September 1948 and closed after only seven performances.

I'd guess our show could have run in Greenwich Village for years, but somebody decided that we should take the production to Broadway. The argument went that our reviews had been so overwhelmingly positive that they would translate into big business on the Great White Way.

Once it was decided to move the play uptown, Lee Strasberg finally came to see it. With him was Clifford Odets. They liked what they saw. Strasberg's remarks to us had only to do with pace and the picking up of cues. Odets suggested that, to make it easier on the audience, a psychological reason be given to explain why my character behaves as he does. I didn't know if he was right, but I was willing to trust him. This was the first time I'd met Odets but I'd read his plays and I'd done some scenes from *Golden Boy* and *Night Music*. He was very down to earth, speaking to Jack and me as equals. For Odets this was a work session among collaborators.

Jack and I were in the middle of a heated discussion as to whether we should try some of the things we were told by Odets and Strasberg, when Calder Willingham walked into the room. Jack told him of Odets's input. Calder's face swelled with anger. "You could stand on your head and piss before I write that kind of bullshit."

Although we worked on Lee's suggestions, we soon decided they hurt the rhythm of what we had so carefully created. We would stick with what brought us to the party. But we ran into problems; a new and more intricate set had to be devised for Broadway along with a more elaborate lighting scheme. And unlike the Greenwich Village production, the stagehands had to be paid union wages no matter what the show was taking in. In the end, we couldn't make a go of it. We struggled for about four months and it was decided to close the show.

After the curtain fell on closing night, none of us walked away. We just wandered around in silence. It was as if nothing would have ended if we only remained onstage. We had worked hard to make something special and now it was over. Finally we hugged and said our good-byes. I left the stage.

The backstage area was dark but as I approached my dressing room I could make out the familiar figure of a man. As I approached, I saw the silver hair. It was Mr. Sinclair. I stopped in my tracks. How often had I thought about finding out where he lived and going to see him. And now he'd come to see me, in the theater, the place I'd learned to love through him. He had tears in his eyes. "Ben," he said, "you've made me very proud." No review I had ever received meant as much to me as his words. Suddenly closing night was a very happy event.

At the time, a lot of actors were going to psychiatrists. Everyone seemed to want to know, Why am I unhappy? I knew *I* wasn't happy. I wasn't even able to enjoy the stunning success I'd recently had. But I wasn't about to see one of those guys who said absolutely nothing while you lay there for fifty minutes a day, day after day, week after week, year after year, free-associating with the hope of collecting the clues that would lead you to an understanding of why your life was so miserable.

No. If I needed to expose myself, I wanted to sit up and look into the man's eyes. I asked around and, lo and behold, what did I find? A psychiatrist who had charm, empathy, and loved the theater. He was also Italian, which made me feel even more comfortable. His name was Dr. Ferruccio DiCori. I liked my sessions with him because whenever I ran out of material about my life, we talked about plays and performances we enjoyed. It was like sitting with a colleague.

The Korean War had been going on for a year or more when I got a notice from my draft board to report for a physical exam prior to induction. I didn't take this too well. I was convinced that if they sent me to Korea I would die; my body would be found under a huge pile of other bodies on Pork Chop Hill or any other of the thousands of hills they had over there. My brother Tony had been eager to serve in World War II, when there had been real villains to crush—Hitler, Mussolini, Tojo. Everyone knew what was at stake. But I don't think anyone knew who the leader of Korea was or why we were fighting that war in the first place. I'm convinced that Dr. DiCori came to my rescue.

After having breezed through the physical part of the exam, I was led into a small office where a distinguished-looking man interviewed me.

– How long have you been seeing a psychiatrist, son?

– About six months, sir.

– Has it been helpful?

– I think so, sir.

– Good luck to you.

And that was that. I was 4F. I didn't have to go and die in a war that few people seemed to care about.

Chapter 6

GOOD LUCK, BAD LUCK

WHEN I WAS CAST TO PLAY BRICK IN *CAT ON A HOT TIN*
Roof, it was a dream come true. Every actor wished to be in a Tennessee Williams play directed by Elia Kazan. Kazan had not been abandoned. He lost friends but he worked in film and in the theater whenever he wanted to. And despite the controversy surrounding him, most actors would have killed to work with him, too. He was the "actors' director," and he had chosen me to work with. I couldn't believe my good fortune.

Four days before rehearsals began I found myself staring at stained yellow window shades in a second-rate Greenwich Village hotel. Louise and I had argued; I spent my days and nights alone in that hotel. All my attention was on the character I would have to bring to life. I'd seen how Williams's plays gave actors the material they could delve deeply into— the glorious Laurette Taylor in *The Glass Menagerie* and the electrifying Marlon Brando in *A Streetcar Named Desire*. How would I pull it off?

When I arrived at the New Amsterdam Roof, near Times Square, where we were to rehearse, everybody was already seated around a large wooden table: Elia Kazan, Tennessee Williams, Barbara Bel Geddes, Burl Ives, Mildred Dunnock, Pat Hingle, and Madeleine Sherwood. Seated nearby facing them were Audrey Wood and the producer Roger Stevens of the Playwrights' Company.

Nobody got up or even said hello. They looked at me in silence. I was

embarrassed because I'd arrived late. I told some lame excuse about the
cab catching a lot of traffic. The truth was that I had taken a subway and
daydreamed my way past the Forty-second Street station. I wound up
way uptown and had to double back.

But once the reading began, all else was forgotten. To hear Tennessee's vivid dialogue being spoken by these fine actors was a revelation.
The play became much more than I imagined when I'd read it on my
own. During the lunch break Kazan suggested that we all go up to Jo
Meilziner's studio to look at a miniature mock-up of the set. Jo was the
top set designer of that time. When I saw what he'd done, I realized why
Kazan thought it important that we see it. The set was simple and it had
power. There were no walls and the stage would be raked: sloping so that
its lowest point reached the third row of theater seats (the first two rows
had been removed). There was an organic reason for the raked stage.
Bringing speeches down front became something like a close-up in the
movies. The audience felt closer to you and could look into your eyes.
Kazan had only recently made a couple of very successful films, *On the
Waterfront* and *East of Eden*. With these films in mind, I realize now
(though I couldn't see it then) that he was playing with space, trying to
bend the formality of theater space. The second act especially benefited
from that set. Almost the entire act is a confrontation between Brick and
his father, Big Daddy, played by Burl Ives, who was big, heavy, and pow-
erful-looking. Kazan staged the act as though he were choreographing in
a bullring. Big Daddy was the torero, prodding and poking, insisting on
the truth about his son's drinking and melancholia, and I, as his son, was
the reluctant bull. At one rehearsal, I stepped out and suggested that we
could get a gasp from the audience if, when Big Daddy pulled the crutch
out from under me, I would be able to fall headlong onto the gallery,
breaking my fall at the very last second. My head would wind up hanging
over the first row of patrons. Gadge looked at me, smiled, and said,

– You want to be a director someday, don't you?

– I never thought about it but now maybe I'll start.

All the action in the play takes place in Brick's and Maggie's bedroom. The only furniture was a bed and a stand where Brick could refill

his drink. He's been injured during a sporting event and he's drinking a lot. His leg is in a cast and he uses a crutch throughout the play. I had to find a way to move like the athlete he was. And I had to make his melancholy and reticence understandable. The audience had to be made aware of his painful secret.

BRICK
> Why can't exceptional friendship, real, real, deep, deep friendship between two men be respected as something clean and decent without being thought of as—

BIG DADDY
> It can, it is, for God's sake.

BRICK
> . . . It was too rare to be normal, any true thing between two people is too rare to be normal. Oh, once in a while he put his hand on my shoulder, or I'd put mine on his, oh, maybe even, when we were touring the country in pro football an' shared hotel-rooms, we'd reach across the space between the two beds and shake hands to say goodnight, yeah, one or two times we—

He's married to a beautiful woman, and I had to make it clear to viewers that rejecting Maggie doesn't come from his dislike or disgust, but instead from the death of Skipper, the friend he'd loved with a love he never admitted, even to himself. The loss of Skipper leads Brick to more and more booze and even greater disgust with people's mendacity, especially his own.

Gadge liked what I was doing. I had heard that he got his nickname, Gadge, from the fact that he often came up with the perfect gadget to make something work. He kept his direction to a minimum, letting me find my own way. I worked on reaching into myself to find the broken part of Brick. On the whole, rehearsals went well, but Tennessee thought that Barbara Bel Geddes, who played Maggie the cat, wasn't enough of a cat, not complex enough. She was much too wholesome for his taste. He was looking for something more neurotic, but I'm sure that Kazan had cast Barbara precisely for that wholesome quality. Theatergoers loved Barbara and therefore she would be able to make audiences embrace this complicated and not always likable character. Gadge was absolutely right about that.

But Tennessee felt there were problems during the scene where Barbara is on her knees embracing my legs and making a plea for me to take her to bed. Tennessee said something like, "Gadge, she's fuckin' with my cadence." He may have thought he was whispering but Tennessee had a deep, mellifluous voice which at that moment was too loud. And he'd been drinking. Well, I looked over and Barbara was gone. She'd run off the stage in tears, so I went after her to console her. When I came back Gadge looked at me for a long time and said, "You're a nice guy." I didn't understand. Wasn't it normal to help a lady in distress?

Mildred Dunnock played Big Mama. When she came onstage you saw a lean, almost frail-looking woman, but her vocal equipment was commanding. In most of her entrances she was followed by Pat Hingle, who played Brick's brother, and Madeleine Sherwood, who had the part of Pat's wife. Here again, Pat was the only southerner in a play about the South. There was an innocence in his performance that made his character's greed less melodramatic. I was shown Millie Dunnock's motherly affection both as Big Mama's son Brick and as Millie's fellow actor Ben. I will never forget her warm, comforting smile.

Before leaving for out-of-town tryouts, we had a run-through on the stage of the New Amsterdam Roof. This was the first time I met Marilyn Monroe. The time she came backstage, she wore no makeup, her hair was windblown, she was girlish and very pretty, and she was ecstatic about what she'd seen. She arrived with Lee Strasberg, who liked it—in fact, he was very enthusiastic, which made me proud.

We opened in Philadelphia to great reviews. William Faulkner came to see it, as did Carson McCullers and John Steinbeck. One day in the bar of the St. James Hotel where we were all staying, they were seated at the same table. Kazan invited me over and as I sat down, I thought, *My God, look who I'm sitting with.* I felt pretty inadequate. But they were pleasant and complimentary about my work. They talked about fishing, hunting, and good restaurants, but not one word about literature. *They do it, so why should they talk about it?*

Only two days before we were to open on Broadway, Tennessee and Kazan came backstage. Tennessee said, "If you like Maggie too much, Ben, then we have no play. If Brick likes her, we have nothing." In those days you couldn't be open about homosexuality on Broadway. It would not sell. So Tennessee clouded the matter masterfully. What probably disturbed him was that I was not cold enough toward her. Gadge said, "Distance yourself from her, Ben."

So I tried something I didn't have much faith in but took a chance on anyway. At the time of the New York opening my performance was still pretty much intact. The play received terrific notices and the critics raved about my acting, using words like "marvelous." But that confused me even more. What the hell was going on? Why were Williams and Kazan asking me to tamper with a good performance? Even though I didn't fully understand what the hell they wanted, I tried to do it. I tried to distance myself, but didn't really believe it, so I never found a believable way to do it.

A month into the New York run, I decided I couldn't make their idea work. I needed to reverse direction to find my original performance. I'd felt that it had always been clear to the audience that Brick won't go near his wife because he's mourning the loss of his friend Skipper. To me, mixing the affection that had once existed between Brick and Maggie was far more interesting than the changes I was being asked to make. But when I tried to get back to that original performance, I found myself being tentative and my vocal energy was low, so low that it resembled my work in the beginning of rehearsals, when I was still finding my way, working to get ahold of my character. One night, from the balcony of the Morosco Theatre, someone yelled "Louder!" It happened on other nights, also. It was the actor's nightmare, the audience demanding something you can't give. I knew Barbara heard it, too. What was she thinking? I felt a hot blush of embarrassment. I was mortified, but I didn't know what to do, where to go for help. Kazan was in Greece on vacation. The character of Brick had been my creation but I felt Gadge and Tennessee had damaged it. In fact I never got it back to what it first had been. I was starring in my Broadway debut and I should have been thrilled. But instead of *Cat* being an event for me to enjoy, it had become a problem. Going onstage was no longer fun. I had to find my way back. I was determined to slow things down, to simplify my movements and remain in the moment until Brick was again fully realized. I knew then that only by going moment to moment would I recapture what I'd lost.

One night, midway through my run in *Cat*, I was leaving the Morosco after a performance and ran into Kim Stanley, who was standing in front of the Music Box Theater and talking to a woman I didn't know. It was Elaine Stritch. They were appearing in William Inge's *Bus Stop*. I knew that Kim was probably the best actress around but I knew nothing about Elaine. Nevertheless I liked her right away. Elaine was outgoing and had an exuberant smile. She suggested we all have a drink at Downey's, a favorite meeting place for actors. These ladies were friendly, they were charming, and they sure knew how to drink.

From that night on, Elaine and I saw quite a bit of each other. She was older than I was and had been acting longer, too. She was determined to have fun, in the process teaching me a lot about the best champagnes, scotch whiskeys, and how to avoid thinking long about anything too serious. Although she was ribald, Elaine was never vulgar. She was loud without being pushy. Gay guys and gals were mad about her, and so was I.

She lived in an apartment in an upscale part of the East Side. The place had a forest-green rug, green drapes, a bedroom lined with bookshelves, but few books. Instead they were filled with expensive-looking dolls of every shape and color.

Her bar, on the other hand, was well stocked. There was scotch, bourbon, gin, vodka, brandy, sherry, and dry vermouth. The refrigerator held at least three bottles of French champagne at all times. We were in the happy, drinking days when booze would simply loosen your tongue, make you talkative, charming, expansive, and amusing, when getting drunk was thought to be truly comical and smoking "didn't" cause cancer.

I spent a good deal of time in that apartment, but I didn't move in. My clothes remained at my place. I did, however, invest in a new razor, a comb, and a toothbrush. And although I slept there regularly we made love only on rare occasions. Being a good Catholic girl, Elaine struggled with a lot of sexual hang-ups, as did many of the Irish Catholic girls I grew up with.

The first time we lay together embracing and kissing, slipping and sliding on her expensive silk sheets, I was very excited. She was nude except for her panties, which I, of course, tried to remove. The dialogue went something like this,

– No, Ben.

– Yes, Elaine.

– I don't think so.

– I think so.

– I have to go to confession tomorrow.

– This is not a sin, it's a pleasure, believe me.

– I know. That's my problem.

And that's more or less the way it went.

The sex when it happened was terrific, but who knew how long it might be until the next time? Here was a woman who loved sex but was afraid of it. Slowly it became less and less important to our relationship. I often thought of those overheated times with another Irish Catholic girl—my childhood sweetheart, Margie Sheridan. She allowed me to kiss and fondle her until both of us were puffing and panting, but then she put a stop to it. This was exciting torture. Inside the grown-up Elaine Stritch was a young girl frightened of going all the way. I guess I enjoyed the challenge. Besides, Elaine kept me laughing.

It was late August and my commitment to *Cat* had come to an end. After my last performance, Barbara Bel Geddes hosted a supper party in my honor at Downey's. The entire cast was present, as were my mother and my brother Tony.

Barbara had been to Sicily, so she and my mother talked about that, particularly the splendid Greek temples of Agrigento, the province my mother was born in. I saw that with Barbara she was making a concerted effort to unbreak her English, to speak clearly. She did very well, too. My mother had taken care to look her best that night, putting on a bit of rouge—something she never did when my father was alive. Here was a woman of another era and culture, mixing nicely with some of the most important theater people of the day. I was proud of her.

Burl Ives brought along his guitar and after dinner, he tuned his instrument and sang:

> *All day, all night, Marianne*
> *Down by the seaside sifting sand*
> *Even little children love Marianne*
> *All day, all night, Marianne*

Burl had made his name as a folk singer. In spite of his lumbering size, his voice was surprisingly intimate and gentle. My brother had seen him in concert years before, and Burl was pleased to hear that Tony was even able to tell him some of the songs he had performed that day.

Barbara motioned to Jim Downey, Sr., the owner, who scurried away. When he returned he carried what I guessed to be a poster or something similar. But it was far more precious than that. It was a beautifully framed Picasso lithograph. "It's called *Inez with Child*," Barbara said. "It's for you, from us."

There was applause. Then Burl took my hand, squeezed it tightly, and said, "I'm going to miss you." Barbara had tears in her eyes when she said, "You're a bad boy to be leaving us." And Millie Dunnock whispered in her embrace, "Take care of yourself."

Two days later, I was on a train headed for El Paso, Texas. Louise and I had finally agreed to a Mexican divorce. The paperwork had been prepared, and all I had to do was get to show up and get them stamped. It would all be quick and legal. Louise made things easy.

When she found out about my affair with Elaine Stritch, for

example, I was expecting a jealous scene, an eruption, an earthquake. Instead, she handled herself with style. Sitting across from me, her legs crossed and arms folded, she said, softly, "She's too old for you." Louise seemed to have no problem with my straying, she just didn't like my choice. She knew also that our marriage had lost any zest it might have once had. Better to end it now.

The following morning a van arrived to drive me across the border to Juarez. Waiting inside the van were three men also on their way to sign divorce papers. One of these gentlemen said to no one in particular, "I don't know if I'm doing the right thing." There was no reply from any of us, just a long silence.

The room where the paperwork would be done was large and seedy with a floor covered by a day's worth of cigarette butts. It seemed that not one woman had made the trip to Mexico to rid herself of a husband. Men alone filled the three long lines leading to the two agents—male, of course—who were authorized to put an end to what had once meant so much to each of us. When all was done, a deep sadness took hold of me and didn't let go for some time.

Heading back to New York, I decided to get my mind off my personal life. I reached into my overnight bag and opened the script of my next Broadway play.

A Hatful of Rain was born out of a couple of scenes that I'd done at the Actors Studio. Playwright Mike Gazzo developed those scenes into a play that dealt with a talented musician down on his luck and drinking too much. But Mike hit a creative roadblock with my character, Johnny, and he wasn't able to move forward.

Then, during one of our many walks through the city, Mike and I started talking about an article we'd read in the *New York Times* about drug addiction. We stopped in our tracks and said, almost in unison, "That's it, Johnny's a junkie." Everything fell into place for Mike—the characters of the father and brother were fleshed out and genuine conflicts were developed. The main conflict of course, was drugs. What were they giving Johnny that he couldn't give himself? What could I do to make the part more powerful than it had been at the Actors Studio?

I had some important work ahead of me in searching out the pain at the base of my character, the missing wounded part that drugs allowed Johnny to forget. Once I found that, the play would spring to life, and become something other than just another story about drugs and the horror of withdrawal.

The Studio production had Anthony Franciosa as my brother, Frank Silvera as our father, and Carroll Baker, my wife. Carroll was an especially attractive blonde in her mid-twenties. When I first met her, she was with Jack Garfein. We locked eyes, and I was ashamed of admitting to myself that I was attracted to my friend's girl. She and I rehearsed for weeks, usually at night. During one of our coffee breaks, Carroll told me that she and Jack had parted. I must say I wasn't unhappy about her news. A couple of sexual escapades soon followed with everything ending as quickly as it had begun. It was a run-of-the-play affair. Afterward I heard the news that Carroll and Jack Garfein got married.

We performed *Hatful* at the Actors Studio to mixed reactions. Lee Strasberg had nothing positive to say. The audience was not overly enthusiastic, either, but I knew we were onto something because the material moved me and I was sure it would move others, too. Some producers saw the show but didn't share my passion, and without a producer there'd be no show. For months Mike Gazzo and I were the only ones convinced it would work. Then we met Jay Julien, whom we convinced to take a chance on us.

Jay had sharp features. He was the sort of guy who had trouble trusting anyone or anything. Being a lawyer didn't help. But Mike, director Frank Corsaro, and I eventually got him to loosen up and to start dreaming with us.

Jay had his office on Forty-fourth Street, up the block from the Belasco Theatre. I dropped in often to prod him into making the necessary phone calls to potential investors. Their names were typed on blue cards, and before I even entered his office I shouted, "Get out the blue cards." I still tell Jay that I coproduced *A Hatful of Rain*.

After much pleading the money was finally raised. We were on our way to Broadway at last. But we had no actress to play my wife. Carroll had been good but not really comfortable in the part. And anyway, George Stevens, one of the top movie directors, had cast her in *Giant*, which also featured Elizabeth Taylor, Rock Hudson, and James Dean. Not a bad beginning for a young actress.

Jay got Shelley Winters to read the play. Shelley had won an Academy Award for her supporting performance in *A Place in the Sun*, also directed by Stevens. After some hesitation, she decided to join us. All this took place before Kazan cast me in *Cat*. Because Mike, Jay, and Frank were friends and depended on my being in *Hatful*, I'd asked my agent, Audrey Wood, to get me out of *Cat* within six months instead of the year they were demanding. I was either very brave or very stupid. They could have said no, we'll get another actor. But Kazan and Audrey, who was also Tennessee Williams's agent, made it happen. I was now free to do *Hatful*.

When we got to Chicago, where I was to change trains for New York, I started feeling sick. I had the sweats, then stomach cramps, then nausea. Instead of the train, I took a taxi to the nearest hotel, where I just made it to my hotel room in time to drop my pants, sit on the toilet, and at the same time, vomit into the sink, which, thank God, was nearby.

I'd been stupid. On my way to the van that would take us back to El Paso, I'd stopped at a taco stand. Big mistake. I was drenched with sweat, sitting on the toilet with my head in the sink. I felt lonely as hell. But while I was going through all that, I was telling myself to pay attention to the agony—how it started and what it felt like. *Who knows*, I thought, *maybe it'll come in handy*.

When the train pulled into Grand Central, I was still in bad shape. I could barely walk the length of the station. When I reached my apartment, I headed for the refrigerator, grabbed a half-empty carton of orange juice, and gulped it down. I stripped, jumped into bed, and stayed there for two days. I rose only to go to the bathroom and to drink water. I must have poured gallons of the stuff into my system.

On the third day, I was feeling pretty good. I shaved, showered, dressed in loose-fitting clothes, and headed for the elevator to the lobby.

I was feeling light-headed but with the most cheerful voice I could muster, I greeted my doorman and asked him to get me a cab. I was excited. I was on my way to the first rehearsal for the Broadway production of *A Hatful of Rain*.

The challenge facing our director, Frank Corsaro, was to take a class project and turn it into a professional event. Shelley was the only actor who had not previously done the play and she was confused by the way we worked. Those of us trained at the Actors Studio always attacked a scene from a variety of angles, which made her nervous. When I first met her, she was friendly but suspicious. She didn't quite trust us—or rather, our approach to acting. When she spoke there was a tremolo in her voice that made her seem on the verge of tears. *She's going to be great in this part*, I thought. Over time Frank won her trust and Shelley grew comfortable with us.

In the third act, Tony Franciosa and Frank Silvera, who played the father, had a scene that led to recriminations and violence: the father hits his grown son. One night in Philadelphia, the method thing was carried a bit far. Tony had told Frank that it would help him if he were really slapped hard. Frank let one go, and actually made Tony stagger, so much that you could see he was having trouble remaining standing. He got through the rest of the act but for the curtain calls I had to drape his arm around my shoulder and carry him onstage. That was probably a first for the theater and certainly a first for me.

Before *Hatful*, a drug addict had never been the focus of a play on Broadway. In preparing for the role, I never took heroin and I never knew what it was like to go without it. However, I read a great deal about the effect the drug has on a junkie. At the end of Act II, my character is in need of his fix. He's in pain. To bring that to life I used what we called sense memory, a favorite exercise of Lee Strasberg's. Arguably the most famous example of the power of the senses to recall moments in our past can be found in Marcel Proust's *Remembrance of Things Past*, in the chapter where in tasting a madeleine and sipping a cup of tea the narrator remembers his aunt, an old gray house, the streets along which he used to run errands, the water lilies in the town, the people, and their dwellings. All from a bite of his madeleine and a cup of tea.

By remembering that squalid bathroom in Chicago where I'd been so ill, the furniture, the colors, the smells in that lonely hotel room, I hoped to be able to recall the stabbing pain in the stomach, my body going from fever to chills, and the trembling in my arms and my legs. I was reaching for the pain, the loneliness, and the need for relief that I prayed for that night in Chicago.

We opened out of town in Philadelphia, where the reaction was soft. Jay and I knew right away what was needed. We had a good first act and a powerful third, but the second act needed a confrontation between Johnny and his father. We discussed this with Frank Corsaro and he agreed. Jay and I dashed over to see Mike and on the spot we improvised what we meant. Mike resisted at first but then wrote the scene as suggested— without it, I'm convinced the play would have failed.

Then without warning Shelley Winters's performance took an unexpected turn. She had asked Stella Adler to help her with the part. Along with Strasberg and Sandy Meisner, Stella was considered one of the most perceptive acting teachers. She was a strikingly attractive woman with wavy blond hair. When I was first introduced to her, I had the feeling she was using her big blue eyes to undress me. Stella was upfront about it: she liked men.

I don't know what she told Shelley, but her attack on the part served the play very well. Stella helped her find the emotional center of the character, the concern for her addict husband. The phone call in the final moments, when she has him committed, was for the first time touching. I was impressed that she'd achieved this so quickly. An actor can go weeks, even months, searching for that center and sometimes it just won't come. But one night, when he's not looking or reaching for it, the center appears. There's no better gift an actor can receive.

In the meantime Elia Kazan called me in Philadelphia to say he wanted me to star opposite Carroll Baker in Tennessee Williams's *Baby Doll.* "Do you think you have a hit?" he asked. "We didn't do too well in Philadelphia," I confessed. He said he was on his way to take a look.

The night he came was also the first performance that included our new scene. To our astonishment, we received a standing ovation. I met Kazan at a restaurant near the theater. The first thing he said was that he liked what I was doing with my part, and we both knew that Franciosa's role was flashier than mine, but if the audience wasn't drawn in by my character the play would never work. Gadge said,

– I know what you're up against. You handled yourself the right way. Simple and easy. Like a good movie actor.

– Thanks, Gadge, it's been a struggle.

And then he flashed his sweet Anatolian smile and said,

– Looks like you've got a hit here.

– Just my luck.

– We'll do it another time, Ben.

But that time never came. We never again worked together.

Hatful opened at the Lyceum Theatre on Broadway and was an overnight smash. The curtain calls were amazing. The entire audience was on its feet. As I stood onstage, soaking up the applause, I scanned the house and found who I was looking for. My mother. She was standing with tears in her eyes, looking up at me with a love and a pride I'll never forget. This was only the second time that a production originating at the Actors Studio received rave reviews by the New York critics and brought commercial success. I'd starred in both of them. This fact has never gotten much notice from anyone. What are you going to do?

One critic noted that my performance in *A Hatful of Rain* was "titanic." The rest of the actors in the play started calling me "Benny the Boat." The part also earned me my first Tony nomination. I'd never heard of the award, much less understood how important it was, so I didn't attend the awards dinner where the Tonys were presented. But I am particularly proud of that nomination because there I was, an emerging actor in his mid-twenties, competing with two legends—Paul Muni in *Inherit the Wind*, and Edward G. Robinson in *Middle of the Night*. Of course I didn't win; Muni did.

My agent Audrey Wood was now a member of Lew Wasserman's Music Corporation of America. She really admired my work and expressed a warm, motherly concern for me. In fact, I was the only actor she even represented. I was flattered to be looked after by someone who was also advising some of the best writers in the American theater.

She brought quite a few producers and filmmakers backstage. They had seen my work in *Cat* and *Hatful* and wanted to meet me. I soon began to get a lot of movie offers but I kept turning them down. The bulk of my important work, up to then, had been done in the theater with people I knew and respected—people I also felt safe with. They were like family. And the high quality of material I had worked on spoiled my view of motion picture writing. By comparison film seemed too spare and simple. I wasn't prepared to look at it objectively. I hadn't yet realized the power of images over words.

The legendary Hollywood producer Sam Spiegel came to the rescue. He decided that *End as a Man* would make a good movie, though it would be retitled *The Strange One*. That really got me excited. Sam was an outstanding producer who had recently done *On the Waterfront* and was about to produce *The Bridge on the River Kwai*. I was happy that our project, which we had developed at the Actors Studio, had come so far.

Richard Sheppard was the MCA agent negotiating my deal for *The Strange One*. He'd persuaded Sam to raise considerably his initial offer but I thought we could go even higher. Sam was adamant that he'd go no further. I was about to call his bluff when I received a call from Dick. He said James Dean was pushing to play my part. Jimmy was now a hot commodity, having scored big in *Rebel Without a Cause* and *East of Eden*. Dick Sheppard told me that Jimmy himself had called Sam to try to convince him that he would be far better for the role than I and that Sam was now talking to Jimmy's agent. Jack Garfein, however, was standing behind me all the way.

– I'll be damned. I thought the guy was a friend of mine.

– He's no friend.

– What do you suggest?

– Let's make the deal.

And so we made the deal, but I never talked to James Dean again.

I think that Spiegel became involved not only because he liked the material but also because Jack Garfein was a survivor of the Nazi concentration camps and Sam wanted to help him.

Born and educated in Vienna, Sam left Europe as Hitler and his hooligans were making it clear that Jews were not wanted. He was a cultivated man who spoke English with a charming middle European accent. The size of Sam's belly was testimony to his enjoyment of good food and wine, which was second only to his love of the arts.

Spiegel dropped in on us two or three times during the filming of *The Strange One* in Orlando, Florida, having flown halfway around the world from Ceylon (now Sri Lanka), where he was shooting *Bridge on the River Kwai*. He took me, Jack, and the rest of the cast to dinner, apparently content with what we were doing.

Jack's command of the film surprised me. It was the first movie for all of us but he seemed especially comfortable and assured. There were two actors who had not been in the Actors Studio production: the young, handsome George Peppard, who I had never heard of, replaced William Smithers, and James Olson played the dumb football player that Al Salmi portrayed so well. Jack got them to blend in perfectly. Peppard brought an innocence and vulnerability to the part that helped the story, and Olson got all the same laughs Salmi had gotten. Arthur Storch, who played the butt of all the insults and hazing, took the additional step of having a dentist fit him for an upper plate of very bucked teeth. Onstage he used no visual device to demonstrate how unattractive his character was, but it was decided that on film it would work well. And it did. Paul Richards's comic take on a homosexual who is writing a book about Jocko was as good as ever. And my sidekick, Pat Hingle, with his fear of flouting protocol, was even better on film than he was onstage.

One day, more than midway through the shooting, while we were on the set rehearsing a particularly difficult sequence, Sam came to town for another visit. Usually he was welcomed by everyone, but this time Jack said in a loud voice, "Mr. Spiegel, would you please leave the set?" He had to ask more than once before Sam left. I was dumbfounded. He had given Jack the chance to direct his first movie. Why would Jack turn on his benefactor? I didn't like it at all. If Sam was asking him to do something he disagreed with, it should have been discussed and remedied in private.

Later that day Sam called me into his office. He gestured for me to sit down but then said nothing. He just stared at me in silence. Finally he said, almost to himself,

– I treated that boy like a son.

– Sam, I'm sure Jack is rehearsing his apology right now.

– I will never again allow my heart to lead me anywhere.

Silence.

– I'm going to bring in a very good director to finish the picture. Will you stand behind me, Ben?

There I was, having to choose between a big-time producer who could do me a lot of good and a friend who had stood behind me.

– Sam, you've come so far. There are only two weeks left to go. Please let him finish.

He stared in space a moment.

– Tell him, Ben, I need more close-ups of you.

I didn't know whether he was serious or stroking my ego to gain allegiance. It didn't matter. Jack would complete the picture. But Sam's vengeance was long-lasting and far-reaching. *The Strange One* was a good movie, very well made, but Jack's film career was hurt badly by his run-in with Sam. He messed with the wrong man, and it hurt all of us. Sam never promoted our movie. It was as though he wanted to do nothing to help Jack Garfein succeed. There was no publicity junket, no screenings for opinion-makers. I don't remember doing even one interview. There was a small ad in the *New York Times* and the movie opened at the Astor Theatre on Broadway to decent reviews, but business was soft. At the same time, though, it had opened to spectacular notices in London—for the movie, and particularly for my performance. Many people in England went to see it. But that didn't help any of us in the United States.

* * *

No matter where in the world our work took us, the Actors Studio remained our home. It was the one place all of us could—and did—come back to again and again. In many ways, Lee Strasberg was our stern but caring father. One could easily mistake his demeanor for sadness, but he wasn't exactly an unhappy man. His life was art, music, and theater, all of which he took very seriously. He seemed to have no time for laughter. The Studio was a place where people who were starting a career could not only mix with but also work alongside fellow members who had already made names for themselves in Hollywood or on Broadway. It was a place where, if you were not afraid of Lee's sometimes harsh judgment, you could play parts that no one else would ever cast you in. The Studio was like a well-equipped gym where you could stretch, tune up, and stay in shape. It was not a school; it was where you worked on your craft. There was no other place like it.

In a session at the Actors Studio shortly after shooting *The Strange One*, I saw Lee Strasberg crying. The night before, we'd all heard the news that James Dean had been killed in a car crash. A lot of terrific things had happened to Jimmy since we'd last seen each other. I was sad that his ambition and my pride had put an end to our friendship. When I heard the news I could think only of the days we'd spent struggling to get any kind of job. He'd had a fantastic moment in the sun.

Suddenly Lee was railing against what he saw as the self-destructive behavior of too many of us, whether it be driving too fast or drinking too much. Although he was addressing the class I knew he was talking to me. Not long before, he'd pulled me aside to ask why I drank so much. I don't know how he found out about it, but he had the facts. Despite my surprise and embarrassment, I was touched by his concern. I don't remember how I answered him but it must have been pretty soft. Lee let it pass. Still, his question was a warning: drinking could bring trouble for an actor. However, it remained an important part of my life. Sometimes it was social, sometimes festive. But, of course, there was also troubled drinking, "poor me" drinking, and, worst of all, angry drinking. It consumed too much of my time and it had begun to take its toll on me. Booze was becoming too good a friend. I didn't think I could be an artist if I didn't live on the wild side, drink heavily, go without sleep, fuck around, or even get into brawls. I wanted to live on the edge. Maybe I'd read too much Hemingway.

One Tuesday, I was sitting in the back row at the Studio with Marilyn Monroe on my right. Lee was now allowing celebrities to monitor our classes. Even though she wore no makeup Marilyn looked terrific. Everyone seemed to like her, too, including me. I think we all respected the fact that the best-known woman in America wanted to learn more about her craft.

That day two actors were performing a scene from "The Cat," a short story by Colette. The actors were in bed, apparently naked under silk sheets—rolling around and kissing with tongues flying into wide-open mouths. But the acting was not very good. Marilyn turned to me and asked if I would like to work on that scene with her. As exciting as that would be, I didn't think it was such a good idea, so I told her I wasn't up to working at the Studio just then. She looked at me sternly and said, "What's the matter, don't you want to grow?" A perfect straight line if there ever was one! I had no easy punch line to come back with.

There was a cafeteria across Ninth Avenue on Forty-fourth Street, and after the studio sessions, Lee and a group of us would often stop there for lunch. On one occasion he spoke about an idea for a class project. He'd always thought that in the productions of *Macbeth* he'd seen, the reason for Lady Macbeth's control over her husband was never made clear. He'd seen the part played well but never with the sexuality that could make her spell over Macbeth entirely understandable. He thought that he might work on it with me and Marilyn. I came close to choking on my tuna fish sandwich.

Marilyn was delightful. She spoke in an adorable little whisper, which worked very well for the movies, but Lady Macbeth would be strutting her stuff on a large stage and it was doubtful that Marilyn would ever be heard past the second row. That didn't deter Lee. He obviously had a mad, fatherly crush on Marilyn and thought he could help her do just about anything. Yes, he thought it, but alas, he couldn't.

— CHAPTER 7 —

DRINKING, DANCING, DREAMING

IN 1957, THE PHONE DIDN'T RING AS OFTEN AS IT HAD IN recent years. At this point, offers from Hollywood would have been very welcome indeed. I was afraid the boat had sailed, that I'd allowed my moment to pass. Even my run of three hit plays in a row was not followed by a new play. Things were slow, and I knew that only another piece of exciting work would heat up my career again. I was determined not to show any anxiety—not even to my family—and I never discussed my disappointment with anyone. My pride was stronger than my pain. Rather than redoubling my efforts, or hiring a PR firm, or admitting to anyone that things were bad, I found a bar.

Harold's Show Spot was home to gamblers, Broadway sharpies, a few actors, and one or two writers, all waiting for their luck to change. No Eugene O'Neill gin mill could compare to Harold's for pipe dreams, for sad and funny stories, where a winner never had a good yarn but a loser could entertain you all night long. Nobody there ever asked, "What's happening? How are things going?" Nobody was doing much so those questions were taboo. They might embarrass somebody. Harold's was a perfect spot for the down and out.

Elaine Stritch was still in my life at the time but she kept me on a long leash. I felt no pressure from her. I played the field, finding women here and there. All this changed one night at a cocktail party on the Upper East Side. A lovely blonde said to me in a charming accent,

91

– I've seen all your work, daahling. You're wonderful.

– I'll bet I know who you are.

– Who am I?

– You're one of the Gabor girls. The prettiest one. You're Eva.

– You're sweet. What are you doing after the party?

Every man's dream.

—I have nothing planned.

– Would you like to go dancing?

So we went dancing. Then had supper. Afterward, we went back to Eva's apartment in the annex of the Plaza Hotel. Sometime during the night she prepared a bubble bath for me. I slid into the tub and she placed a tray of cheese and fruit on a stool nearby. Eva sat on the edge of the tub and fed me, slowly and playfully, one grape at a time. That was a first for me (and, I might add, it hasn't happened since). She was rewarding me for the pleasure she'd had. Lying in the warm water, I felt like a pasha. But did I need a reward? It was a pleasure to be with a woman who enjoyed sex as much as I did.

With Eva the champagne flowed at places like El Morocco, where we would dance, 21, where we would dine, and Chez Vito, where we would have our nightcaps surrounded by serenading Hungarian violinists. The music often brought tears to her eyes.

– Oh Ben, I try not to cry when I hear these songs, but I always do.

– It's got a lot of feeling.

– Daahling, I want to take you to Budapest.

– We should do that someday.

I was living a playboy's life and loving it. But I told myself all this was only temporary, that my work awaited me. I'd be broke soon anyway. More than once I wondered how much longer my meager savings would last. Thank God for dinners at the Gabors.

These took place in the town house Magda Gabor owned with her husband, Tony Gallucci, who had made his fortune in construction. Magda was the oldest of the three sisters, followed by Zsa Zsa, then Eva. I must have had dinner with the sisters half a dozen times at that town house, along with their mother, Jolie, whom they adored. I never heard a cruel or sardonic remark from any of the sisters toward one another, either. A lot has been said and written about the Gabors, but I've never come across anything that mentioned their warmth and generosity. They were a family and they loved each other.

Once at the Gabors I met Marlene Dietrich, to whom I made the mistake of calling someone a narcissist. One of her eyebrows went up, she gave me a withering look and said, "Well, Ben, everybody in this world needs a good share of narcissism to survive." Eventually, but very slowly, she warmed to me.

Since Eva and I saw each other only at night, I had no idea what she did with her days. I was therefore taken aback one day when she invited me to a preview of a play she was doing off-Broadway. It was Franz Wedekind's *Lulu*, and it was at precisely that moment I realized we'd never discussed our careers.

I was told to go backstage, where Eva would see to it that I was seated properly. The place was abuzz with activity. The door to Eva's dressing room was open. She stood in front of a full-length mirror and there, kneeling on the floor, fiddling with the hem of her gown, was Marlene Dietrich. To my surprise, here was a legend helping a friend through opening-night jitters. Marlene was there to lend her support.

Eva didn't have the emotional depth or physical size to do the role of Lulu full justice, but the audience seemed to like her. Her sweet voice and Hungarian accent lent her a warm stage presence. I still remember the line of hers that brought down the house: "I wish I had been born a man so that I would have the pleasure of knowing me."

Later, en route to Magda's town house, I said I was proud of her but jealous of her performance. Ever since I was a boy, the sound of applause made me want to get onstage. *I have to find a play to do*, I thought.

When we reached Magda's, the actor George Sanders was there. Though he had recently been divorced from Zsa Zsa, he was still family as far as the Gabors were concerned. He said little and ate even less. He wasn't at all the urbane and imperious man he portrayed in *All About Eve*. Instead I sensed a profound sadness in him. Years later, he killed himself, leaving behind a suicide note that read simply, "I'm bored."

Many people dropped in to congratulate Eva on opening night. One of the guests was Noël Coward. Although I had met him a few times before, I wasn't prepared for his charm and friendly wit. At one point he sat at the piano and started playing softly. Eva walked up to him and whispered in his ear. Noël nodded, then Eva called for everyone's attention and said,

– Daahlings, Noël is going to play some songs from his new musical *Sail Away*.

Everyone was excited, none more than me. We gathered around the piano, standing and sitting wherever we could fit in. Noël proceeded to perform the entire score. Some songs were good, others not so good, but here was a master entertainer at work. It was one of those evenings one never wants to come to an end.

Still, the highlights of my visits to Magda's house were actually the times I spent alone with her husband. Tony cried a lot. I think that in me he thought he'd found a kindred spirit—an Italo-American he could level with, who would understand him. In his gravelly voice he would talk about his dead mother, sip some scotch, and cry. He told me all about his father, also dead, sip some scotch, and cry. And sometimes he talked about how he had built his good fortune, sip some scotch, and cry.

Some weeks later, Eva and I attended a play at the Royale Theatre, across the street from Harold's. At intermission I suggested that we go over for a drink. Well, Harold put on the dog. He treated her with the respect and deference reserved for royalty. She asked for a glass of champagne and he had Ray open a bottle of Dom Perignon. "On the house," Harold said. At first the rest of the boys watched in awed silence, but they soon had Eva in conversation. She fell right in with the humor and camaraderie of the place. Harold gave Eva a sort of code name. She was Hungarian so he decided on "The Goulash." That way, when he would ask after her, no one would know to whom he was referring. He was protecting my privacy.

Audrey Wood and Lew Wasserman were excited by Metro-Goldwyn-Mayer's interest in me starring with Elizabeth Taylor in the movie version of *Cat on a Hot Tin Roof.* Wasserman suggested I come out to the coast to meet George Cukor, the famed director who was slated to direct it. He said the studio heads at M-G-M were also anxious to get a look at me.

In those days, airports wheeled aluminum stairs up to the plane when it rolled to a stop. As I descended, Wasserman was there waiting. He was a tall, lean man and had a long, Lincolnesque face. I was more than a little surprised that he had come to meet me. He suggested that we keep my luggage in his car and drive directly to lunch. He took me to Romanoff's, where Hollywood big shots gathered.

Michael Romanoff himself led us to a booth where two middle-aged men were waiting. The graying George Chasen and the dark-haired Ed Henry were the top motion picture agents at MCA. We said our hellos, and while the waiter was taking our orders, Gregory Peck stopped by the table to say hello, followed later by Lana Turner, John Huston, and Humphrey Bogart. Wasserman got an awful lot of respect.

He turned to me.

– I thought you should meet George and Ed. They'll be looking after you.

Ed said,

– We expect big things, Ben.

George gave me a friendly look, smiling expectantly.

– There's no doubt in our minds that you'll be a superstar.

Ed was very serious when he said,

– That'll mean a considerable amount of money. I hope you have a clever business manager.

George added,

– With taxes like they are, he's going to have to come up with some creative deductions.

Holy Christ, I thought, *is this really happening?* While they went on talking, in my mind I was already spending the money. I would move my mother to a building with a doorman. She'd also have a maid who'd do the cleaning and the laundry that she'd been doing for too long. My mother wouldn't have to find the sun in that place, it would shine through every window.

And I started dreaming about traveling. I'd go to Italy. I'd finally see France. Spain. The Hawaiian Islands. India. Katmandu. You name it. What a time I'd have!

The waiter brought a bottle of red wine. He poured a little into Wasserman's expensive-looking crystal glass, waiting for his approval. Lew twisted the glass back and forth and stared into it, as the dark red liquid rolled around. He put his nose to it, then took a small sip. He nodded his head, and the waiter served everyone. I drank a bit of that wine, and thought, *I'm in the same room with so much glamour and power. And they're telling me that I'll soon be part of it.* It seemed like only yesterday that I'd been in a cellar on the East Side of Manhattan, helping my father make a wine that I swear was much better than the expensive stuff we were drinking.

After lunch, Ed Henry drove me over to M-G-M in his beautiful blue BMW. Benny Thau, the head of production, had his office in the Irving Thalberg Building. Thau liked me and was pushing hard for me to costar in *Cat*.

When we walked in his office, three men were awaiting our arrival. They rose. The only face I recognized was that of George Cukor, director of stars like Garbo, Joan Crawford, and Katharine Hepburn. I had seen his photo many times. Benny Thau introduced himself and the others. Among them was Eddie Mannix, who had a lot of clout in the company. Thau couldn't have been more gracious and enthusiastic. He had seen my performance in New York and was very impressed; I was sure he wanted me in the film. Mannix was friendly but less demonstrative. He had not seen the play. Neither had Cukor, who said he'd heard from friends that I had been wonderful. The meeting ended on an upbeat note and Cukor asked me to come with him.

He led me down a long, narrow corridor into a very small office. It was barren and obviously not in use. It was dark but he didn't turn on the lights. He sat down and started peppering me with questions about the Broadway production. He was most interested in how Kazan handled the homosexual themes that are made explicit in the play. When I told him that the word was never mentioned by anyone, ever, he smiled. We talked for about fifteen minutes, and as he shook my hand he said, "See you soon."

I walked back to the main entrance, where Ed Henry was waiting. I found myself whistling, which I rarely ever did. I was happy. Ed was obviously ecstatic, too. He thought they wouldn't even demand a term contract, which was the norm when a studio offered an important role to an actor.

I was back in New York for only a few days when Ed called to say that he was close to making the deal and would call me the following day. Where would I be at about seven P.M. Eastern time? I told him that I'd be at my mother's. He took the number and I wished him luck.

My mother was about to put the spaghetti into the boiling water when the phone rang. I knew it was L.A. Ed Henry's voice told the story. Before he even began the explanation, my stomach turned over twice. He told me that Cukor had walked away from the project, so everything had been put on hold. He didn't know what was going to happen. He explained the problem to me. Cukor was angry that the brass at M-G-M intended to get rid of all hints of homosexuality in *Cat*.

If the picture was made, he said, Benny Thau would fight for me to be in it. But we did have a problem with Eddie Mannix, who was pushing for Paul Newman, who M-G-M had under contract. Ed encouraged me to hang tough, that it would still happen. Nevertheless I had a dark feeling that it was really over. I was right, too. Richard Brooks directed it and Paul Newman starred. That was hard to digest. I'd created that role, lost the character, struggled and suffered to re-create him, and now a stranger to the play and the character of Brick would inherit what I'd done to bring Brick to life. It broke my heart. Never had I been so devastated in my career. What would happen to me now? Or all that money I'd dreamed of having, all those places I'd travel to? Would I get another chance, or was that it?

Jay Julien helped my situation by asking me to join the national company of *A Hatful of Rain* for the last six weeks of its run. I was at loose ends so I agreed, and I joined the show in Milwaukee. Watching my first performance from the wings was Nicholas Colasanto, the actor who years later played Coach in the TV series *Cheers*. He was one of the understudies.

Nicky had a pushed-in nose, a big smile, and plenty of opinions about everything. That was familiar. I grew up with a lot of guys like that. One of them was Iggy, who drowned in the East River when he was a kid. He'd had the same boxer's nose that Nick had and he, too, felt he knew everything. Iggy was always trying to teach me something. "Do this, do that. . . ." When I was all of eleven years old he gave me some important advice. He told me that when I was with a girl, I had to be careful. That I should only use a "cundrum" called Ramses because those were the ones that didn't break. We didn't know how to pronounce *condom* in those days. Iggy gave me my first and only lesson about the birds and the bees.

Nick reminded me a lot of Iggy. One night in a hotel bar in San Francisco about one in the morning, Nick was pretty drunk. A woman was sitting across the way in a black dress, pearls around her neck, gloves, and a hat—very chic. Nick sent her a drink. As the bar was closing, she rose and as she wiggled into her coat, she smiled and nodded in our direction. I told Nick I was going to bed and that he should, too. Of course I knew he wouldn't. Being on the road, touring from one town to another, can be a lonely experience.

I was in one of those deep, dreamless sleeps when there was a thunderous banging on my door. Before I could ask who was there, I heard Nick's voice, "Ben, are you awake?" I was too tired to say anything. I walked slowly to the door but when I opened it, I knew there was a problem. Nick's clothes were askew and he was hyperventilating.

– Ben, I gotta tell you what happened. You won't believe it. You'll think I made it up.

It seems that the lady invited him to her house for champagne. They got into the taxi and she told the taxi driver *Nob Hill* or whatever. They arrived at an old brownstone. They walked in and kissed and rolled on the floor and started tearing each other's clothes off. He heads down where all the honey is, and he starts going crazy, thinking, "Oh, she's so beautiful." Soon he hears, "Would you like another drink, darling?"

He looks up and there she is, across the room. He'd been chewing on the green rug; he had green rug all over his mouth. So, he spits out the pieces of rug and she hands him a glass of champagne. "I want to show you something," she says.

He follows her to what he describes as a steel door. She opens the door and there's a coffin, a glass coffin like St. Valentine's in Italy, or like Lenin's in Moscow—and inside is a body looking as if it were made of wax. She said,

— Isn't he beautiful?

— Yes, he's a good-looking guy.

— That's George, he's been gone for ten years, but I'll always keep him with me.

— Will you excuse me a second? I'll be right back.

And Nicky ran. He got his pants, almost forgot his shirt—no socks, grabbed his shoes, and jumped in a cab.

Oh, that lonesome road. You can never tell where it will lead—too much booze, grabbing hold of anything so as not to be alone.

In New York, Harold's was an oasis for the lonely. Mike Gazzo decided to write about the place and its habitués. Again, I performed some of the first scenes he wrote at the Actors Studio. You might say I'd become Mike's male muse. The scenes were well received, which gave him the confidence to continue and to turn the material into a play.

So in 1958 I went into rehearsal for *Night Circus*, a play born of loneliness. It was during those rehearsals that I started seeing less of Eva and a lot of my leading lady, Janice Rule. Being with each other every day at rehearsals, talking and flirting, kissing her full, soft mouth during our love scenes, aroused me as much as it did her. A torrid love affair soon followed.

Janice and I played two people who fall in love. She had incredible presence onstage, with her shapely legs and long auburn hair enhancing the effect. Our stage intimacy found its way into our private lives and not considering—or perhaps not caring about—the consequences, we headed for trouble. Janice was married to the talented writer Robert Thom.

Our homes were close enough for Janice to walk from her apartment to mine, on West Seventy-fifth Street. There we'd meet to make love for a few hours almost every afternoon. Sometimes we'd have drinks or even an early dinner in out-of-the-way places, hoping to avoid running into people who knew us.

On most nights, after our performance, I'd drop her off by cab a half-block or so from where she lived. One night, though, our kissing and the touching wouldn't stop, and we did something stupid: we went to my place. It was about half past midnight when I finally put her in a taxi to head home. As I reentered my apartment, the phone was ringing. I picked up the receiver.

– Ben, this is Robert Thom. Have you seen Janice?

The blood rushed to my face. My ears were on fire.

—The last time I saw her, she was at the theater. When I left, she was still there.

– Well, she may be with friends and have forgotten the time.

– If it gets too late and she's not home, please let me know.

– Thanks, Ben.

I was touched by the man. Here I was caught up in a betrayal. I had to find the strength to end this affair. Mike Gazzo would've smiled knowingly at the kind of trouble I was in.

CHAPTER 8

THE BABY

I THINK IT WAS THE DAY WE WERE TOLD THAT *NIGHT Circus* would close that Otto Preminger offered me a very good part in *Anatomy of a Murder*. It wasn't the key role in the movie, but it was flashy enough that I said yes. Otto was a very savvy producer so I knew that the picture would get topnotch promotion, as I think Otto was an even better producer than he was a director. He knew exactly how to package his product.

Anatomy was shot in the Upper Peninsula of Michigan. On the first day of shooting he showed the cast the ad that would be used for promoting the movie. In other films, that would be done after the final cut, when all was finished. Otto understood that good publicity began from the first day of shooting. The ad was designed by Saul Bass, who'd created the highly stylized titles for *The Man with the Golden Arm*. Otto also hired Gjon Mili, who was a top photographer for *Life* magazine, to take photos during the filming. He hired the esteemed Boris Levin as the production designer and Sam Leavitt as the director of photography. He got even Duke Ellington to do the music.

Our cast was full of enormous talents, too. James Stewart played the leading role. Otto also cast George C. Scott, who had never done a film before, but Otto had been impressed by him in the theater and sensed his potential. Lee Remick played my unfaithful wife and I played the husband who kills her lover. Otto also pulled off another coup by getting the famous lawyer Joseph Welch, who had gone toe-to-toe with Senator Joseph McCarthy recently and beaten him, to play the judge.

My trial for murder was the centerpiece of the movie. Insisting on authenticity, Otto shot in the courthouse where the trial actually took place. Courtroom scenes are often static and monotonous—but not with Preminger. Otto filmed it simply and yet was able to give it a sense of fluid movement.

In his role as my lawyer, James Stewart handled himself with effortless elegance and ease. Watching him up close was an eye-opening experience. His easy way with dialogue, even the legal jargon, was delightful, and the humor he found in his part was an important reason for the eventual success of the movie. George C. Scott's talent and intelligence were immediately evident, too. When he interrogated me in the witness box, I knew that I was working with a contender. I looked into his eyes, and there I saw it: real thought. Here was an actor who'd been working off-Broadway in a couple of Joseph Papp's productions of Shakespeare performed in Central Park, and his smooth technique was already in place on his first movie.

Strangely enough, Lee Remick and I had no scenes together. The catalyst for the story was her infidelity, driving me to kill another man; and yet we never appear together in the movie. Otto had originally wanted Lana Turner for the role, but there were disagreements about wardrobe and makeup, so Lee was cast. When she was on the stand and I sat at the defense table, I could feel what she was doing with her character. Easy and natural, she never pushed or exaggerated.

Preminger had the reputation of being the latest in a line of Germanic directors who wore jodhpurs and a monocle, and wielded a horsewhip. He was known to be hostile, if not downright cruel, to actors. On *Anatomy* I saw that happen only once. A character actor from the West Coast was obviously not giving Otto what he wanted. After about the fourth take, Otto became insulting, accusing the actor of not doing his homework. What caused it, I think, was Otto's frustration in not knowing what to say in order to help an actor. He expected you to bring everything to a role yourself.

James Stewart, whom I'd idolized as a boy, befriended me during the shooting. Between setups, Jimmy would disappear from the set. Rather than schmooze with the other actors, he stayed behind closed doors with his assistant, learning his lines, which he had plenty of, and working on his performance. He knew how to use his time better than most of us. When he got in front of the camera, he was letter-perfect, and always knew what he was doing. His acting was so natural that if you turned your back, you couldn't tell if it was Jimmy talking in life or Jimmy talking in the movie.

I had a good-sized scene with him in the county jail where I was held awaiting trial. If your concentration had a tendency to wander— and mine did—Jimmy's presence cured that. The manner in which he looked at you and conveyed his thoughts, carried you along. If you were to remain alive in the scene, you had to pay attention or he'd leave you behind. I wasn't going to let that happen. I wanted to earn his respect as a fellow actor.

Our scene together went very well. I felt even better when Jimmy asked me if I'd have dinner with him that night. *He must have liked what I did*, I thought. We went to dine in the very charming country inn where the cast and crew were lodged.

As I was about to leave my room for dinner, the phone rang. It was Janice. She was pregnant. She said that it was my child, no doubt about it. I asked her what she intended to do, and she said that she would have the baby. *Holy Christ*, I thought. *She's married and living with another man*. What the hell had I done?

– You sure you want to do this, Janice? It could be a lot of trouble.

– I'm sure.

Look at the chance she's taking, I thought. *Her feelings for me must be more serious than I was aware*.

—I'll call you when I can, Benny. I love you.

– I love you, too.

As I headed toward the dining room I realized that I'd never told her to leave her husband. Nor had I said what I would do if she had the child. We didn't discuss running off together. We didn't talk about marriage. Things were left to work themselves out. If there was hell to pay, it would have to be tomorrow.

I was worried when I sat down at the table and I hoped it didn't show. I told myself to push it out of my mind. Jimmy's presence had a calming affect. He never hurried anything. He seemed to think before he said something important. I was sure he would have thought ten times before he got himself into a mess like the one I was in. I wanted to ask his advice and was certain that he would have the answer, but I said nothing.

He asked why I decided to become an actor. *From watching you, Jimmy,* I thought. And that was the truth. And not only Jimmy, but Clark Gable, Spencer Tracy, Gary Cooper, and Cary Grant. There are a lot of very good actors today, but those guys had size. And then there were the glamorous women, the ones in sunken bathtubs, munching on chocolates while they talked on white telephones. "It was the movies, Jimmy," I said. "That's where I started to dream."

He told me that he never had an interest in becoming an actor. It didn't happen until, as a lark, he appeared in a play at Princeton University; when he heard the applause he was hooked. *Just like me.* There's nothing quite like being applauded, enjoyed, even loved by an audience.

Jimmy and Henry Fonda had been at Princeton together. He spoke of his concern for his friend, whom he called Hank. He told me that although Fonda was currently the king of Broadway, with his enormous success in *Mr. Roberts* and *The Caine Mutiny Court-Martial,* he was very unhappy because his film career had slowed down. That got my attention. If it could happen to Henry Fonda with his beautiful body of work, maybe I should think ten more times before continuing in this racket.

Aside from Stewart I also became fond of Joseph Welch. He was now retired from legal practice and he did the movie for fun. In the early fifties, Senator McCarthy and his chief counsel, Roy Cohn, went too far when they attacked members of the United States Army, which pissed off a lot of people in Washington. A well-known lawyer from Boston was hired to represent the Army against McCarthy. And like all bullies when they are cornered, McCarthy lashed out stupidly. He publicly accused the young lawyer, who was Welch's assistant, of having belonged to left-wing organizations. More than a big mistake, this was the final act that ultimately led to McCarthy's downfall.

A few years earlier, I'd been in a restaurant on Eighth Avenue when I heard McCarthy's familiar voice. I looked up to the television screen and caught the unforgettable moment when Joseph Welch, defending his young assistant, turned to McCarthy and said, "Let us not assassinate this lad further, Senator. You've done enough. Have you no sense of decency, sir? At long last, have you left no sense of decency?" Welch's words were the stake in Dracula's heart. McCarthy was finished. Friends and colleagues of mine were punished and suffered under McCarthy's accusations, so I would've liked to have spoken with Welch about those sad days. However, I decided not to reopen a chapter in his life that he likely did not want to revisit.

Welch and his wife became my friends. They loved gin rummy, so we played while waiting to be called to the set. He had great humor, too, about winning or losing.

When Duke Ellington arrived on the set, I felt like a kid in a candy store. I was going to meet the Duke himself. I'd seen him and his band in the movies, but the one and only time I'd seen him in person was when I was a boy, in one of those stage shows that followed a movie in a Broadway theater. He was impeccably dressed for that performance, and I remember thinking that his music sounded unusually sophisticated, not like any jazz I'd ever heard. I became a fan on the spot.

Otto got wind that it was Ellington's birthday so he arranged a luncheon celebration. The cast and crew toasted the Duke in a modest, local Italian restaurant. Duke rose to say a few words, which I expected would be about the film or his music. Instead, he talked about a diet he'd been on. He'd lost fifty pounds on the old grapefruit-with-everything diet—grapefruit with beef, lamb, pork, eggs, chicken. Cholesterol didn't exist in those days, as far as we were concerned.

I first met Colleen Dewhurst in Michigan, too. It was cold, snow up to your eyeballs. Nobody's wife or mistress or girlfriend showed up, but

Colleen did. She came to spend a few days with George C. Scott. George and I had become buddies; I considered him a brother-in-arms. In the 1940s, he and I would have wound up in those Warner Brothers pictures, the good ones, starring James Cagney or John Garfield or Edward G. Robinson or Humphrey Bogart, that made me believe it was possible for me to act in the movies. All of those men had imperfect features, and whether they were gangsters, or private eyes, or running a gambling joint in Casablanca, they were always outsiders. They had little respect for the ways of the world. I could relate to those guys. Like George they could have come from my neighborhood.

Work continued on the movie. Almost everything took place in the courtroom where, while others were being questioned, I would have little to do for long stretches. My biggest challenge was to remain alive, to keep thinking and feeling. Watching Jimmy and the work of the other fine actors made the job easy.

I was sorry when *Anatomy* came to an end. I'd formed attachments that I hated to let go of. There was no wrap party, no end-of-production celebration. Everyone packed, said their good-byes, and left Ishpeming, Michigan. I didn't know if I'd see any of them again. I liked everyone on that movie so much that it was a sad parting.

When I got back to Manhattan, to my new apartment on East Fifty-third Street, it seemed emptier than ever before. It didn't help that there was very little furniture, a minimal amount of artwork, and uncarpeted parquet floors. However, there was a big bed, which is where Janice and I spent most of our time.

While I was away on location she had found herself a Freudian analyst. After her sessions she would drop in on me. I'd make her one of my famous omelettes and we'd talk about everything—everything, that is, except what was worrying us. We never talked about her husband. Mentioning his name might have reminded us of how selfish and deceptive we had become.

Nor was I going to tell her what to do because I knew that any decision she made had to be her own and made freely. I never pressed her to leave her husband, but I think she knew that if she ended her marriage I would stand by her.

The lovemaking was intense but bittersweet. Our time together was burdened by too much past, but I told myself to go on. For me it was a matter of honor; I would stay if she had my child. But why was she doing this? She never spoke badly of her husband, whom I liked and admired. I was flattered that such a striking woman might be willing to turn her life upside down for me.

I always found that dealing with personal problems was far easier when I was working on a project I liked, and with actors who were gifted. Fredric March, who probably never gave a bad performance in his life, was about to star in a film, *The Young Doctors*. Stewart Millar and Lawrence Turman were coproducing and they asked me to costar. It would be directed by Phil Carlson and shot entirely in New York. It was hard to say no—I was going to work with another one of my favorite actors.

March had starred in the Broadway production of *A Bell for Adano*. When I played his part, Major Joppolo, at the Boys Club, I kept his photograph in front of me while I put on my makeup. His manner of dress in that film was the look I wanted—the cut of his mustache, the thickness of his eyebrows, the way he wore his uniform had mattered greatly to me. Now I was going to work with the man after whom I'd modeled myself.

When I played my first scene with him, I couldn't help watching his performance so intensely I almost forgot what I was doing. He had all the moves. The way he threw a line away was often more interesting than when he framed one. He knew how to use the camera; it was his friend. I on the other hand was still having trouble with it. I was comfortable when the camera was placed some distance away, but when it got too near, I felt nervous. During close-ups, I felt the pressure of being watched by this big machine, and this made it difficult for me to feel that I was in a real place. It stared at me. It seemed to be saying "All right, wise guy, show me what you've got."

March seemed to have blinkers on when he played a scene. His eyes zeroed in on me as though they would never look away. Everything else around him was shut out. When I told him that I had trouble concentrating when the camera was up close, he suggested I think of the camera as another piece of furniture. I started to do that and it helped a lot. When it was time for my close-ups Freddy could have gone to his trailer and waited to be called for the next scene, but he insisted on being there, off-camera, to play the scene with me. He would perform it as fully as he did for his own close-ups. That was a courtesy that not all stars were prepared to extend to younger actors.

The story of *The Young Doctors* involved the pathology department of a respected hospital. I played the idealistic young doctor trying to bring new and more precise methods to the work; March represented the old guard. He's distrustful at first but eventually he comes to respect what I'm trying to do. Here was an actor in command of his craft. I felt like a boxer in the ring with the champion. I had to go the distance and show what I had while doing so.

Ina Balin was a talented young actress who played the nurse I was in love with. She develops a tumor on her leg and it's decided that the leg must be removed. But then it's learned that the cancer has spread to other parts of her body and she will die. When we shot the scene in which she learns that her leg will be amputated, the set was absolutely silent. Phil Carlson was seated on a small crane directly above us. The camera was pointing downward, favoring Ina as she talked about us and our future together. She doesn't know that she will not live long. Something began falling on my head. It felt like drops of water. The scene was playing well so I kept going. The drops became more frequent but it was not until I heard a choked, gurgling sound that I looked up. Phil was weeping. His cheeks were soaked with tears. He was the best audience the movie would ever have.

I liked Ina very much. She had a warm, welcoming face with a big friendly smile. I often told her that she was the kid sister I wished I'd had. Many years later I was having dinner with a group of friends when one of them mentioned casually that Ina Balin had died. This hit me so hard that I was surprised by how badly I took the news. I hadn't seen that lovely girl for some time and yet there, in front of everyone, I began to cry. I left the table and walked outside to the street for some air. So many things about those days with Ina entered my mind, among them that last scene we'd played together. How shallow my performance had been, I then realized, compared to my feelings when I heard about her death.

Janice and I met as often as possible through most of 1959. But now she was in L.A. shooting a film called *The Subterraneans*, based on a book by Jack Kerouac, with the screenplay written by her husband. I was touring the summer theater circuit on the East Coast, playing the title role in *Epitaph for George Dillon*, by John Osborne, who only a few seasons before had caused a sensation with *Look Back in Anger*. Aside from everything else about the character of George that I'd have to worry about, I had to manage an English accent. How would I make it believable? It was a challenge and I worked very hard at it. My costar was Meg Mundy, a terrific actress, and we were directed by John Stix, whom I knew from the Actors Studio.

It was to be a short tour, playing for one-week stands in about four or five theaters, one of them on Cape Cod, where Joseph Welch and his wife had their summer home. I tracked them down, and they were delighted to hear from me. I was invited for lunch and the first thing I saw when I entered their charming home overlooking the harbor was Mr. Welch playing gin, this time with a local fisherman. Mrs. Welch said she had a surprise for me. She'd remembered my telling her while we were in Ishpeming that I'd never tasted homemade Boston baked beans. She had them waiting for me.

Mr. Welch and I kept in touch until his death in 1960. While he was in the hospital, I sent him a telegram: "Dear Mr. Welch, you have got to get well. You are the only one I can beat at gin rummy." Mrs. Welch called me later to say he chuckled at that.

On August 15 it was my turn to receive a telegram. "The Arab arrived. I'm naming her Elizabeth. I love you." Janice and I had always joked that, being Sicilian, I must have more than a few drops of Arab blood in me.

So my daughter was born—but would she ever really be mine? Would Janice tell her husband? And what would happen if she did? I knew that our secret was coming to an end and that decisions would have to be made.

I counted the weeks, the days, anxious for Janice's return, and yet I wanted to run far away from it all. Janice told me that when she got back to New York from Los Angeles, she intended to pick up her analysis where she had left off. She was obviously struggling to make a decision and I was sure she wouldn't get much advice from her Freudian shrink. Advice was not his line of work. I thought it might be best if we broke things off and she continued her life with Thom. The few times I met him I was struck by his sensitivity, his vulnerability. I had taken advantage of that. He invited me into his home and I slept with his wife.

John Frankenheimer helped me put things on hold. While he was in New York he offered me the starring role in a TV drama. In those days, *Playhouse 90* was considered the most prestigious of all dramatic shows and John had become the program's unofficial director-in-residence. In five days' time I would have to be in Los Angeles to start rehearsals. My reunion with Janice would have to wait; she'd be coming east as I'd be going west.

I checked into the Beverly Hills Hotel. This was my first acting job in Hollywood and I was determined to live well. I rented a shiny, red convertible and bought my first pair of sunglasses. Driving down Sunset Boulevard with the wind blowing through my hair and the radio playing, I felt like a real, important movie star. Often when I stopped at a red light, I'd get waves from people. *Amazing*, I thought. Only three years before I would have been the Invisible Man, and now, three thousand miles from home, people were saying hello. That's show business.

Frankenheimer liked actors so it was a pleasure to work with him. He spoke in a fast, excited fashion and was full of energy. *Playhouse 90* was a ninety-minute television drama that rehearsed for one week before being broadcast live.

My show was called "The Troublemakers." It had many good things going for it but something was missing in the relationship between my character and that of Barbara Rush, who played my girlfriend. We were only a couple of days from going on the air and something had to be done. The author of the piece wasn't around—he had never come out to California—so John put in a call to Rod Serling, who said, "Come on over and we'll see what we can do." Well, John and I went over to the Hotel Bel-Air and, seated under a palm tree on the patio of Rod Serling's suite, we sort of acted out what we thought was needed. Serling nodded, then went to work. In one pass, he wrote two scenes that really excited us. They turned out to be the best in the show.

I was tired when I got back to the hotel; I intended to take a long bath, order a light dinner from room service, then go right to bed. But when I opened the door, I saw a telegram on the secretary. It said simply: "There will be a party on September 15th. Please come. I love you. Janice." I didn't get much sleep that night.

At rehearsal the next day, the same question danced through my brain over and over. If Janice were to remain with her husband, wouldn't it be better for me not to go to that party, not to see my little girl? Once I saw her, wouldn't losing her be too painful? My thoughts went back and forth and it was hurting my work. I made a deal with myself. I'd make my decision on the flight home.

Only I didn't make a decision until I was already home and inside my apartment. I would not go to that party.

On the morning of the fifteenth, I rose very early and settled into my morning routine of coffee and the *New York Times*. I couldn't concentrate. My left leg was bouncing up and down, tapping out a nervous tattoo. I stared out at the quiet East Side skyline and I felt myself weakening. Maybe I *should* go. At least I'd see my daughter once. *Should-I-or-shouldn't-I?* went on for the next half hour. At last I decided in the shower: a definite No.

The party was in full swing when I entered. Janice met me at the door. She led me by the hand through the crowd, introducing me to the many people I didn't know. She led me toward her husband, who was seated on the floor. I told Janice that I would rather say hello to him later.

I left her with other guests and headed for the bar, where I poured myself a very stiff scotch. I stuck my head into the kitchen nearby and spotted my brother Tony. I hadn't seen him in a while and he'd put on weight. (He's the only person I've ever heard declare he didn't like to be thin.) Tony now sported an important-looking mustache, much like our father's.

Dan Lavezzo, owner of my favorite East Side watering hole, PJ Clarke's, was there, too, in the midst of exploring one of his many theories about the reasons for self-destructive behavior. The only thing he liked more than playing the horses was discussing Freud. Dan had read everything the man ever wrote.

Listening to Dan, or rather pretending to, was my pal Edmund Trzcinski, who'd heard it all before, just like the rest of us. Triz had written *Stalag 17*, the play inspired by his imprisonment by the Germans during World War II. Triz and his collaborator, Donald Bevan, took a comic slant on those events, and enjoyed a big success on Broadway. Triz had been trying for years for an encore. No luck. In spite of that, he remained always hopeful. That night, he was wearing his signature ascot and sipping a very dry martini, which, he told me, was the only thing that would calm the tremor in his hands. Robert Loggia, one of the only actor friends I had at the time, was there also. His father was born in a Sicilian village very close to that of my own father's.

I sat down across the table from my brother, thinking how thoughtful it was of Janice to invite people I knew and was comfortable with. Then from out of nowhere Janice handed me our daughter. "Here she is," she said, and left the room. I looked down at Elizabeth, who smiled back. Was she really mine? She had black hair and she had brown eyes, so far so good. Her mouth and nose looked like they could be mine, too. How happy my mother would have been with this little girl. While my brother was in the army in Italy she asked him more than once to bring home an orphan girl. My mother was already in her sixties but still dreaming of having a daughter. It never happened. But here was the granddaughter she would have fussed over.

I heard a voice. "What have you done, my brother?" Triz raised his glass and said, "Well done, old chap." Dan Lavezzo cackled. And Bob Loggia gave me his melancholy Sicilian smile. I think he knew the mess I was in and the trouble I'd see.

There I was, at an age when life should be free and unburdened, when all of my energy should have been devoted to craft and career, mixed up in a drama sure to hurt someone very badly. Could I take my happiness at the expense of someone else's? I didn't know what to do. If I ran, I would lose my child and, of course, Janice. If I stayed, there would be a lot of pain, possibly more than if I left.

Janice and I continued seeing each other, knowing full well that our situation would have to be resolved immediately. Then something came my way that helped delay any decision. I was offered a movie in Italy with the great Anna Magnani and Totò, an Italian comic genius. The entire film would be shot in Rome. *Perfect*, I thought. *Time and distance are what I need, what we both need.*

Risate di gioia (literally Laughs of Joy) would be directed by Mario Monicelli, who'd directed *Big Deal on Madonna Street*, a hit comedy all over the world. I was honored that Monicelli wanted me to be in his movie alongside Magnani and Totò. The movie was bought for American distribution by the powerful producer Joseph E. Levine, who immediately retitled it *The Passionate Thief*, after my character. I played a young rogue who has persuaded Totò's character to assist him in stealing from New Year's Eve revelers. Magnani plays Totò's date who has no idea what we are up to.

Monicelli was a very serious, unsmiling man but a master at directing comedy. As Totò and I weaved through what must've been a thousand people—men in black ties, women in evening gowns—our attempts at lifting things from the other guests were truly comical. As he did in *Big Deal on Madonna Street*, Totò found the humor in his own ineptitude.

That production gave me a lasting lesson in freedom and improvisation. Magnani and Totò came from a background of theater and variety shows, where dialogue was often improvised or rewritten, and they were forced to use their imagination and their wit. They kept me on my toes but I learned fast, and despite the fact that I acted in English while they spoke Italian, the timing never suffered. I'd always spoken the Sicilian dialect with my parents, never a word of English, and that was a big help in understanding my costars. I never missed a cue.

I first saw Anna Magnani in Rossellini's *Open City*. The raw realism of her work in that 1945 movie was an eye-opener. Whenever I could, I used to go to the World Theatre on West Forty-ninth Street, which showed foreign movies, usually Italian or French, in the years after World War II. A few directors who were part of a new movement called Neorealism, had started making terrific pictures. I was still a kid but I knew that these movies had something that American films lacked. Neorealism *was* a new realism, shot often on real streets. In some scenes the directors had nonprofessionals playing scenes with professional actors, who didn't seem to be actors either. Magnani's Roman roots were evident in her passion and in her humor. Her talent bowled me over.

Totò was born in Naples. Although he was illegitimate, he was recognized at age thirty by his blood father, *Il Marchese* Giuseppe DeCurtis. I don't know how that made him a prince but that's what he became, *Il Principe* DeCurtis. Straight out of Dickens.

Totò wore dark glasses. It was said that he was going blind but when he was called to the set he took those glasses off, and when the scene started he seemed to see everything.

He'd written a very famous Neapolitan song—a lament to love and betrayal called "Malafemmena." Totò had once been in love with a very beautiful and famous actress and she left him for someone else. He wrote, "Woman, you are an evil woman . . . You've intoxicated my soul . . . I love you and I hate you . . ." Decades later, people are still singing it:

Femmena, tu si na malafemmena,
Chist'occhie 'e fatto chiagnere
Lacreme e 'nfamità
Femmena, si tu peggio 'e na vipera . . .

One night we were shooting in a beautiful Baroque church. Totò, Anna, and I were seated outside near the entrance. The street seemed deserted. It was August, holiday time, and most Romans had left for the country or for the beaches. I asked Totò to sing me the song. He looked at me from behind his dark glasses. He didn't so much sing the song as talk it, with a reality and an immediacy that I'd never heard before. At one point, Anna joined him in harmony. An extraordinary night.

I'd been in Rome for six or seven weeks and was never happier. Attilio Belfiore was my driver for the entire shoot, and that was good, because he spoke no English and I had to speak Italian. Attilio's face might have been used to stamp a Roman coin. On my days off he'd take me to one museum after another, to the Roman Forum, the Colosseum, the catacombs. At night I'd take Attilio and some other people, even complete strangers, to dine outdoors in Trastevere, the old and colorful part of Rome. There'd usually be guitars or mandolins and real voices singing beautiful songs. I ate it up.

Janice called to tell me that *The Subterraneans* would be shown at the Cannes Film Festival. She was flying over without her husband. I don't know how she arranged it but she came to see me in Rome. *Risate di gioia* was shot entirely at night so my days were free.

It was a joy exploring Rome with Janice. We went to the Vatican Museum and headed straight to the Sistine Chapel in order to see Michelangelo's work. It was the first time I'd entered that stunning space, and when I looked up at the enormous ceiling, picturing so simply and powerfully the creation of man, I could only wonder how one person could possibly have painted that masterpiece. We then walked across the Tiber River to see the extraordinary works of Bernini, a sculptor whose larger-than-life figures seemed to move, even to breathe. I was an American boy seeing these things for the first time and I was knocked out.

At dinner, I asked Attilio to send over a guitar player to sing those lovely Roman and Neapolitan songs that I liked so much. I wanted my evenings with Janice to be storybook romantic, and they truly were.

When it was time for Janice to leave Italy we agreed to see each other when I returned home. *But should I?* I wondered. If she remained with Thom could I live with that? My time away from New York had only added to my confusion and worry.

Magnani had not been very warm to Janice. Here was a very lovely, some said beautiful, young girl at the beginning of her career. Anna had hit midlife and was not happy about it. She was living in Rome but preferred Paris. Her personal life was not happy, either. As far as I could see she had no lover. None of this affected her spirit when she worked, however. She was full of energy and always gave 100 percent. She was also not shy about going after what she wanted, and she wanted me. I enjoyed that about her, too.

But the fact that she was an older woman, that she was a legend, and that she was Italian made it impossible. It would have been like being with one of my aunts. The first time Anna called me in Rome to invite me to dinner, I asked Attilio to tell her that I was not feeling well. He didn't think that was enough. He said that I had a severe case of the *caccarella*—diarrhea. "Poor thing," said Anna. On another occasion, when Attilio could think of nothing else, he told her that I was suffering from the same malady. Anna became concerned, and advised Attilio to make sure that I eat *in bianco*; that meant white stuff only—rice, pasta, or potatoes with only a bit of olive oil to give it some taste. We had turned a corner. I was no longer sexually appealing for Anna. Instead, I became her son. As a matter of fact, when the filming was over, she embraced me and said just that: "Good-bye, my son."

I was back in New York only a day when Janice came to visit. She had told Thom that he was not the father of her child. He had fallen to his knees and clasped both ears in an effort to shut out the horror. It was his nightmare and my bad dream come to life. In my old neighborhood they would have called me a prick. And that's what I was—young, selfish, and without much conscience. But I suddenly had a very attractive woman who loved me and wanted to make a life with me.

— CHAPTER 9 —

THE MARRIAGE

JANICE AND I MOVED IN TOGETHER. AT FIRST, TIME WENT by happily. I was now with my daughter, whom I could lift in my arms, take to the park, push on a swing, kiss her goodnight. I could be there as she grew. I could talk to her about her dreams and she could talk to me about anything, including my work. I wanted her to be proud of me.

Janice's divorce had been quick and clean, and with some nifty legal maneuvers we were able to get Liz's birth certificate to read Elizabeth Gazzara. That meant a great deal to me. She had my blood and now she would share my name.

Janice had another child with her former husband, a daughter named Kate. She was four years old when they divorced, and Kate was baffled and shaken by her parents' breakup. It was difficult to have any impact at all on her. She probably blamed me for her parents' breakup.

Thom was determined to have a major say in how Kate would be raised. Initially his phone calls were infrequent, but as time progressed and his wounds healed the calls came more often. Janice never refused to speak to him. He had tapped into her guilt, and she would stay on the phone with him, listening to his problems for far too long. I understood the man's position but his steady, almost daily, calls became an intrusion. There had been no real honeymoon and no period of celebration for

Janice and me. All the pulling and pushing, resentments and guilts about the past put a damper on our household.

After about a year of these calls, Janice came to me with a suggestion. She thought that it would be best for the girls if we allowed Liz to accompany Thom on his visiting days with Kate. She'd discussed it with her analyst and he felt it best we didn't separate the sisters on those occasions. I bowed to the experts and consented to her plan.

When the day finally came for Liz to join Kate on her first outing with Thom, I felt that familiar sadness in the pit of my stomach. I couldn't even say good-bye. After the nanny had dressed Liz in her leggings, her dress, her little coat, her mittens, and her knitted cap pulled over her ears, Liz followed Janice and her taller, blonde sister with little steps to the door. I had to turn away. I didn't want her to walk out that door. I was afraid that these visits would only create confusion and distance between my daughter and me.

One sunny Saturday morning, Janice suggested that it might be fun for Liz if I took her to the Museum of Modern Art. There was an exhibition on that was suitable for children. I was sure Thom would get around to seeing that show with Kate so instead I took Liz, who was two years old, to Harold's. I thought she'd have a better time there.

The only thing Harold disliked more than children was a man in a suit and tie wearing brown shoes. In fact, once, when Harold was drinking, which was almost always, he refused to serve a guy dressed like that. Harold himself was fastidious, always in a dark suit and, of course, shiny black shoes. He was born in Paris and used the most expensive French cologne, which he must have poured on, not sprayed, because come midnight his scent was still much stronger than the scotch, bourbon, and beer that had been spilling on the dark mahogany bar since morning.

It was just before noon when we walked into the place. Dinah Washington was singing "Drinking Again." You had to be very good to make it to Harold's jukebox. He lifted Liz up, placed her on a tall barstool, and said to Ray the bartender, "Give the young lady anything her heart desires, give her one of your 'Shirley Temples.'" Ray went to work and put a large, bright red creation in front of my daughter. All attention was now on my little girl, and she ate it up.

It was the beginning of July 1961, and I had a picture to do on the West Coast entitled *Reprieve,* which would start shooting in mid-August. I was feeling out of shape so I thought it would be fun to put together a softball team from among the regulars of Harold's bar.

Harold was excited about having a team representing his establishment. We went to work making up the roster, choosing the players and what position they would take. It was a true dictatorship. Harold had the final say. If you wanted to play, you had to follow his rules. I would play center field, Joe DiMaggio's position. While Ray entertained Liz at the bar, we made our plans.

On our way home, I told Liz that on the following Saturday we might visit the museum. "No," she said, "I want to go to Harold's." She had good taste even then.

The softball games took place in Central Park. We lost our first game 24–2. There were a lot of charley horses and strained muscles, too. I was only thirty years old but it took a solid week to get rid of the aches and pains. We lost the second game, and the third. We finally won the fourth and went on to win the next two. Then the betting began—heavy betting. Ringers were brought in; these were top athletes who augmented the squads. All the teams were suddenly doing it because there was now a lot of money involved.

To my left and right in the outfield were Dick Lynch and Lou Corleone of the New York Football Giants. I knew I had to be faster to keep up with those guys. When I was a kid I used to imitate DiMaggio, picking up a bat just the way he did. Or I'd assume his stance, legs apart, and try to swing the bat with his grace. In the outfield, I concentrated on getting a jump on the ball so that I would have time to move as quickly as he did. Joe never hurried to the ball but always got to it. I was going to show the big boys, the ringers, that I could keep up.

I went to Davega's, a big sporting goods store, and bought steel cleats, which I was told would give me more speed. That Sunday was my first time in cleats. It was the bottom of the seventh and last inning and we were losing 5–3, the bases were loaded, and I ripped a line drive down the left-field line. I rounded first base and as I headed for second I saw I'd get in easily, so I thought I'd showboat a little and slide gracefully like Joe D used to do. I heard it before I felt it; my ankle snapped in two. An ambulance drove right onto the field and up to second base. I was in a cast for nine weeks. My baseball career was over.

Millard Kaufman, who was to direct the movie I'd committed to doing, had to postpone shooting for a month. *Reprieve* told the story of John Resko, who had been convicted of murdering a man during an armed robbery in the 1930s. Resko was sentenced to the electric chair but Franklin D. Roosevelt, who was then governor of New York, commuted his sentence to life in prison only hours before he was to die. It was in prison that Resko learned to paint. His work caught the eye of a civilian instructor, who took up his cause. Resko was released after he had served thirty years.

I was to play Resko. This would be my first film shot in Hollywood. Millard assembled an impressive cast: Sammy Davis, Jr., Rod Steiger, Ray Walston, Stuart Whitman, Vincent Price, and Timothy Carey.

We shot on location, too, in Folsom, a maximum-security penitentiary that housed scores of lifers. Before shooting started, the warden took us on a guided tour of the prison. We walked through a cellblock, looked into the mess hall, crossed the exercise yard to a kind of structure where the prisoners made California license plates, then walked by the gas chamber, which had been inactive for a time, and into what they called "The Hole." That was where they put what they considered the incorrigible prisoners—most of them black or Latino. Resko himself was with us in the tour. I wondered how, after having spent thirty years in prison, he had the stomach to go back there, however briefly.

We shot scenes in the license plate factory using real prisoners as extras. We also shot in a cellblock and on the yard. But we were authorized for only one week of filming at Folsom and had to head back to L.A., where sets had been built to simulate the prison corridors and cells. My first scene in the studio was with Sammy Davis, Jr., who was determined to be a good actor. This probably explains why I never saw the entertainer in Sammy; he never clowned around on the set. Before every take he'd go off to a deserted corner of the studio and try to concentrate and immerse himself in his next scene.

Since joining me in Los Angeles, Janice and I had talked a lot about marriage and by this time we got serious. We decided to fly up to San Francisco over a weekend and marry there. We chose San Francisco because I'd never been there. Janice's sister, Emily, was matron of honor and Emily's husband, Dennis, was my best man.

When we arrived back in Hollywood, I found out that *Reprieve* had been retitled to *Convicts Four*. Clearly the wrong people had taken control of the picture. Kaufman was a very talented writer but he'd never directed before. By his side at all times was an elderly man named Doane Harrison, who had worked almost exclusively with Billy Wilder as his adviser on editing. He, in effect, was dictating where the camera should be and how the picture would be cut. In the end, the movie lacked passion. *Convicts Four* was "professional," but it was an editor's movie. By this I mean that an actor's behavior and movements would rarely, if ever, be allowed to vary from one take to the next. If you picked up a cigarette it would always be at the same moment, take after take. If you laughed during a scene you would be expected to do it at exactly the same point, take after take. That way, the editor would have an easy time matching the takes. I had a hard time working under these conditions and at the risk of being a total pain in the ass I resisted it as much as I could. But my resistance was futile. Everything cut together well, but in the end the film had no real life. It's not easy to give 100 percent to a lost cause, but I did my best. Most actors do.

* * *

When I got back to New York I received a call from Robert Lewis, who said that a young producer named Norman Twain had offered him an intriguing play, *Traveller Without Luggage*, written by Jean Anouilh; Lewis was going to direct it, and he thought I should play the lead. I was flattered. His work in the theater was highly respected, having directed such big Broadway hits as *Brigadoon* and *Teahouse of the August Moon*. It would be exciting to work with him. I felt a new surge of energy. Theater is where I came in. It had been only three years since I'd been on the stage but it seemed like far more time had passed.

At the first rehearsal Bobby Lewis was terrific. He was an actor himself, a bit flamboyant, short, with long legs and a barrel chest. His head was completely bald and shiny. I swear I once saw my face it. When he squinted he looked Asian, and as a result, he often played the cruel Japanese officer in those World War II movies Hollywood cranked out in the 1940s.

In vividly describing his idea of what *Traveller Without Luggage* was about, he took the opportunity to act out all the important moments, playing everybody's part. A director who gives line readings, demonstrating how he'd like the dialogue to sound, is not usually appreciated by actors, but Bobby made it fun. He performed with such delight that you couldn't help but enjoy him. His enthusiasm and style were so over the top that they would be hard to imitate. An actor wouldn't even try, and I don't think Bobby expected us to. He was simply hoping to inspire us with his vision.

The Riverside Drive apartment Janice and I occupied overlooked the Hudson River and the Seventy-ninth Street Boat Basin. Though Janice had lived there with Thom, she liked it so much she didn't want to give it up. So I bought it and went about redesigning the place. I also bought the apartment next door, broke through the walls, and combined the spaces. I had the kitchen and the bathrooms redone, bought new furniture and rugs, and had the rooms painted fresh new colors. All in an attempt to make the place mine, but it never was. Other people's ghosts seemed to be hanging around.

Dealing with plumbers, painters, and construction workers who are generally out to screw you is no way to prepare yourself for an opening on Broadway. I should have been wholly concentrated on rehearsals because *Traveller Without Luggage* was not easy for me. I couldn't get a handle on my character, an amnesiac who is found in a railway siding at the end of World War I and spends the next fifteen years in a mental institution where he's given the name Gaston. The play begins when a family is brought to see him in the hope that Gaston may be the son they lost in the war. At first he has no idea who they are, but gradually he learns through them that sensitive Gaston was once arrogant, aristocratic Jacques, who had done a lot of naughty things, including sleeping with his brother's wife. He can't bear even the thought that he was once this person, so he chooses instead to walk away.

I tried many different attacks, but nothing fit. My fellow actors seemed to have had no trouble finding the vocal and physical energy to perform in a way that to me seemed much too stylized. They were all good actors and what they were doing was effective but I found their performances unbelievable. I was trying to find a simpler way to deal with my character's dilemma.

Bobby was supportive. He tried to help but his emphasis was on how things should *look*, while I was searching for answers to why things were *done*. Nor did our set help. The play was staged in a highly theatrical set designed by Oliver Messel: the walls, windows, doors, and furniture swirled in the curved art nouveau style. In this environment I had trouble keeping my performance grounded in reality. I was "acting." Here was proof that if you're not able to think genuine thoughts onstage, if you only mimic feelings and emotions, you're simply presenting the character, not revealing him.

At a midnight meeting with Bobby, I suggested that perhaps if we played with the staging, loosened it up, that might help me. I felt that the staging, like the set, was too formal and interfered with any real behavior or feeling. But it was too late. The other actors were comfortable with their parts and there simply wasn't time to start over. Ever since, I've felt that we missed the chance to do something special with that play. I'd avoided confrontation out of respect for Bobby, who was one of my fathers, you might say. I felt grateful to him for being one of the people who made it possible for me to have a life in the theater.

Bobby was one of the original founders of the Actors Studio, but left when it became clear that Elia Kazan and Cheryl Crawford were not interested in using the studio as a pool of talent for mounting productions. Bobby was not interested in teaching as much as he was in putting on a show. So, in 1951, Lee Strasberg replaced Lewis and introduced what became known as the Method, an outgrowth of the Stanislavsky system, which was sort of a blueprint for the actor as he attempts to build a character.

Strasberg was the opposite of Bobby, who was outgoing and expansive. If there was any problem with Lee as a teacher, it was that there was no joy. He was perceptive, with a great eye for falsehood—for what was indicated, not felt—and he rarely gave compliments. Well, that's not exactly true. He had a lot of good things to say about the dead, people like the great Italian actress Eleanora Duse, but never about the living.

Bobby would have been very happy with Rip Torn. Rip came to my apartment one morning in 1962 to hear what I thought of the idea to launch an Actors Studio Theatre. His pitch got me excited. He must have visited a lot of other members and got them interested, too. Obviously, he and some fellow members had convinced Kazan and Strasberg to give it a go. I don't know why Eugene O'Neill's *Strange Interlude* was chosen for the first production, but somebody must have decided it would be an audience pleaser. Well, it was. And what a cast was assembled: Geraldine Page, Franchot Tone, Betty Field, Pat Hingle, William Prince, Jane Fonda, Geoffrey Horne, and me. Our director was José Quintero.

Almost the first thing José did was to set up a lunch with O'Neill's widow, Carlotta. He wanted her blessing for the production. As the play was long and often repetitious, he intended to make cuts but wanted to make sure that Carlotta would not be looking over his shoulder, dictating what could or couldn't go. José was from Panama and spoke with a pronounced accent, yet had come to be known as the leading interpreter of

O'Neill, who was very much an American writer. José's production of *The Iceman Cometh* had resurrected an interest in O'Neill's plays.

He brought me, Gerry Page, Jane Fonda, and William Prince along to that lunch. Gerry was already a full-fledged star, both in theater and film. Jane was still struggling to make a name for herself apart from being Henry Fonda's daughter, and William Prince had been considered a fine character actor for years. We all turned on the charm, and José got what he wanted. Carlotta gave him a free hand.

Strange Interlude could have turned into a high-class soap opera, but Quintero got his actors to avoid melodrama. Even though Franchot Tone and Betty Field were from another generation, they joined us in imbuing the play with a relaxed naturalness. The production was theatrical, of course, but the acting was grounded in reality. Nothing was pushed just to make a point, as was the case with *Traveller Without Luggage*, where the artifice of the otherwise brilliant set seemed to infect the actors so that many moments were indicated rather than felt.

I worked hard at becoming onstage a person who belongs to the upper classes, who drinks and dines at country clubs, takes part in regattas, and sleeps with beautiful and intelligent women. The character would have to speak the English language clearly and beautifully, and seem to belong to that society. This wasn't too difficult to achieve, as I have a good ear and never really had a New York accent anyway.

José Quintero staged *Strange Interlude* beautifully, but the play presents a special challenge. Apart from normal dialogue between the characters, their inner thoughts are also spoken aloud. José led the way for us in solving the problem. All previous productions of *Strange Interlude* had the actors turn out front to speak their inner thoughts; we did the opposite. We spoke our thoughts looking directly at the other actor, as though the lines we said were a continuation of the conversation. It was believable and it worked. I guess it did because the audience appreciated the humor in the real thoughts of the characters, thoughts that are usually censored. Even with cuts, the play ran five hours, so the curtain went up at six; there was a one-hour break for dinner at eight, and everybody was back in their seats at nine and by midnight on their feet, applauding.

Strasberg came backstage on opening night and did something I'd always thought he was incapable of doing. He embraced me. I was taken aback because it was not his style. But he put his arms around me and gave me a hug. I think now that Lee was simply relieved that the performance had gone so well. He'd felt that the reputation of the Actors Studio, *his* Actors Studio, was at stake with that production. But in that moment I was dumbstruck. I couldn't say anything.

There was a lot of enthusiasm that night. I was particularly pleased when Edward Albee came backstage after the show to congratulate me on my performance. I knew then I was doing something right.

I took a special liking to the people in the cast of *Strange Interlude* and thought it would be fun to mix them with some of the habitués of Harold's—including Harold himself, of course—so I gave a party at our Riverside Drive apartment. I even invited Harold's bartenders, Ray and Scotty, with instructions that I expected all guests to be loose and happy by the end of their second drink. So it was done, and things got off the ground quickly. The blend of people was perfect and, as I expected, the Harold's regulars were getting most of the laughs.

But when I recall that night my most vivid memory is of Jane Fonda, a product of private schools and a privileged background, seated on the floor at my mother's feet, looking up and talking to her for almost the entire party. Here was my past blending with my present. I could've hugged Jane then and there. She was having the time of her life with my mother, a woman who had only four years of schooling and arrived in America in steerage.

A few weeks later my mother died. It was Good Friday 1963. She had brought her favorite sister, Carmela, home from the hospital and made sure that she was comfortable. My mother was seventy-eight years old; Carmela was eighty-one. She walked the four blocks home from Carmela's apartment and on the way bought a fish that she was going to bake for us that evening. She put the fish in the kitchen sink and slowly ran cold water over it, took off her dress—she was wearing a full satin slip—and lay down on her bed. She telephoned Carmela to check in on her once more. And while they were chatting, my mother died.

I got the news on Riverside Drive. It was late morning and I was alone in bed; Janice was shooting a TV show in Florida somewhere and had taken the kids with her. The phone rang and it was my brother Tony. He gave me the news: "Mama died." The night before, I had been drinking into the wee small hours and was suffering a very bad hangover. The news took time to seep in.

I hopped a cab to East Fifty-seventh. My brother opened the door, and there were tears in his eyes. Dr. Finger, my mother's doctor, was there and appeared saddened. He said, "You can see her now," took his hat, and slipped quietly out the door. I stood there but couldn't get my bearings. Between the pain in my head and the pain in my heart, I couldn't move. I never walked into that room. Tony and I sat at the kitchen table and, for what seemed like hours, said nothing.

Finally, he spoke.

– We'll take her to Abundi's.

– Are they still in business?

– The sons took over.

We sat in silence, a long silence. Neither of us seemed to know what to do or say next. I hadn't cried. Like when my father died, again no tears. I figured that if I couldn't cry for my mother there must be something wrong with me—an impediment, a blockage in my brain. My brother asked,

– You want me to pick out a coffin?

– It's gotta be bronze, like Papa's.

– She'll be next to him in Calvary.

– Is there room?

– Oh yes. Mama made sure of that. There's room for us, too.

I forced myself to go to the theater that night. I'd always heard that the show must go on and so forth. Pat Hingle and I were sharing a dressing room. This was the third play we'd done together. When I saw his kind face with that sweet dimpled smile, it happened. I broke down. I cried for a long time—I just couldn't stop. Pat was concerned I might not be able to go on, but in the nick of time, I pulled myself together. In those days, if something dramatic happened in your life and you were doing a play, someone was sure to say, "Use it." I never consciously thought about that but it's true my performance was never better than it was on that night.

Sadly, *Strange Interlude* was the last work I would ever do with the Actors Studio. It was becoming a foreign land to me. When I had joined, members were required to pass two very tough auditions, the first judged by a respected and reputable professional, and, if you passed, you auditioned again for Kazan, Crawford, and Strasberg. Now people were just walking in and sitting down, mainly successful Hollywood people. That amused me, because in my day some of us, stupidly I might say, turned down movies in order to remain clean and untainted theater actors. Strasberg's idealism was one of the driving forces behind those decisions. All that had changed. I think Lee enjoyed the publicity and prestige of being mentor to people like Marilyn Monroe. As a matter of fact, I think that Strasberg's most important contribution is not to the theater but to film acting. The Studio's approach was responsible for the relaxed simplicity and the seething and surprising emotion you see in many motion picture performances.

CHAPTER 10

TELEVISION AND TEARS

IN THE EARLY SIXTIES, TV WAS ALWAYS A SECOND CHOICE for actors because many people thought it put a real damper on an actor's chances in the motion picture industry. But film offers weren't forthcoming, so I decided to gamble that somehow, somewhere, the big screen would once again be a part of my life. The theater certainly hadn't made me rich, so I agreed to do something I'd sworn I never would do—a TV series. It was to be produced by Universal, which at the time was owned by MCA, whose CEO was still Lew Wasserman.

Janice didn't think I should do it. She always let me know how much she respected my talent, and never urged me to do anything I didn't want to be part of even where the money was tempting. But by this time I was tired of worrying about money so I decided to take advantage of the offer. I was going to be out on the Coast at least a year, so we rented a charming house in Westwood. It was early October when Janice and the girls and I left a dark and cold New York for the bright Los Angeles sunshine.

The series *Arrest and Trial* was the forerunner of *Law & Order* and many other similar cop shows you see today. I played a detective who made arrests and the first forty-five minutes of the program covered that portion of the story. The last forty-five minutes covered the defendant's trial, at which the lawyer for the defense was played by Chuck Conners. Chuck had been a professional athlete who had played first base for the

Brooklyn Dodgers, and he later had also starred in a successful TV series called *The Rifleman*, which I'd not seen. I didn't know what he looked like. But as soon as I stood next to his six-foot-six-inch frame, I knew I was in trouble. I'm barely five-feet-ten. So I devised a survival plan. I "helped" the director come to the realization that the most interesting way to stage the scenes between Chuck and me was to keep us as far apart as possible. When we were required to sit near each other, at a table, for instance, I had the prop man place a thick, hard pillow under my der-riere. It was a lot of fun trying that kind of stuff but it didn't always solve the problem, because sometimes we'd have to stand up and there we were—the giant and me.

Mickey Rooney guest-starred in the second episode. It was November 22, 1963. We started shooting on a particularly hot California day in the San Fernando Valley. Again I was working with an actor who was a familiar part of my youth; how often I had seen and enjoyed his movies. He hadn't lost a beat—his ease in front of the camera and his ability to make rather ordinary dialogue come alive was a testament to the command he had of his craft.

When it was time for lunch, Mickey and I decided to forgo the studio food, and we headed over to a nearby restaurant, where we ordered Bloody Marys in a corner booth. Then a news flash appeared on the TV near the bar: John F. Kennedy had been shot. Mickey and I moved to the bar to listen to Walter Cronkite, who was covering the event for CBS News. He was fighting back tears when he told viewers that JFK was dead. Mickey and I turned to each other with what must have been lost looks. Although the restaurant was packed with lunchtime customers there was total silence. Then a woman began to sob into a man's arms. Other patrons also broke down and wept. Right then the assistant director poked his head into the restaurant and said to us, "Ready on the set, gentlemen." "You must be mistaken," I said to him, "Mr. Rooney and I are going home." I shook Mickey's hand and said I'd see him the next day.

I was terribly saddened that this handsome young president was gone. To me he was like a prince, his wife, Jacqueline, a princess. They'd brought style and glamour to politics. I'd become a big fan.

Everyone showed up for work the next day and the day after that, too, but it wasn't easy. Watching the funeral was especially hard. Yet I couldn't stop. After every take, I would run to look at the TV. The funeral cortege was led by a big, black, muscular stallion—with saddle but no rider. A strong-looking marine held him by his bridle but had trouble controlling the nervous animal. It seemed to be carrying all our anger. Behind the caisson bearing JFK's flag-draped coffin were Robert and Teddy Kennedy, Lyndon Baines Johnson, and a phalanx of European leaders led by France's imposing Charles de Gaulle and Ethiopia's diminutive Haile Selassie. It was a moving sight but it wasn't until Jacqueline Kennedy appeared—standing calm and erect, with her two children—that my tears flowed. What style and courage. No queen could have handled herself more gracefully.

That evening friends gathered at my house for food, drink, and the TV networks' constant replay of John F. Kennedy's funeral. I got to bed about midnight because I had to be awake by six A.M. I said goodnight to Janice and the remaining guests and slipped away. But I couldn't sleep. At half past one I saw that Janice was not in bed so I got up and walked to the door. Music was playing. I thought, "What the hell, maybe a glass of wine will help me sleep." I put on my robe, opened the door, and headed downstairs.

As I approached the landing, I heard pained moaning coming from the living room. In the dark I saw two figures, dancing ever so slowly and kissing ever so deeply. The man was a friend who, along with his wife, had been a frequent guest in our house. The woman was Janice. I said goodnight to them, telling them both to continue. I locked myself into the guest room. Soon there was a knock. I didn't answer. I couldn't. I was crying.

I slept in my bungalow at the studio for the next couple of nights. There were calls from Janice but I refused to take them. The man I'd seen with my wife came to me with a cockamamie story about how the Kennedy stuff made him and Janice so emotional that in their need for comfort they got carried away. "Please forgive us," he said. I looked at this guy, who was not a particularly good-looking fellow, and thought, "If she would fuck him, she would fuck anybody." But I said nothing. I simply nodded and walked him to the door.

When Janice and I were alone, she started her version of the same story. They had rehearsed it very well. I watched her carefully. *She's really a hell of an actress*, I thought. I felt like getting out of my chair and backhanding her across the face. I wanted to shout "You betrayed me, and now you can go fuck yourself. I'm leaving." But I was more hurt than angry. So instead I said, "I understand."

Our lives after that went downhill very quickly. The first thing to go was the good-morning kiss. Then the return-home peck on the cheek disappeared. The biggest casualty was the long and passionate kiss promising love and pleasure. The sex act itself, however, was easier. It was less personal.

Soon I began to have trouble caring about anything. It was tough to pump up enthusiasm even for my work. Those long hours at the studio or on location became boring, then unbearable. I was relieved when *Arrest and Trial* didn't get picked up for a second season.

We packed up the family and moved back to New York. During the months that followed I didn't work much, but my one-night stands never stopped. It was as though I were looking for as many good reviews for my lovemaking as I could get.

My trysts took place in strange apartments, hotel rooms rented for the night but used only in the afternoon, the backseats of moving limousines. Even the ladies' powder room was not off-limits. I was on a sexual rampage. It seemed I would rather get laid than get a job. I didn't know what Janice was up to and didn't ask. We had a tacit don't show, don't tell, don't get caught, don't care arrangement.

In time Lew Wasserman came calling again with a new project—*Run for Your Life*, a series created by the highly respected Roy Huggins, who would also produce the show. Paul Bryan, the character I would play, is found to have a terminal illness and has only two years to live, so he chooses to live life to the hilt. I thought it could be a lot of fun.

When we arrived in California, I went right to work. I told Janice to look for a good, livable house. We would be there for at least a year and if the show was successful, three or four more. She decided to again rent the house we'd lived in during my work on *Arrest and Trial*; that didn't bother me in the least. The choice made my life easier. The house was only a twenty-five-minute drive over Coldwater Canyon to Universal Studios. It was in pleasant surroundings, it was comfortable, and it had a pool for the girls to splash in. There was also an excellent elementary school across the street.

Despite the fact that my love for Janice had been mortally wounded, I'd decided to stay with the marriage. What was I going to do—live by myself? Be a weekend father? I became lonely at just the thought of it. I told myself that maybe I'd meet someone else. The marriage lasted for another fourteen years, and for a good part of that time, Janice and I were friendly and civil to each other. We had sex during those years but it was without romance, much like my one-night stands. And yet I remained with her by choice. I feared being alone more than being unhappy. I had to find a way out.

Over the years I'd noticed that life was far more lively and seemed to go more smoothly when there were people around. Soon there were lots of people coming and going. On Sundays, which has never been my favorite day, we filled our place with more than forty people. I fed them, wined them, and dined them—some friends, some not. But what the hell, it was action. It got my mind off things, including *Run for Your Life* and its fourteen-hour workdays.

In some respects doing a TV series is like factory work. Keeping your enthusiasm high is not easy. The weeks, months of playing the same character, with predictable reactions to mainly predictable situations, was getting me down. After endless hours of unsurprising material, it was soothing to have a drink or three in my well-appointed bungalow at Universal. It became a meeting place for friends—actors, directors, writers who were not exactly overjoyed with what they were doing, either. But most complaints were mixed with humor. No crybabies were allowed in Bungalow A.

Often I stayed late. Sometimes I didn't go home at all. If a lovely lady and I struck each other's fancy, I would invite her to have dinner with me and perhaps spend the night. Those nights with strangers were now the center of my sex life. They were usually pretty good performances without very much romance. I would let the ladies touch my skin, but I never let them get under it. I didn't like what I was doing. The preoccupation with women and sex took up too much of my time. I knew that the only way this would ever change would be if I fell in love, but everything I was doing made my chances of doing so pretty slim.

Things turned around for me when I started to direct some of the episodes. My mind and my imagination became engaged. My sadness started to lift and I began to feel useful. As an actor I was responsible only for part of the whole but now the entire presentation would depend on me. Each of those small movies would stand or fall on my vision.

In some of the episodes I directed, my prejudices and sympathies became clear. I was drawn to stories about the loser. I still am. My father's life probably had everything to do with that. He made it possible for me and my brother to succeed but he himself never succeeded, in a country that never became his.

In one show, a man falsely convicted of murder goes to the gas chamber despite the confession of the real killer. The confession came a minute too late. We cast the young Tom Skerritt as the falsely accused and Robert Duvall as the true murderer. I, of course, played the running character, an attorney who becomes involved in the plight of the condemned man. It was a pleasure to work with such good actors. All it took was a suggestion now and then to get them to top form. Directing is fun when you can lead an actor to discover things he didn't suspect were there. But in order to do that you've got to make an actor feel comfortable, set up an environment where he feels he can do no wrong. You've got to let him know that you don't expect him to be better than he is, only as good as he is.

Another episode dealt with abortion. It starred Kim Darby, who most often in her career played sensitive waifs. I didn't want her to pump up the pathos in the story. I felt that if she played against it, found the humor in the character, the audience would be more deeply touched. A few days after that show aired I received a note of thanks from Kim. She said she'd never before seen herself so convincing on the screen.

One Friday night, Frank Gehry, a shy, young architect friend of mine, showed up on the Universal backlot with a friend of his who had just arrived from New York. His name was Robert Rauschenberg. I wasn't aware of his work, but if Frank was with him, you could bet he had talent. And there I was, groveling in the mud, escaping from something or someone in yet another segment of *Run for Your Life* that I was not directing. Needless to say, I was embarrassed. They had come to see Ben Gazzara doing something interesting and all they got was a mud-covered actor, slithering along the ground.

Later, we went to my house, where I could show off some real talent. I made pasta with a puttanesca sauce that, if I do say so myself, was extraordinary. The booze flowed all night and at two in the morning, Janice, Rauschenberg, and I were dancing on the pool table, while Frank looked on with his adorable smile.

Although Frank was then fairly unknown, and therefore having trouble getting assignments, he never seemed beaten. He remained passionate about his work and especially supportive of the efforts of other artists. He was encouraging and comforting when they were down, proud and happy when they succeeded. Frank made my years in L.A. more bearable by bringing some gifted artists to my house—John Altoon, Ed Moses, Bob Irwin, Billy Al Bengston, from the so-called California school. Altoon and Moses became my friends, too. I still have their paintings hanging on my walls.

John Altoon lived in a loft near Venice Beach and it was always a pleasure to visit him there. The place breathed creativity. I've always envied the painter, the writer, the composer: they need no one but themselves. Actors depend on too many other people before they get a chance to show their wares. The waiting for a call from an agent. The waiting for a good offer. The waiting for a good part. The waiting for a good director.

This sucks out your energy. I've often thought how great it would be to wake up, have a cup of coffee, walk across the room, and start painting. Nothing to limit you but your talent and imagination.

Frank and those artists were a big help in getting me through the three years it took for *Run for Your Life* to run its course. The work had been hard but the show allowed me to live in a large house with a pool, a blond pool man to service it, a Japanese gardener to care for the grounds, three cars in the garage, children in private schools, and a wife in psychoanalysis—the whole thing.

The day I finished shooting the last segment of *Run for Your Life* I ran into John Cassavetes on the Universal lot. He called to me, "Hey, Ben, did Marty tell you?" Marty Baum was our mutual agent at the time. "Did he tell you we're gonna do a picture together?" "Not yet," I said. "He will," said John. We waved good-bye. I forgot about John's remark because actors hear that kind of thing all the time, and almost nothing ever comes of it.

I knew John only slightly from the New York days when we were both struggling actors. I got lucky in the theater and sometime later he made *Shadows* on a very small budget. And what an impact that film had on the French New Wave and, by extension, on young directors everywhere.

Only a week before speaking with him on the Universal lot, he had invited me to a screening of his new movie, *Faces*. I'd never seen his work before so I was curious.

He had shot the movie up at his house, and financed it entirely himself. *Faces* starred Gena Rowlands, John Marley, Seymour Cassel, Val Avery, and Fred Draper; none of them household names, to say the least. The screening took place at midnight in a big movie house in downtown Los Angeles. When I got there the place was packed. People were seated in the aisles. I was surprised to see so many people show up late at night for a little art picture. I didn't want to sit on the floor so I thought I'd wait until the lights dimmed and then slip out. I'd see the picture another time.

But when the movie started, I saw filmmaking of a kind that was entirely new to me. The black-and-white photography was grainy yet beautiful. I'd never seen the camera go so close and remain so long on an actor's face. And I'd hardly ever seen an actor's face project as many thoughts and feelings on-screen. It didn't take more than five minutes for me to realize I was watching a major piece of work. I started to get jealous. How could Cassavetes have this kind of talent? Where did it come from?

The characters' behavior was totally unpredictable. I'd seen most of the actors before, in movies made by other directors, but in those pictures their work had not been nearly as surprising or multilayered. *Faces* had structure and yet, as in life, things were never resolved neatly. Nothing seemed acted or directed or even written. It just *was*. I was knocked out. *I have to work with this guy*, I thought.

A few days passed, and John called me. "You want to meet me for lunch at Hamburger Hamlet on the Strip? I want to tell you the story of our movie."

The first thing I said to him when I got there was,

– John, before we start, I gotta tell you that *Faces* is terrific.

– I think I've got myself a distributor.

– They should stand in line.

– Let's talk about our movie.

He proceeded to tell me about three men whose best friend dies, and the impact his death has on them. The third actor was going to be Peter Falk, who was about to go to Italy with John to do a gangster picture. John said,

– I think I can get the money from the Italian producer, Bino Cicogna.

I was about to go to Prague to do a war film. Then John said,

– As soon as we're back in the U.S., we start the picture.

– What's the title?

– *Husbands*. What do you think, you like it?

– Being a husband or the title?

– Take your choice.

– I hope my character has more fun than I'm having.

– That's up to you. You can take him anywhere you want to.

– You've got a deal, John.

CHAPTER 11

HUSBANDS

IT WAS THE SUMMER OF 1968. THE AIR-CONDITIONING IN the International Hotel in Prague was not working. I had all the windows open and I started hearing strange rumblings, then jet planes zooming overhead. I looked out and saw tanks—lots of them—moving into position below us. Not only there but on other streets, too. I called the front desk to ask what was going on. The kindly telephone operator told me, "It's the Russians. They've come like the Germans did in 1939. They've come to kill our freedom." She was crying. "Poor Czechoslovakia," she said.

The next day found the entire company, actors and crew, seated on the three long concrete steps in front of the International Hotel, which was built in the cold, block form imported to beautiful Prague by some somber Stalinist stooge. We were waiting for automobiles to take us across the border into Austria. Up until then we had been shooting a movie about a famous World War II battle called *The Bridge at Remagen*. It was produced by David Wolper and directed by John Guillermin. George Segal and Robert Vaughn were my costars. The Russians were not about to let us continue to make our war movie with bombs bursting, machine guns rat-tat-tatting, and American and German tanks rolling through the countryside. We had to get out.

All the Russian tanks in front of the hotel were surrounded, mostly by women, who were weeping and screaming at the young, mud-caked

Russian soldiers to get out of their country. The young Russians were shocked. They had been told they were being sent to liberate these people.

A young Czech woman who had been part of our production sprang up and screamed something at the Russian soldiers. In no time at all she was on the second-floor terrace where the flags of all nations were flying, with the Soviet one smack in the middle. She tore it from its pole and flung into the street below. It landed at our feet. She was saying some nasty things to those Russian boys. Then I saw it, but I couldn't believe my eyes. The tank on our left was turning the cannon on its turret toward us. "Holy Christ," I said to Robert Vaughn, "they're gonna kill us." You never saw people run so fast. Most of us headed to the back of the hotel and prayed. We heard later that the Soviets got a big kick out of their little joke.

I rushed to my room to gather my things when the phone rang. It was John Cassavetes. He had already heard about the invasion and he said, "Ben, don't get killed, I got the money." I think I laughed out loud. It was nice to get some good news.

In the lobby, I dropped my suitcases among those of the other actors and I headed for the dining room. Early each morning we all ate breakfast there before going to work. We had decided to help a young waitress get out of Czechoslovakia, our plan being that she would ride in the car with Robert Vaughn and me, headed for neutral Austria. She would carry no luggage, only her identification papers. Her name was Apolina. There'd been no hanky-panky between her and either of us, we simply liked her style. She was very pretty and smart. I went to the dining room to see if she still intended to go. I felt like I was in a spy movie starring Humphrey Bogart. I was even wearing a trench coat, although it wasn't raining.

Acting completely relaxed and nonchalant I walked into the dining room, looking neither left nor right. The room was empty but for the headwaiter. I'd become very fond of him, too. He was a man in his sixties who wore white tie and tails and took pride in serving even the meager fare available during those sad days in Prague. He usually had a wide-open smile when he greeted me, but not that day. He approached me, took my hand, and said, "Go, American. Go quickly. We are finished."

Tears filled his eyes. As he walked away, Apolina appeared. She simply nodded. She would go with us.

A caravan of cars appeared in front of the hotel. As everyone was pouring into their ride, we squeezed Apolina into our car. At the checkpoint into Austria—Gmund, I think it was—she crouched on the floor and hid beneath our legs. We were in luck: the Russians hadn't yet taken over that checkpoint. The Czechoslovakian guards took a cursory look and waved us through.

We arrived in Vienna that night. Apolina told us she had a friend who she could stay with. She thanked us, kissed me on both cheeks, and waved good-bye. I've often wondered what happened to that Czech girl.

The movie was finished near Rome on the lake at Castel Gandolfo, right under the Pope's summer residence. The Italians built a replica of the real bridge we used in Czechoslovakia and you couldn't tell the difference.

I had a happy time in Prague with Vaughn and George Segal. A strong location palship had formed among us. We worked together on the picture all day—riding tanks, firing light and heavy weapons, running and jumping and ducking while being shot at. That picture got me into good physical shape. At night we dined together, always laughing a lot.

Our camaraderie continued in Rome. There, any one of us would have sworn that our friendships would last forever. There's an expression in our business, "I love you but the show closed." We haven't seen each other for decades.

John Cassavetes and his wife, Gena Rowlands, had rented a villa in Rome on the Appia Antica. Attilio was again my driver and we were singing as we drove up the long driveway to the big, beautiful, rust-colored villa. I had those butterflies of excitement in my stomach. I couldn't wait to work with John. He embraced me at the door, then walked me through a spacious marble foyer that led to a cozy library. He introduced me to the gray-haired, dimple-faced Al Ruban, who was to be our producer. In the corner of the room was Bino Cicogna, a tall, wiry, soft-spoken man who was going to finance the picture. Peter Falk seemed really happy to see me. He smiled and shook my hand.

Peter, John, and I sat and read the screenplay—or rather the material, because it resembled nothing like the movie we finally made. We met several more times. After each reading we'd have intense discussions, throwing out ideas about character and story. I was breathing fresh air again. I had been away from this kind of work for too long.

Still, the three of us remained on guard with each other. We'd all had experiences where our expectations for a project were high and the results turned out low. Besides, I barely knew Peter, and was just getting to know John better. We couldn't be sure how well we'd work together, whether one or more of us would turn into a prima donna, whether we could trust each other.

The first sign that we were headed in the right direction was the fact that John wasn't afraid to change the script. All he cared about were the characters and finding out what each would really do under his own particular circumstances. He rewrote on his feet, dictating to a secretary, and he'd continue working even after Peter and I were gone. There were always surprises—some good, others less so—at the next rehearsal.

I finished my war picture, John and Peter finished their gangster picture, and we headed back to New York to prepare to shoot *Husbands*. Bobby Greenhut, who later went on to produce some of Woody Allen's movies, was the production manager who made many of the New York deals for equipment and locations. Fred Caruso was doing the same in London. Al Ruban would finesse and finalize those deals. Sam Shaw was more or less John's confidant. He'd listen to John's ideas at any time, for no matter how long. Sam was a fine photographer and he was very good with graphics, too. John and he planned the publicity campaign together.

We rehearsed in a very large room in the Piccadilly Hotel, located in the middle of New York's theater district. At our first meeting, John and a secretary who was a whiz at dictation sat across from each other, and Peter and I sat at either end of a long wooden table. Once we began to read the new script I saw, right away, that my part was richer and funnier than it had been in Rome. So was John's, and so was Peter's, too. In fact, it was almost an entirely different script. This was a lot of fun for me. For three years during *Run for Your Life*, I played a character who showed little color and now I felt as if I'd been let out of jail. Nothing was off-limits as far as John was concerned. His delight when one of us did something surprising gave me the feeling I could go in any direction with my character and it would be all right with him. I had gotten hold of something that would be all mine. Here was my long-awaited chance to create a character from the inside out, using as many parts of myself as I could, to make him come alive.

I even chose the name for my character one night over dinner at Frankie and Johnny's, one of our favorite restaurants. To get there, you climbed two long flights of stairs (it had been a speakeasy in the Roaring Twenties), and from the dining room you could see the lights blazing from the theater marquees on Forty-fifth Street.

John had intended to use our actual names for the characters we would play. Peter and I voted against that. We felt it would give the critics more ammunition to use against us if they disliked the movie. John then told us to pick names instead. I'm convinced that John's willingness to share the creative process with Peter and me was in no small part responsible for what made *Husbands* a really good movie.

Al Ruban had told me that Bino Cicogna was causing problems, that he hadn't sent the checks to pay for the weeks of preparation. By John's behavior, Peter and I would never had known it. He ordered the best food and wine Frankie and Johnny's had to offer. I guess the wine made me a little nostalgic. I thought over the names of guys I grew up with. One was Harry Ackerman, the only Jewish boy in that neighborhood. Anti-Semitism was alive and well on Twenty-ninth Street. I saw Harry fight his way home more than once. I chose the name Harry. It had hardly come out of my mouth when Peter yelled "Archie!" I didn't think he looked like an Archie but I joined John in saying,

– Great.

Then I remembered a Greek family in my building on Twenty-ninth Street and the sons' names were Nick and Gus. I told John that I'd always liked the name Gus and you hardly ever heard it anymore. John smiled and nodded. So that's how it happened. I became Harry, John became Gus, and Peter became Archie.

The picture was scheduled to film for twelve weeks, six in New York, six in London. We were ready to go, but the money hadn't arrived. Bino still hadn't sent the checks for the weeks of preparation. It was clear to us that he was nervous about his investment.

John had to hang tough to get *Husbands* made, and Peter and I hung with him. We showed up at rehearsal day after day even though it looked like the movie would never be made. John was being advised by friend and foe alike to take a pay-off and walk away. No dice. He wasn't going to let this go. I had the feeling that John was even trying to drum up a way to finance *Husbands* outside of Bino. He wasn't going to give up the film.

Peter and I were often up in the production office in the West Forties, but we weren't there on December 31 when Bino and Ralph Serpe (who for many years had been, and still was, Dino De Laurentiis's right-hand man) stormed in to say they were shutting the picture down. We were supposed to start shooting in ten days' time.

Al Ruban was alone when Bino and Ralph appeared. Thinking quickly, he locked the door from the inside and got John on the phone; he couldn't reach Peter, but he got to me and to my lawyer, Jay Julien. He told Bino and Ralph we were on our way and that it was best if they explained themselves to all of us. John was already there when Jay and I arrived. So was David Begelman, who was the agent for John, Peter, and me. He and Freddie Fields controlled the most powerful artists' agency of the time, ICM. David had brought Harvey Orkin, who had become an agent after a lifetime of struggling to become a writer.

There was a lot of pacing, arguing, and intense but quiet conversations that afternoon. John concentrated on Ralph Serpe. I had known Ralph for a long time. In 1956 he was in the room when Dino offered me the costarring role opposite Audrey Hepburn in *War and Peace*, one of the films I should not have turned down. Henry Fonda played the part and looked lost. Even his costumes seemed to make him uncomfortable.

Ralph was a troubleshooter for almost all the Italian productions that planned to shoot in the States. Bino must have thought he was just the man to get him out of our deal. Rumor had it that he was connected with the Mob.

It took hours, but the climate slowly changed from hostility to friendliness. John pulled me aside and said,

– I think we got a deal.

– Great.

– But we've got to take a gamble.

– I hope the odds are good.

– It'll make it easier on Bino if we only take expenses, no salaries, until the picture's sold.

– What if we don't sell it?

– We'll sell it. And when we do we'll get a much better payday.

He made me believe it and the work we'd been doing convinced me that we might create something special.

John finally got Peter on the phone. He explained the situation and Peter said he would go along, too. So that was the deal. Serpe, Begelman, and Orkin left. And on that snowy New Year's Eve John, Al, Bino, Jay, and I hammered out a new contract. Jay was an enormous help because he was the only one who knew how to type. John went over every point. He refused to find himself on the short end of any transaction. He'd become as tough and demanding a businessman as he was an artist.

January was very cold but none of us cared. One of the first scenes we shot was the funeral of our friend, which opens *Husbands*. John chose a cemetery in Port Washington, Long Island. I knew his older brother was buried there and, while I'd never heard John mention him, I knew he felt deeply about his brother.

When our characters arrive at the cemetery, there is a very long line of limousines and hundreds of mourners. John was establishing that our late friend Stuart had been a popular, much-loved man. This scene sets up the rest of the film. It becomes clear to each of our characters in his own way that Stuart was not being mourned properly, that the atmosphere with all its formality was cold and unfeeling. So we decided to have our own wake—drinking, singing, laughing, vomiting, and making fools out of ourselves.

From the cemetery, the three of us go to a gym. Our characters, who love basketball, rent gear, running up and down this big space. Soon we're out of breath and we fall to the floor, backs against the wall. Stepping out of character, Peter asked John to cut the camera and John did.

– John, is my eye straight?

He wanted to know if all the running around had moved his glass eye. And John asked me,

– Ben, what do *you* think?

I took a hard look. And said to Peter,

– I think you gotta straighten it.

Peter looked at both of us for some time.

– Okay. Turn around.

Neither of us did. Peter paused and said,

– I never even did this in front of my wife.

And I said,

– We love you more than she does.

I was joking, but maybe it was true. Peter took the eye out without a mirror and replaced it in the right position, looked at us, smiled, and said,

– Okay. Let's shoot.

We played another scene in an empty bar where the three of us are drinking heavily and singing our favorite songs. When we saw the dailies for these scenes, John laughed hysterically. I thought the scene was flat and rather boring. *What was he laughing at?* I wondered. He then said, "This is the worst piece of shit I've ever seen." I'm sure Peter was as relieved as I was to find we had a director who didn't kid himself.

The next day we reshot the scene. This time John found a new bar and arranged to have a dozen extras included in the background. These people didn't know what they were in for. John pulled four tables together and placed all the extras around us. The tables held pitchers of real beer and shots of whiskey, which were actually iced tea. This was the only scene in the picture that was entirely improvised, which meant that none of us had any idea whatsoever what was about to happen. John looked around and said,

– All right, people. We're going to have a singing contest. I'd like every one of you, one at a time, to sing your favorite song.

Peter and I looked at each other in astonishment and I said,

– What are we doing when all of this singing is going on?

– If you don't like the song, if they don't think they put enough feeling into it, you let them know.

It was all about feeling, the ability to express it, to get it out, which tied in with our characters' trying to find a way to mourn our friend. It occurred to me that this whole movie might have been John's homage to his brother Nick. Did he feel that he'd never mourned him properly? I wanted to ask him, but we always seemed to stay away from personal things. As much as I loved John, we got to know each other well only through what we revealed about ourselves as actors and how we faced pressure in our lives.

As a director, John hardly ever told his actors what to do, where to go, when to sit, when to get up, what to think, what mood to be in. But somehow he created the atmosphere for everything to fall into place. This drove Peter crazy, because he wanted clear direction and John would talk and talk, but never get to the point. Peter would often stare at him, then turn to me and say, "Do you understand what this man is saying?"

"Yeah, he wants you to go over there."

"If he wants me to go over there, why doesn't he say, 'Go over there'?"

John smiled, and I walked away so Peter wouldn't see me laughing.

The scene after the singing contest, when all the patrons have left the bar and the three of us husbands linger on until closing, was the moment when Harry feels such affection for Gus and Archie that I took them one by one in my arms and kissed them both smack on the lips. It was completely unscripted and unprepared. But when I did it I knew it was perfect. Peter stared at me dumbfounded and said:

– You are amazing.

John giggled and said,

– Get away from me, you fairy.

That pleased me so much that I shouted gleefully,

– Fairy Harry! I wish I were. I might be better off.

That was a perfect fit for the story. Harry's life at home was not a happy one, to say the least.

Months later, when John screened a rough cut, people thought the drinking scene was too long. John thought the opposite. He knew that only in taking time would the scene really touch audiences. You might not enjoy it, it might make you nervous, it might even bore you, but you wouldn't be indifferent.

Working with John, I never felt the presence of a camera. It always seemed to be far enough away that I'd almost forget it was there. That changed when he started using a handheld camera. That camera became another actor, moving and then lingering, seeming to listen. John always seemed to capture your best moments. He was waiting for surprises—for you to surprise yourself—and he was always there to capture that moment.

In the story, the three husbands leave their wives behind and go to London. There, they gamble, pick up women, anything that spells life for them. We shot the gambling sequences at a casino called the Sportsman's Club. It was an elegant place, and we were drawn back there even when we weren't filming.

Our wives—our real wives, that is—came with us to England. Our kids came, too. I found a charming apartment in Cadogan Gardens, which is in the Chelsea district of London. The place had a little flower-filled garden and was in walking distance of the King's Road, which offered a lot of life and activity that Janice, Liz, and Kate enjoyed. The girls had brought all their Beatles records to London and we bought even more for them there. I think we enjoyed those records even more than the girls did. When I'd get home to our apartment, or rather when I *could* get home, I'd hear "Yesterday," "Lucy in the Sky with Diamonds," "Eleanor Rigby," and all the rest. During dinner they'd still be playing that music, but at a lower volume. After dinner, Janice and I would sing along with the girls, attempting to learn the words to the music. I still remember the lyrics to a Beatles song Liz sang to me in London, when she was nine years old.

Hey Jude, don't make it bad,
take a sad song and make it better.
Remember to let her into your heart,
then you can start to make it better . . .

And so on, very sweetly.

John and Gena, and Peter and his wife, Alice, found apartments in other parts of town. I think that during the eight weeks we were in London, the families may have gotten together only twice. Our wives, unlike their husbands, weren't in need of each other. But they let us devote whatever amount of time we told them we needed to make the picture. Wisely, our wives never came to the set. I guess they knew that making a movie is like being in the middle of a love affair. There's no room for people who are not involved.

At the end of our day's work, we'd often go home, shower, put on some good clothes, and return to the craps table at the Sportsman's Club. The first time we played there, no other customers were at the table. It just wasn't anyone's game. But once we began, our enthusiasm and passionate expletives attracted players from the roulette and blackjack tables to watch these loud Americans.

One night John, Peter, Al, and I broke the bank. Al, especially, had so big a night he was able to buy himself a Jaguar. I don't know what John and Peter did with their winnings, but I bought Savile Row suits and a lot of shirts at Turnbull & Asser. Eventually we lost a lot of the money at the very same table where it had been won. But that night was special. We were winning at such a rate that there was not enough money to cover us, so they had to close the craps table. That was the happy opposite of the movie. In the movie, Gus, Archie, and Harry can't seem to win anything. What were we doing, spending night after night together? Not one of us ever talked about it but it could have been that life was imitating art and that our camaraderie was a part of the making of *Husbands*.

After one week's shooting in London, disaster loomed again. The money ran out and Bino wouldn't send any more, not even our expense money. He's seen the dailies, too, and had gotten cold feet. I don't think he understood what the hell was going on in this movie anyway. But what did John do? He kept shooting. Bino would either have to give us the money or lose the movie. We would then own it and he would never be able to get the film back. Eventually he must have realized that this could happen so he returned to the fold for good. I'm sure that the fact that we stuck together—John, Peter, and I—made that happen.

For the pickup scene, John told Al to find the biggest space in London he could locate. In the story, Gus and Harry have found their girls and Archie is still searching for his. Al located an old, abandoned railroad station called the Round House. John asked to have a bar constructed that was at least one hundred feet long. He wanted a lot of people standing there, drinking and having a good time. Archie was to walk past scores and scores of tables with every seat full, looking for the right girl to pick up and take back to his hotel room. This is where he finds his girl.

John also built a stage where there would be clowns, acrobats, fire-eaters, and trapeze artists swinging from above. This elaborate set was constructed to impress David Picker from United Artists, who would be visiting the set, as would people from Columbia Pictures. John knew that Picker would find these flashy production values appealing. He had no intention of putting that scene in the movie. His scheme worked. Both United Artists and Columbia wanted the picture. The film was sold to Columbia and Bino received his investment plus some, and we three had ourselves a very good payday. We'd made an independent movie, and I thought we'd be lucky if we got some small distribution company to handle it, but now it was going mainstream. That was exciting, because it meant our baby would be promoted properly and would be seen nationwide.

People who see *Husbands* often tell me they believe that John, Peter, and I had been lifelong friends. Not at all. Those friendships were formed during rehearsal and solidified with the making of the movie. If that picture succeeded, it was because in playing those three characters, we ourselves came to trust and like and even love each other. We had become real friends through the process.

It was tough to say good-bye to that movie. The experience of creating Harry and living with him meant that I'd never get him or the film out of my mind. I'd grown to like my character, mainly because of this friendship with Gus and Archie, and I loved making *Husbands* mainly because I'd made new friends in John and Peter. And now it was coming to an end. I knew what that meant—there'd be promises to keep in touch but an almost certain drifting apart. That's probably why the last day of shooting was very emotional for me, more so than on any film or play I'd ever acted in. It was the scene when Archie and Gus say good-bye to Harry before they return home to their dull, predictable lives. Harry, whose wife has left him while he's in London, decides to stay in England. God knows what's in store for him at this fragile point in his life. His friends are all he has and they're leaving. As a farewell gesture he brings a small group of women of all ages to his suite. He orders bottles of Dom Perignon in an attempt at gaiety. Gus and Archie join him, and the three have a very unconventional good-bye. When we shot the scene, the camaraderie, the affection among these men really got to me. While performing on film, I was living a moment I'd dreaded in real life: the end of our friendship.

John was unafraid of a long running time. He had trouble telling his stories in the customary hour and a half or hour and forty-five minutes. He shot an awful lot of film and spent many months in the cutting room, where he changed the entire focus of *Husbands* from one screening to the next. At some screenings Peter's character would dominate things, at others John's, and at still others, mine. Of course the latter was my favorite version. The first time he ran the movie it was a little over four hours long. In spite of the length, I still think that version was *Husbands* at its best. It told the story of the three men fully and was even more entertaining than the final cut. John was obligated contractually to find a way to tell the story in only two hours and fifteen minutes. I know it hurt him to lose so much extraordinary material. But seeing some of my best moments disappear drove me crazy, and at one point it brought about a bad confrontation.

Peter and Al were with John in his office when I stormed in to say that I thought what he was doing in the editing room was ruining the picture. My anger made John furious almost to the point where blows would be exchanged. Instead, I made a dramatic Broadway-style exit, slamming the door behind me. Peter chased after me, and as I got into my car, stuck his head through the window and said,

– Ben, it's gonna all work out.

– I doubt it.

– He's not finished yet.

That stopped me. I suddenly felt awful about what I'd just done. I knew I'd been selfish, but I couldn't control myself. I was human, after all.

Two weeks passed when, early one morning, Al phoned to say that it was time to deliver the final print to Columbia Pictures in New York. John came on the line and said he thought it was important that I be there in order to present a united front. Neither of us spoke of our furious disagreement; I simply had to go. The picture was so good and we'd worked so hard on it that I put my concerns aside and joined them.

We took the red-eye from Los Angeles that very night in order to show the film the next morning to the bosses, Stanley Schneider and Leo Jaffe, in their fancy screening room. Peter couldn't be there because he was shooting the pilot for *Columbo*. Well, the men at Columbia liked what they saw. So did I. I think by then I'd seen about ten different versions of the movie and this was the first time the picture was about three husbands instead of one or two. With so much material to work with, John had spent close to a year in the cutting room. Late into many nights, long after his editor had gone home, he was still at the Moviola trying various ways to bring a scene to life. If he slept, it wasn't for long. He was the artist who would not let something go until it was right.

◀ My first Communion.
New York City 1936.

▶
With my mother and father on
Easter Sunday at my uncle
Jack's house.

◀ Mr. Sinclair seated in front
of our acting group at the
Madison Square Boys Club.
My friend Jackie Passalaqua
is at my right.
New York City 1946.

▶

A Bell For Adano, 1947.
Starting to grow up.

▲ With Claude Rains *in Jezebel's Husband,* 1952. I will never forget his kindness to me.

▲ Performing in *Danger*, 1952. In my first paying job, actor Marty Ritt made playing the role easy for me.

◀ With me, Pat Hingle, and William Smithers in *End as a Man,* 1953. We were a smash.

Starring on Broadway as
Brick in the original
theatrical production of
Cat on A Hot Tin Roof.
New York City 1955.

▼ With Barbara Bel Geddes in the role of Maggie in *Cat.*

WRITHING WITH AGONY, PLAY'S HERO (BEN GAZZARA) IS HELD BY BROTHER WHO QUIETS HIM WHEN CRAVING FOR DRUGS CANNOT BE SATISFIED

Film, Play
on Addicts

From two directions the problems of drug addicts hit the entertainment world. Broadway offered an engrossing new play, *A Hatful of Rain*, whose hero is an ex-G.I. victimized by dope peddlers. From Hollywood came an impressive new movie, *The Man with the Golden Arm*, whose hero, acted by Frank Sinatra, is an ex-addict who succumbs again. The film

kicked up a rumpus when the Motion Picture Association of America refused to approve it because it dealt with the taboo subject of drug addiction. United Artists resigned from the association and will show the movie anyway. Meanwhile *Hatful* was sold to 20th Century-Fox for $250,000, which indicates confidence that the ban against the subject will be lifted.

FIT OF CRAVING, THE MOVIE'S HERO (FRANK SINATRA) BITES TOWEL TO HELP HIM THROUGH TORMENT WHEN HE IS DEPRIVED OF DOPE

▲ Sharing a page in *Life* magazine with Frank Sinatra. I was starring on Broadway in *A Hatful of Rain* and Frank's movie *Man With the Golden Arm* had just been released. Actors playing drug addicts were a novelty in 1956.

◄ Shelley Winters and me in
A Hatful Of Rain, 1956.

▼ Acting with my second wife,
Janice Rule, in the play
Night Circus.
New York City 1958.

▼ Looking for a new play to perform in.
New York City 1957.

With the marvelous James
Stewart and Lee Remick in
Otto Preminger's film
Anatomy of a Murder, 1959.

◀ With the splendid Anna Magnani in
The Passionate Thief, 1960.

▼ Performing with Aline McMahon and one of my childhood idols Frederic March in the movie
The Young Doctors, 1961.

▲ Enjoying my daughter Liz by the sea. Connecticut 1961.

◄ If I could have picked a sister she'd have been Ina Balin, who acted with me in *The Young Doctors*.

►
My brother Tony and me in my West 75th Street apartment. New York City 1957.

▲ Sharing a laugh during rehearsal for *Husbands,* New York City 1969. I was loving the work.

▲ Peter Falk, me, and John Cassavetes in *Husbands,* 1970.

▲ John and me on the set of *Husbands*.

▶
Losing too much money in *The Killing of a Chinese Bookie*, 1976.

▶
Even in bad trouble, Cosmo introduces his players. *The Killing of a Chinese Bookie*, 1976.

▶
With Zohra Lampert and Gena Rowlands in *Opening Night*, 1977.

▲ With Peter Bogdanovich in a scene from *Saint Jack*, 1979. What a time that was.

▼ With Audrey Hepburn on the set of *Bloodline*, 1979. Things between us had become complicated.

▶
With my wife, Elke, shortly after we met, on the Grand Canal, Venice 1981. Italy soon became a second home.

▼ Chuck Barris, John Cassavetes and me watching a Knicks game in Chuck's bedroom at the Wyndham Hotel, 1983.

◀ Drinking and laughing with
Charles Bukowksi, whom I
portrayed in the film *Tales
of Ordinary Madness*.
Los Angeles 1984.

▲ Playing a saint in *Don Bosco*.
Rome 1986.

▶

Gena Rowlands, Aidan Quinn,
Sylvia Sidney and me in
An Early Frost,
the first television movie to
tackle AIDS, 1985.

▲ Taking to an off-camera David Mamet in his film *The Spanish Prisoner,* 1998.

▼ Working with Nicole Kidman in *Dogville,* 2002. I have a lot of respect for her.

▲ Elke and me on our terrace in Vourpia, Italy 2003.

Although they loved *Husbands*, the guys in distribution at Columbia seemed confused about how to market the picture. John of course was going to oversee that phase of the movie, too, to make sure they took care of our hard work. For weeks, a day did not go by that he didn't say, "Come on, let's go up to Columbia." And off we'd go, John, Al, Sam Shaw and I, to 711 Fifth Avenue. We'd walk into the office of Joe Ferguson, the head of publicity, who would call the head of distribution. We had two questions for them: "What theater are you going to open in? What will the ad campaign look like?" In one particularly contentious meeting, I remember that we were told that the small, marginal Festival Theatre on West Fifty-seventh Street was the best house available. We were also shown some terrible ads of Peter, John, and me holding champagne glasses with balloons floating around us. We knew we'd have to fight for something better.

We were opening in a week and had to move fast. I don't know who got to him, but the man who booked the Cinema I—the most prestigious house in New York City—was shown the picture and said that we could have his theater in ten days. We convinced Columbia to go along with this, and that theater was where we screened the picture for the critics. Our reviews were glorious. Newspapers and magazines raved. Aside from the money Columbia was going to spend on advertising, John was able to get an additional $250,000 to aid us in promoting the picture.

On opening, December 8, 1970, John and Sam ran a two-page ad in the *New York Times* with all the magnificent quotes both the film and the acting had received. Columbia thought we were crazy. But it worked. The picture opened to terrific business at Cinema I.

With that, we sort of retired from promoting the film. Peter, John, and I made some appearances with Dick Cavett and Johnny Carson, but the time came at last to let *Husbands* go, to let it walk on its own.

I felt empty, deflated, a kind of postpartum depression. I had just lived through the making of a movie from its start to finish. It was an experience that led to deep, personal friendships that would last a lifetime. Could that ever happen again?

* * *

Nobody became wealthy from the critical success of *Husbands*. Al Ruban came to me one day and said that John was a little jammed up and could use a few bucks. I didn't have much left, but still I asked "How much?" And Al said that ten grand might help a little. So the next day I wrote out a check and sent it over to John's office with a note that said, "It's nothing, John, it's money." The next day John called.

–Would you like to go to Vegas?

– When?

– Tonight.

– Okay.

We landed in Las Vegas and went straight to Caesar's Palace, where we headed to the craps table. It didn't take long for me to realize that things were not the same. We'd always had fun at the craps table before but now the game was cold and businesslike. Gambling had become about making money. Neither of us was having any fun.

We won and we lost, we lost and we won, but there was none of the passion or laughs we'd had in London. It was hard work, and finally we ended up without a dime. On the morning flight back to Los Angeles there was not one word spoken about the long night we'd just spent. John broke the silence,

– Have you ever been to Venice, Italy?

– I sure have.

– How would you like to do a picture there?

– I'd pay to do it.

– Well, I have an idea.

And for the next hour he told me a fascinating story that I knew he was making up as he went along. John always had to be in action. If he wasn't shooting a movie he had to be dreaming up one.

Within a week I received a ten-thousand-dollar check in the mail and attached was a brief message: "Don't ever lend me money again."

CHAPTER 12

OTHER GIGS

QB VII WAS BASED ON LEON URIS'S BOOK OF THE SAME title and took me to England, Belgium, and Israel. Abe Cady, my character, is an American writer who accuses a doctor of performing cruel experiments on Jewish prisoners while he himself was a prisoner in one of Hitler's concentration camps. The accused doctor is a Christian who has been knighted recently by the Queen of England. He sues Cady for defamation and a trial at Queen's Bench VII follows.

The show was the first American TV miniseries film ever made. It ran six hours and aired over four nights in one-and-one-half-hour installments. The cast included Anthony Hopkins as the doctor, Leslie Caron as his wife, Lee Remick as my wife, Anthony Quayle as my lawyer, Robert Stephens as the doctor's lawyer, and Jack Hawkins as the judge. Also appearing were Dame Sybil Thorndike, John Gielgud, Joseph Wiseman, and Sam Jaffe.

The segments depicting Cady's life as a young man were shot in Los Angeles. One day, while shooting a scene in which I taunt my father for his rigid Orthodox beliefs, the assistant director told me I was wanted on the phone.

It was Janice with very sad news. Thom was dead. He had rented a motel room and taken a lot of sleeping pills. I asked how Kate took the news, and Janice said that she was being brave but it was clear that Kate was shattered. I said that I'd rush home right after the last shot was completed. As I walked back toward the set, I wondered whether I had given the man one of the wounds that led him to kill himself.

The funeral was held two days later. I asked Janice to invite everyone to our house afterward, including Thom's wife, Millie Perkins. She and Thom had two daughters together and they were there, too. There were also our friends and, of course, Kate and Liz. However, I continued to feel conflicted over his death. Here I was, hosting these people in my home, yet I felt like an intruder. I couldn't even bring myself to say the name of the person we were mourning.

At one point, Kate came to me behind the bar where I was mixing a dry martini. Her big, blue eyes were swollen from days of tears. Kate had allowed me to raise her as my daughter—that is, to pay for her upbringing—until she was thirteen or so, at which time she decided to return to her father, who had since remarried. This pained Janice terribly and I didn't like it either, but I never resented her for it. I respected Kate's choice. She admired her father; Kate and I had never really "bonded." Her longing for her father had precluded that. Thom's funeral was the beginning of the end of what little relationship remained.

– Thank you, Benny, for inviting everyone.

– Thanks are not necessary. We're family.

– What a family!

She had me there. I could've told her how tough it had been for Janice and me; that our beginning was overly complicated; that maybe Kate and I never really had a chance. Instead, I said nothing. As I stirred the Bombay gin, I considered how I'd handled myself when Kate was with Janice and me. I'd made sure that she was always on equal footing with Liz. How often I'd felt a young father's desire to squeeze, hug, and kiss his daughter, but I was held back by Kate's pain at not being with her father. In order to compensate for that I tried to show her that my affection for Liz was no greater than what I felt for her. I never complimented one girl more than another, nor rewarded one over the other. My intentions were right but the effect was wrong. In a foolish attempt at being even-handed, I robbed Liz of the simple and uncomplicated beginnings a father and daughter should have.

I went around the room making small talk—very small indeed. This was not my crowd. I felt out of place. Liz came up to me. Thom's death wasn't easy for her, either. She had been very fond of him.

— When are you leaving, Dad?

— Tomorrow.

She embraced me.

— I'm gonna miss you.

She said the right thing at the right time.

The day after Thom's funeral I was on a plane for England. The courtroom sequences for *QB VII* were shot at Pinewood Studios in London. I made quick friendships with all the terrific English actors in the cast. Quayle, Hawkins, Hopkins, and I would have lunch together practically every day. Jack had been blessed with a warm, distinctive voice, but he had developed cancer of the throat and a good part of his vocal chords had been removed. He spoke through a device inserted into his trachea. I was touched by the charm and good humor with which this fine actor faced what to him must have been horror.

One day he said, quite matter-of-factly, that in America they had devised a way to return full voice to people in his circumstances. "As soon as I finish here, I'm on my way," he said. Well, he did just that, and as a result of the operation, he died. I think he understood the risk but he was first and foremost an actor. He wanted his voice back. He wanted to be whole again.

Hopkins, who could do a very good imitation of Jack, dubbed his performance under a pseudonym. Watching Quayle and Stephens, with their beautiful vocal equipment, square off against each other was very exciting. And even dubbed, you felt the sardonic humor in Jack's performance. In spite of his challenges, his craft was very much in evidence.

I had the honor of acting in one scene with Dame Sybil Thorndike, whose tenderness was very touching. Although our acting styles differed (she played Saint Joan in George Bernard Shaw's original production of *Saint Joan* in 1923), I watched her and her fellow English actors with respect and admiration. Their craft, the subtle ways each actor choreographed his or her performance, was thrilling. They were like ace three-card monte players: you think you've seen real thought and it's not there, you think there's real feeling but no—look again. They do it so well that I wondered why we Americans go through all that struggle and suffering trying to live the characters we play when we might have more fun and satisfaction taking the British actors' advice: "Oh, just act it, for godsake!"

From London, the cast and crew went to Israel to shoot scenes where Abe Cady has chosen to live. We shot in Tel Aviv and Jerusalem, where I saw an especially good-looking girl on the set one day. Her skin was bronzed by the sun, and she had high cheekbones, sparkling eyes, and a lovely figure. I introduced myself. She smiled warmly and said her name was Sara. She was on leave from the army. I liked her a lot on the spot and she liked me, too. Together we toured Jerusalem, including the Arab quarters where we weren't particularly welcome. She knew which restaurants were good and which to avoid.

One time, at lunch, she told me that she had earned quite a few medals in the army, honors for shooting, among them. I told her I'd love to see them, and asked her to wear her medals that night. She later appeared at my hotel room door, her medals strewn across the left side of her uniform. No sooner had she stepped into the room than we started undressing. I unbuttoned her shirt but before she could take it off, we were all over each other. There I was, rolling on the bed with a sharpshooter.

This twenty-two-year-old Israeli girl made me happier than I'd been in a long time. I had a hunch that if I remained in Israel long enough, I would fall for Sara. But I wasn't trusting enough, and figured that if I remained at arm's length I wouldn't get hurt.

Sara and I had the classic on-location romance. Everything we said to each other was tremendously interesting and amusing. Our passion and abandon was the stuff of fantasies. We had a beautiful beginning, free and unburdened, then later a tender ending, but like most on-location affairs there was no middle part. And that's not always bad, because often it's the middle that kills you.

When it was time for me to leave Israel, Sara drove me to the airport. We said au revoir, but we both knew it was good-bye. It was the first time since meeting Janice that I had allowed myself to be emotionally involved with a woman, unlike the many other women I'd had affairs with. Sara had really touched me. If my stay had been longer there's no telling what might have happened. But my feelings for Sara were proof that romance was still alive and kicking inside me. If I wasn't overly careful, I might be able to fall in love again.

In 1975 I got a call from Stuart Rosenberg, a director and an old friend who I hadn't seen in years. He was about to direct a picture in Spain, *Voyage of the Damned*, and wanted me for it. Stuart had already assembled one hell of a cast—Faye Dunaway, Max von Sydow, Maria Schell, Malcolm McDowall, Lee Grant, Julie Harris, and Orson Welles, among others.

Voyage of the Damned told the story of a ship, *The Spirit of St. Louis*, and its departure in 1939 from Germany with a boatload of Jewish passengers. Goebbels had cynically allowed the boat to sail for Cuba, betting that they would not be allowed entry. Sure enough, they were not. The captain then turned the ship around and sailed for New York, where the Roosevelt administration also refused to accept its cargo. And so *The Spirit of St. Louis* was forced to return to Europe, where the great majority of its passengers were sent to Hitler's death camps.

In the movie, Welles played the official responsible for deciding who got into Cuba, and I played an American lawyer pleading the case of these desperate people. We had a seven-page scene to do together, and I wanted to see how Orson worked, so I went to the set where he was shooting another sequence. I noticed that he would get half a line into the scene with the girl, then stop to ask the director a question. He did this repeatedly. I could tell that he just couldn't remember his lines. I thought, *Jesus, it's going to be a long day tomorrow.* Then I had an idea. I went to see him at our hotel later that night.

– Orson, my name is Ben Gazzara.

– Oh, yes, Ben, of course I know who you are.

– I have a problem remembering lines. I don't know what's happening.

– Really? Why don't we rehearse then? Meet me in my suite tomorrow morning at seven. We have an early call, you know, and that's a long scene. But don't worry about it. We'll rehearse and rehearse.

– Gee, I appreciate that, Orson.

So I knocked on his door at seven, he invited me in, and told me breakfast was on the way. I told him I'd eaten. He said,

– Well, give me a moment.

The breakfast—two cartsful—arrived shortly: a pitcher of orange juice, six croissants, four fried eggs, bacon, yogurt, bread, chicken.

– Will you have some, Ben?

– No, no.

– All right then, let me pick at this.

About a half-hour goes by, he devours the entire meal, and says,

– Let's read it.

So we read it. Whereupon he says,

– Let's read it again.

When I reached the set I was feeling flutterings in my stomach again. I was about to act with the man who made *Citizen Kane, The Magnificent Ambersons, Touch of Evil*—all classics. And Orson was a classic by himself. To my surprise, we shot our scene in one take. Orson had learned his lines that morning by talking them to me for an hour. I tricked him and it worked. One of my proudest moments.

While the crew was relighting for another set up of the scene, Orson and I discussed a mutual friend who some studio executive had said was too old to direct a certain motion picture. The friend was fifty-five. Orson was around sixty and I could see how deeply the situation offended him. Years before, the major Hollywood studios had turned their backs on him, refusing to give him a dime to make a movie. From then on it was tough going for Welles. He had to scheme and struggle too long and too hard to raise money in order to continue making movies.

* * *

When I returned from Spain, I learned that Janice had developed a nerve problem that sent pain up and down her left arm. Doctors were unable to determine the cause and her suffering worsened. A couple of experts recommended surgery. After much thought and discussion, Janice decided to try it. For a couple of weeks, she was pain free but later the problem returned, as severe as ever. A neurologist prescribed Percodan to assist with the pain. In time it became her best friend.

Liz graduated from high school and decided to study art, art history, and photography in Florence. I thought it was a terrific choice. Her mother's condition precluded travel so when the time came, I would accompany Liz to Italy in order to set her up at her school.

When Liz and I arrived in Florence, we hunted for a place for her to live. Nevertheless we found the time to go to the Uffizi Gallery, enjoy cappuccinos in the Piazza della Signoria, and dine in charming little restaurants. Our favorite spot was Camillo's. During dinner, after we'd been there on two or three occasions, Liz became red in the face.

Embarrassed, she said, "Dad, they think I'm your girlfriend."

"I've never been more flattered," I said.

One morning, walking along the Arno River, we ran into Robert Rauschenberg, who was in Florence preparing a showing of his works at Forte Belvedere. He suggested we come there that afternoon and spend time with him. Liz was excited by the idea.

We were greeted warmly, then sort of hung around as Bob determined the placement of his works. He had assistants, but he handled and moved many of the pieces himself. They were spectacular works, many created with found objects. You didn't have to be an expert to see that Rauschenberg was and would be an important modern artist.

I found Liz an apartment in a picturesque neighborhood where artists and artisans lived and worked. School began two days later and it was time for me to go. Liz and I had really gotten along well and had enjoyed each other's company. It was the longest uninterrupted time I'd ever had with her. Between my work and other professional

commitments, I'd never had an opportunity to take leisurely trips with
her. Now that she had grown into a young woman, I realized how
quickly time had passed. I left Florence with a heavy heart.

If the L.A. house was lonely before Liz left for Italy, it now became
impossible. Janice's condition had worsened. To kill the pain, she'd taken
to mixing her Percodan with vodka, a combination that altered her per-
sonality. Where once she had been simply opinionated, now she was strident. Where once she had been passionate, now she was loud. Despite
her problems, she pulled off a coup: she was accepted into the Los
Angeles Psychoanalytic Institute to study to become a psychoanalyst.
Very few people who are not M.D.s are accepted into such an institute. I
admired her for the discipline it took for a person in her condition to
fight through the drugs and the booze and accomplish what she did.

When she first told me about her intentions, I was surprised. Janice
had always been a determined and talented actress. She had recently done
a couple of very fine pieces of work. Her performance in *The Chase* with
Marlon Brando was particularly good. I enjoyed her in *The Swimmer*
with Burt Lancaster, too; although she was already suffering nerve pain,
her performance was alive and quite touching.

I don't know whether the situation for women in film has changed,
but in the 1970s it was a difficult profession for women, especially after
age forty or so. They were offered parts less frequently, and those roles
that came along were usually uninteresting. Janice decided that she wasn't
going to sit around and wait. I respected her for that but her decision also
had its downside. The guests in our house were no longer artists, they
were analysts. The talk was no longer outrageous and funny, it was
serious and sober. These analysts derived satisfaction from studying emotions; I became an actor in order to express them.

When Marty Fried, a director I knew from the Actors Studio, called to
say there was a guy from Chicago who had a beautiful new theater and

he wanted to open with a production of *Hughie*, by Eugene O'Neill—with me as the star—I thought it might prove to be a way to escape an increasingly somber situation.

I picked up a copy of the play without knowing anything about it and found the writing terrific. I was ready to get out of Los Angeles, and in the fall of 1976 I left for New York, alone. Hughie went into rehearsal in a small theater in Queens on the site where the 1964 New York World's Fair had been.

My days and nights spent at Harold's Bar had furnished a lot of good material I could use to create the character of Erie. He's a Broadway sharpie, a gambler, and a loser, but he has a way of turning reality on its head so that the ending is always a happy one. He's a dreamer—a pipe dreamer—and God knows I'd rubbed elbows with plenty of those guys. I devised a strident walk I thought would be right for Erie, along with a vocal rhythm. I tried to demonstrate the pride and dignity that kind of person would have.

Hughie was virtually a one-man show. The action takes place in the lobby of a third-rate hotel near Broadway. Erie enters late at night after a two-day binge of gambling and boozing. He claims he's tired and must go to bed but instead regales the desk clerk with stories about a friend named Hughie. His tales may or may not be true. Peter Maloney played the desk clerk brilliantly. He had only a dozen lines of dialogue but the way he listened, with an utterly exhausted and forlorn look, was riveting.

We opened in Chicago to splendid notices. Jay Julien thought it might have a chance in New York, so we took it there. But we had a problem in terms of the show's length: can a one-hour play fill a Broadway evening?

Val Avery, who gave such terrific performances in Cassavetes's *Faces* and *Minnie and Moskowitz*, invited me for lunch at the Players, a club in a lovely town house in downtown Manhattan. The Players had started as a private club for actors but now took in writers, journalists, and even critics. I was chatting with Val near the library when through the corner of my eye, I saw Brooks Atkinson seated in a burgundy-colored uphol-stered chair. As theater critic for the *New York Times* for many years, he had always given me glowing reviews. Although retired, he still wrote an occasional Sunday piece.

I approached Atkinson and introduced myself. I told him that I was planning to appear in *Hughie* on Broadway, adding that I wondered if we might need another play, a curtain raiser, to fill out the evening. He thought we did. That was all I needed to hear. I informed Jay of Atkinson's opinion and we decided to look for something that would work. I read quite a few one-act plays over the next week, but no luck. Nothing seemed to fit.

The one that fascinated me most was *The Man with the Flower in His Mouth*, by the great Italian playwright Luigi Pirandello. This title character looks at life in a completely original manner, able to see and enjoy things that had seemed ordinary only a short time before. The flower the man is carrying in his mouth is cancer, and despite his anger at having this affliction, now he lingers where he used to hurry, looks where he used to glance. He marvels at every move a shop girl makes as she ties a string around a package. He's stopping time. He's making everything last longer, perhaps even life itself. I found the play powerful and moving. It would be a great challenge, but I realized that if we did this play, it ran the risk of dominating the evening. O'Neill's *Hughie* might suffer by comparison. We decided to keep looking.

Then one day, Marty Fried suggested a play by David Scott Milton he had directed at the American Place Theatre. We read it, liked it, and we decided to use it.

Duet deals with a man who thinks he's being followed by the Russian secret police, but in fact is chasing himself. This meant playing two characters, with constant appearances and disappearances, changes of costume, speech rhythms, and accents. It was a good thing I was in shape because it was hard work. It was a physically exhausting play to do.

Although I got great reviews and earned my second Tony nomination, we did no business. People didn't seem to want to see a revival of a one-act O'Neill play, no matter how well we filled out the evening.

John Cassavetes attended a performance of *Hughie/Duet* near the end of our run. After the show we went to Frankie and Johnny's for supper and halfway through the meal he said we'd be starting a new picture together soon. I figured he was just trying to cheer me up, because he knew I was pretty upset about my show closing, so I didn't take him seriously. In fact, I forgot about it.

After *Hughie/Duet* closed and I was back home in L.A., David Scott Milton was the first person I called.

– Hello, David, you wanna go to the gym?

– Ben, where are you?

– I'm here. I'm in my house in L.A.

– Is there a problem? Did something happen? What about the show?

– The show closed.

There was a long pause.

– I'll be a sonofabitch. How could it close with those reviews? It should've run at least two years.

– I don't know, David, but nobody came.

– Sonofabitch.

– I feel like playing some racquetball. Wanna meet me at the Century West Club?

– What time?

– In about an hour?

– I'll be there.

We embraced each other at the door. I saw he was fighting back tears. The play had meant a great deal to him and now it was no more. I felt bad enough for myself, but I felt even worse for him. I'd relied on pride to get myself through the weeks of playing a show I knew would have a brief run. I made it fun for myself, trying new things, making changes in my performance, never allowing myself to become depressed, but the look I saw on David's face gave me my cue. I started crying. Every feeling I'd bravely suppressed came pouring out in tears.

CHAPTER 13

SHOULD WE KILL HIM?

CASSAVETES SURPRISED ME AGAIN. ONLY TWENTY-FOUR hours after I'd landed in L.A., he called to say he'd be ready to shoot a movie, *The Killing of a Chinese Bookie*, in about two weeks. "Are *you* ready?" he asked. I sure was. If ever I needed an ego boost it was at that moment. I liked working with John so much because he wanted nothing more than for his actors to do well. I think it's safe to say that most actors who appeared in a Cassavetes movie have never given better performances.

Husbands had been a liberating experience, freeing me to create from scratch the man I played. Since then I'd appeared in highly commercial projects in which my characters were set in stone. I was grateful to have another chance to be part of the creation of my character.

Exactly two weeks later I was playing Cosmo Vitelli, the owner of a strip joint whose club is not only his home but his life. He directs all the shows with a panache that the great Florenz Ziegfeld would have applauded. The sketches are not especially sexy or funny, but Cosmo pours his heart into them. They're his sole source of happiness. But gambling is his weakness and it soon lands him in trouble with some unforgiving gangsters.

In the first scene of the movie, Cosmo pays off a large debt to the loan shark played by Al Ruban, who was also producing the picture. That first scene was also the first sequence we shot, because John liked to shoot his films in order. Directors hardly ever have that luxury but it was John's money—raised by him alone—and his prerogative. Shooting in sequence is a joy for the actor. You have a chance to feel your way around and get to know who and what you are before having to play scenes that take place in the middle or even at the end of the movie. I think that many of the things John did as a director came from how he wished he had been treated but hadn't been when he worked as an actor.

The production felt strange that first day. I wasn't enjoying myself, which was unusual for me on a Cassavetes picture. Everything seemed businesslike, impersonal. I called Al that night and told him that I hadn't enjoyed shooting our scene. "It wasn't you, Al. You were terrific. But is something wrong with John? Is there a problem?" "Not that I know of," said Al.

The next day we shot a night scene in Cosmo's club. The scene takes place just prior to showtime, which is Cosmo's favorite moment. He visits his girls and Mr. Sophistication, his gay master of ceremonies, while they're dressing for the first show of the night. Cosmo comes to rally his troops, to bolster them into giving the best show that's in them. He hopes to lift their spirits by telling them a story about the danger of tainted food. "Botulism can result and you don't fool around with botulism. It ain't no joke." Cosmo goes on and on, tossing off his amusing theories. I expected the scene to run simply with me telling the story while others listened. Not in a Cassavetes movie. John had told the girls and Meade Roberts, who played Mr. Sophistication, to interrupt me when they felt like it, to agree or disagree, be interested or bored as they saw fit. He knew I'd fight through their reactions no matter what, which I did. At last I began to have fun on that picture.

What a pleasure to work with such freedom. With the pressure off, an actor didn't have to bring in a scene prepared and ready to go, with no elbow room either for small or drastic changes.

The next day Cosmo rents a big limo and picks up three of his star strippers to keep him company when he goes to a private gambling casino. Well, he loses. His debt is $25,000 and he can't pay it. He's lost to the wrong people and, after many threats, he's told they'll take his club and the slate will be clean. These guys know that the club is Cosmo's life and after letting him sweat, they propose a solution. If he were to kill a certain Chinese bookie, the score would be settled.

It was while shooting the sequence where I dropped the girls home after this awful night that I came to understand for the first time the picture I was making. I had just walked the last girl to her door. John was kneeling on the floor of the limo holding a handheld camera, following the action. When the scene ended and he took the camera away from his face, I saw that he looked sad. Out of the blue, he started talking about dreams and how they were the most valuable things people have. Not everyone was a dreamer, however. At the opposite end of the spectrum, there were the killers of the dream, the people who were the "nuisances" that make it difficult to go on. This must have touched John deeply because his eyes suddenly filled with tears.

It was then that I understood. The picture could have been a metaphor for John's life: a man with a dream having to battle people without vision. I knew at that moment what had made me uncomfortable that first day of shooting. John was outside the scene, behind the camera. In *Husbands* he'd always been beside me, in front of it. Here, in the back of that limousine, talking about his feelings, John had stepped out from behind the camera to join me in the scene.

John liked to take chances. The girls he cast as the strippers were not actresses, and yet three of them had scenes throughout the movie. One of the three—a tall, beautiful, very shapely black girl—played my lover. When we were driving to the gambling casino where Cosmo goes into debt, I saw firsthand how John got performances from amateurs: he did nothing. He told them jokes; we laughed together. They told a few jokes and we started shooting. John was sitting on the floor of the limo pointing a handheld camera at us. If the girls ever had stage fright, they were over it. They were themselves, simple and honest. There was no acting.

Working with the actors who played the gangsters was different. They were professionals and John expected them to bring him something special. One night, while shooting in a car parked on Sunset Boulevard, he didn't think his actors were putting enough thought into the work. It was the first time during filming that I saw John become angry. It may have been real anger or it may have been his way of jump-starting the scene, but whatever it was, it worked. The next take was terrific.

One element that helped reduce pressure was John's decision to remove the lighting. He turned to Al and said, "Let's do this with only the lights of the passing traffic." The interior of the car was concealed by total darkness. Three of the gangsters sat in the back, one in the driver's seat, me in the middle next to him, and another gangster on my right. There were some good actors in that scene, too: Seymour Cassel, Timothy Carey, Robert Phillips, Morgan Woodward, and John Red Kollers. Their characters instructed Cosmo on how to enter the compound where the Chinese bookie lived, get to him, and kill him. It wouldn't be easy; the place is guarded by armed men and ferocious dogs. I had a hard time seeing the faces of the other actors and found John's approach to be a futile experiment, especially since the camera couldn't be seeing much either. The next day at the dailies, I was proven wrong. The scene had a sense of foreboding and menace it could never have had otherwise.

John wrote what's probably my favorite scene in the movie on the morning we shot it, in a hot dog joint on the Sunset Strip. We didn't change a word. It's night. Cosmo is on his way to kill the bookie and stops at a gas station. He goes into a telephone booth and calls his club. He wants to know how things are going there. Is the Paris number being performed? At the other end, Vince, the manager, doesn't understand. At that moment I thought that to make myself clear it would be fun to sing Vince the song from the sketch—"I can't give you anything but love, baby"—and therefore juxtapose the life-and-death mission that Cosmo is about to undertake with his childlike concerns about his club. The moment is classic Cassavetes, touching and amusing at the same time.

John loved what I was doing with the material so much that he picked up the handheld camera and practically jumped into that phone booth with me.

— Sing the whole song, Ben.

— I don't know the whole song, John.

— I don't care. Hum what you don't know.

So I did what I could and John covered that scene up and down and in and around. It's my favorite scene of the movie.

Finally, the night arrived when we shot the killing. The crew set up at a house in the Hollywood Hills. Meanwhile John and I had dinner in an Italian restaurant on Sunset Boulevard. He turned to me and with an I'm-not-kidding look in his eyes, he said, "Do you think we should kill him?" "Who?" I asked. "The bookie," he replied. The picture is called *The Killing of a Chinese Bookie*, and he's thinking that it might be more interesting not to kill him—and on the very night we were to shoot that scene. Maybe the picture would find a more interesting direction, he suggested. Should-we-or-shouldn't-we went on for some time. Then Al appeared, pointing to his watch. "John, everybody's waiting." John looked at me and sighed. "Okay," he said, "let's go up and kill him."

It was the first time I'd laid eyes on the actor who played the man I was supposed to kill. He was wading in an indoor swimming pool, talking in Chinese to a beautiful Asian girl. An elderly man, delicately built, he looked like a gentle college professor. I could see why John was having trouble killing him. He had cast entirely against type and found it hard to harm the kind of man he'd chosen. We killed him anyway.

—— CHAPTER 14 ——

THE THEATER

THE DAY AFTER *CHINESE BOOKIE* OPENED AT MANN'S Westwood Theatre in L.A., I went into rehearsals for *Who's Afraid of Virginia Woolf?*, costarring Colleen Dewhurst and directed by Edward Albee. We decided to rehearse in Los Angeles, because I was living there and Colleen was finishing up a movie in town. But I wasn't thrilled to be acting in one of the great American plays. As a matter of fact, I felt pretty down. *Bookie* had gotten indifferent notices. My feelings were hurt by the critical response and remained so for some days. Oddly, this actually helped me with the part of George in Albee's play. A major reason for the war between George and his wife, Martha, is a lifetime of hurt feelings. I knew firsthand that when mixed with whiskey those feelings can lead to dangerous, if not savage, behavior—albeit dressed up in highly literate and witty banter.

Our cast of four read the play for Albee. It tells the story of two unhappy couples whose relationships unravel in the course of a booze-sodden evening together. George is a history professor at a small New England university; Martha is the daughter of the university's president. She invites Nick, the new young faculty member, and his neurotic wife, Honey, home for a two-in-the-morning, postparty drink. The ambitious young couple is gratified by the attention of these influential figures, but the event rapidly turns into a nightmare of recriminations, accusations, and attempted seductions. Everyone's dirty laundry is remorselessly dragged out—the hysterical pregnancy that led to Nick and Honey's lifeless marriage, the imaginary son George and Martha have invented to keep their own marriage from falling apart. Dawn finds all four stripped of their masks and illusions, and maybe ready to face life without them.

When our reading ended I expected Edward to do what most playwrights would do at this point, to explain to us the backgrounds of the troubled people we were to play. He didn't. He might've also indicated how his play should look and sound. He didn't. Instead he started putting the play on its feet.

I'd never played a character who possessed George's intellect and dark humor, and yet I felt at home. Edward had a large hand in that. I was pleased and surprised when he told us he didn't want to repeat or duplicate the staging from other productions of the play. Our staging would be tailored specifically to our cast. I simply cleaned up my diction and let the witty and acerbic dialogue carry me along.

Even though Edward obviously knew his own play inside out he never tried to push us toward what he thought we ought to do. Rather, he allowed Colleen and me to find our own way. In effect, rehearsals were used to help make us comfortable with the language and its intricate rhythms. He trusted us to find the inner lives of the characters through the process of acting. Here he was the director, not the writer.

The very talented actors Maureen Anderman and Richard Kelton played the young couple who innocently walk into the verbal fusillade. Their characters listen and watch with open mouths as the war rages between George and Martha. Colleen and I worked well together and found not only the vitriol to make sparks fly but, more importantly, the humor at the heart of the play. I knew that Edward was pleased by my performance because his notes to me were never about my handling of his dialogue—they almost always concerned tempo. Once that was on target, the play took off.

One of the reasons Edward and I never had a lengthy conversation about my character, I believe, was because he didn't want to discuss the feelings that gave birth to his play. I would have to discover those emotions myself. As a result, we were polite but rather distant toward each other. Was it shyness on both our parts? I don't know. We might have gone even further and deeper had we shared our thoughts about the play, but those conversations never took place.

We got splendid reviews in Boston, which was to be our only out-of-town tryout before opening in New York. James Karen was standing by for me, meaning that if I were run over by a truck, which was the only way I would have missed a performance, he would go on for me. I'd known Jimmy since my early days at the Actors Studio. He was already a member when I joined, and he was one of the actors who appeared in our adaptation of *Catcher in the Rye*. Jimmy and I now became the friends we should have been years earlier. He made the road less lonely.

I'm sure that Ken Marsolais, Colleen's companion and our producer, saw in *Virginia Woolf* a vehicle for Colleen's tremendous talent and stature as an actress. In addition, she had that wide-open smile and bright eyes look in her that betrayed vulnerability—all perfect qualities for the role of Martha.

We opened in New York to good reviews from everyone, including Clive Barnes of the *New York Times*, God bless him. I received my third Tony nomination for that performance.

Colleen and I enjoyed ourselves together enormously onstage and after the curtain came down we'd sit in her dressing room—the closest dressing room to the door that led to the street—and I'd almost always linger. I liked Colleen so much and I was warmed by her affection toward me. Jimmy Karen was usually there and friends popped in, too. We amused each other, telling stories, having laughs—with the help of some very fine scotch whisky. But there was more to my lingering than simply having good times. I was stalling. I just didn't want to go home. It was empty there.

During the runs of *Virginia Woolf* I lived alone in our New York apartment, as I had done when I did *Hughie/Duet*. It was pretty quiet and lonely. It would have been nice to have some people around. My nights with strange women were not filling the bill.

The night Cassavetes came to see the play, Colleen was struggling to hold on to her voice. She was often hoarse, but this time she had no voice at all. There was no understudy for her so the only choices were to cancel the show or to let her go on and hope for the best. Well, she went on. It was both an act of bravery and wishful thinking.

That performance was demanding work for everyone. I could barely make out the words Colleen was saying onstage and I knew the people seated in that packed theater were hearing even less. I worked harder that night than I ever had as an actor. We were a team and the play would collapse without both of us. I tried to fill in what I was sure the audience was not hearing. It wasn't easy. I couldn't wait for the play to end. When the curtain fell, there was thunderous applause and when we came out for our curtain calls, we got a standing ovation. Go figure.

Cassavetes came backstage and he, too, joined the revelry in my dressing room. After everyone had cleared out, he mentioned that he had written a screenplay about the theater, and in it he'd created a great part for me. He wanted to start shooting the movie in three months.

In the early spring of 1978, I moved west again. I still had my house with Janice in Westwood. Her condition had not improved and she was over-medicating herself in the tried-and-true way. Despite her excess, she went to her office every day. She was now a full-fledged psychoanalyst and had a couple of patients. I had the impression, however, that it was more of an impassioned hobby than a profession, and that if she were offered a part in a movie that would take six months to shoot on the island of Bora Bora, she would have swum there, ready for hair and makeup.

Again, John Cassavetes had to finance his picture himself. He knew his work had been marginalized by the powers that *were* at the time. He never bothered to show the script of *Opening Night* to any of the major distribution companies; he knew they didn't understand him. Neither did most American audiences, for that matter. In France, Germany, Spain, and Italy he was highly respected and considered an artist who had revolutionized cinema, and, probably more than any other American director, had given filmmakers all over the world a chance to dream about making their own movies, but at home people hadn't caught on. That was yet to come.

Nevertheless Cassavetes was able to finance *Opening Night* and we started shooting soon after my return to L.A. I played the director of a play that was to open on Broadway after an out-of-town tryout, and John played the show's leading actor.

The interior theater sequences were shot in the Pasadena Civic Auditorium. When I arrived on location for the first day of shooting, Al Ruban was already on the set, busily instructing the crew where to place the lights to illuminate the enormous space. It didn't take me long to realize that Al would be the director of photography. All along I'd thought he was mainly a numbers guy, the person who made the deals in order to make John's movies possible. No one, including Al, had ever told me that he'd mastered the craft of cinematography. That revelation taught me an important lesson: never pigeonhole anyone. The person next to you may be capable of things you never thought possible. It was one thing for Al to act in a scene while producing a movie, but here he had the responsibility of photographing the entire motion picture himself.

The handheld camera that John often used made Joan Blondell very nervous. She had starred in films since the late thirties, but in a Cassavetes picture she never knew when she was being photographed. One day she said, "I hope he doesn't follow me to the bathroom." Paul Stewart, who'd belonged to Orson Welles's Mercury Theatre and who appears as the butler at the beginning and the end of *Citizen Kane*, played the producer in our film. Decades earlier he had worked with Welles, the most innovative young rebel of his day, and here he was again, working with another. He was obviously a good judge of talent. It must have been galling for Paul to have been typecast in gangster roles for much of his career.

Gena Rowlands played a star who is having a very tough time accepting old age. In one particularly brilliant dressing-room scene, Gena's character, Myrtle, shows up drunk for the opening-night performance. As her director, I have to make Myrtle up and get her ready to go on. We never rehearsed or even discussed the scene. Neither of us knew what the other would do and I had only a rough idea what I would say. This gave the sequence the look of spontaneity, that it was happening for the first and only time. Gena was wonderful. It was not until we did that scene that I realized the depth of her talent. She was simple, easy, quiet, and yet I could almost read her mind. It was screen acting at its best. The scenes John played with Gena in the play-within-the-play, however, were tightly scripted. He and Gena brought an elegance and an irony to the material that didn't seem acted, either. I never saw them rehearse those sequences but they were letter-perfect, natural, and funny. They must have taken their work home with them.

For the setting John didn't choose a modest theater the size of a Broadway house—like, say, the Music Box or the even larger Broadhurst. No, he chose something the size of Radio City Music Hall and filled it with real people who would be our audience. He took out an ad in the local paper and the citizens showed up, gratis, and they were entirely believable as a real audience—which, of course, they were. When we shot the opening-night sequence, they arrived in their finest attire, some men even in tuxedos and many women in long evening gowns. But it was their reactions to the events onstage that felt so genuine—natural could never get that kind of authenticity from professional extras.

One day, near the end of shooting, John had an unbreakable appointment. I'm sure it had to do with money—those appointments always did. *Opening Night* was costing more than he thought it would. Budgets were getting tighter. But it was a shooting day and John asked Peter Bogdanovich if he would kindly direct a particular visual sequence while he was gone.

I'd met Peter at a dinner party some years before, around the time he was going to Texas to shoot his second movie, *The Last Picture Show*, which became a big success. He had seen *Husbands* and peppered me with questions about John and how he worked with actors. Peter had been impressed with the freedom of our performances. I was not in the sequence Peter was going to shoot, but I came on the set to say hello, and he asked me to hang around and have lunch with him.

During that lunch, I made Peter laugh over and over. I was having one of my good days. That night the phone rang. It was him.

– Listen Ben, I'm gonna do a picture in Singapore. It's based on a book by Paul Theroux. It's called *Saint Jack*. I want you to play Jack.

I kept my cool.

— Is there a screenplay?

— Yeah. I've been working with a friend of mine, Howard Sackler, who wrote *The Great White Hope*, and we've got a first draft. Why don't you come to the house tomorrow around noon, pick up the script, and we'll talk.

The meeting went well and I was invited on board. And that was exciting. I was about to work with a man who'd been written and talked about as one of the truly important directors of the 1970s. His work, along with that of William Friedkin and Francis Ford Coppola, had started the decade off with a bang. However, even though Roger Corman was producing *Saint Jack* and it was guaranteed distribution, we'd in fact be making a no-frills independent movie. I don't think Peter had more than a million-dollar budget. Within five weeks' time we would start filming. Three days after the end of the last film I'd ever work on with John Cassavetes, I was on a plane to Singapore.

—CHAPTER 15—

SAINT JACK

BY THE TIME I ARRIVED IN SINGAPORE, IN APRIL 1978, Bogdanovich had already been there for a few months while *Saint Jack* was in preproduction. In order to get a better grasp of the setting of the story we walked the streets, seeking out the kind of places Jack, my character, would have frequented—brothels, Boogie Street, the Chinese section, the quays, the Raffles Hotel. In the process we discovered that the screenplay did not work. It needed to be entirely revamped. As if that weren't plenty to do, we would have to start shooting in three days.

I was anxious on the first day. Where Jack should have been relaxed and serene, I was nervous and irritable. I loved the part, but I didn't know my character well enough—yet. He hadn't taken over. The problem was that I was working too hard to find him. I didn't have to chase after him; he'd come to me if I just relaxed. That meant being brave enough to keep my performance simple until I understood enough about Jack to make points, to frame moments. One brief scene that was giving me special trouble involved my letting a wealthy Chinese client know that his favorite prostitute is back in town. However, I couldn't relax into it and the more I tried to lighten up, the worse it got.

Peter, finally, printed the scene and we went on to the next shot. At the end of the day, he suggested we have a drink in his suite. I knew he

181

was concerned. So was I. After the drinks arrived, he started talking about a brilliant performance he had seen in 1953.

– I was fourteen years old and I was working as a critic for my high school paper, my first assignment. It was the first review I ever wrote. I was bowled over by what I saw. I saw you, Ben, at the Theatre de Lys in *End as a Man*.

He said that he was telling me this to remind me of my gifts and that the camera would love me if I didn't fight it. He then changed the subject and we started talking about our personal lives. Here was a man whose first three big studio films, *The Last Picture Show*, *Paper Moon*, and *What's Up, Doc?*, had all been smash hits. Now he was dealing with material that was more difficult and not as easily accessible to audiences. He was also working with a budget far smaller than he had during those heady days, and he had no superstar to carry some of the weight of the picture. His personal life was in free fall, too. He and his girlfriend, actress Cybill Shepherd, were coming to the end of their relationship. With all this to face, Peter also had to overhaul the screenplay. I felt if anybody could make our film a success it was Peter, and I told him I would help him accomplish that. I think it was on that night that Peter and I began really to trust each other.

It's standard procedure for an actor to be given a finished script. He shows up every day to shoot a predetermined scene with a predetermined number of pages. Afterward he goes home and studies the material for the next day. Not here. Almost every night, I sat in Peter's suite with him and his friend George Morfogen. George had worked with Peter before and Peter trusted his opinions, especially on story. He was an especially perceptive and creative man.

We bounced ideas off each other and Peter would write the scene to be shot the next day. An exciting way to work. That's when I saw him at his best. We filmed in the Chinese district where Peter let the life on the streets continue while I wove through it. Finally my first major scene arrived; I was pleased to learn that Peter intended to film the entire scene in one shot. He did this often during the course of filming. His camera would move slowly from a full "master" shot of the scene to closer angles of the action, which would include close-ups of the actors, too. Those three elements were traditionally done separately and we actors would have to wait for the director of photography and his crew to reset their lights. With Peter it was done all in one.

Denholm Elliott, a brilliant actor who originally was from the theater, felt equally at home with Peter's way of working. Before filming, Peter would rehearse a scene thoroughly without the camera present. This allowed actors a chance to get to know the material so well that it became a more natural part of us.

The picture deals with Jack's friendships with William, the character Denholm played, and four English expatriates who are Jack's drinking buddies. Peter made sure that before we worked together we spent a good deal of time in each other's company—wining, dining, and laughing. As a result, the first time on the set felt like a reunion of old friends. The same with the girls, all nonprofessionals, who played the prostitutes Jack manages. It was important that I liked them and vice versa. Peter worked hard to make these connections among his players happen; he also picked up a lot of dinner checks, getting those girls to feel free and comfortable with me.

I became especially comfortable with one girl in particular, a Malaysian woman named Rita, who had long, glistening black hair and a smile that lit up the room. Her boyfriend or husband, I don't remember which, was working on an oil rig in the South China Sea. She was obviously lonely, so she wound up at my place one day for an on-location romp. I told her to make herself at home, to take a bath, order room service, whatever she liked. I'd be back in an hour or so.

Peter was rewriting the scene we were to shoot the next day and asked me to be there. Well, I got caught up in the work and one hour became three. When I got back to my room, I was sure she'd be asleep, or even gone. But no, there she was, eating satay and having a glass of white wine. She gave me that million-dollar smile. She was lovely.

I don't know how long we were at it but I didn't get enough sleep and the morning was rough going. When I got on the set, my daughter Liz was there. She had been hired by Peter as a production assistant after Liz had called me from Florence.

– Dad, do you think you can get me on that picture you're doing?

– What are you interested in? What would you like to do?

– An assistant of some kind. Maybe work with the set designer?

– When do you have to be back in Florence?

– Oh, I don't have to be back until September.

– Promise me one thing.

– What's that, Dad?

– That you won't become an actress.

– What do you have against it?

– It's too hard, unless you're really talented and very lucky.

– You don't have to worry, it's not my thing.

– I'll talk to Peter, I'm sure we can find something.

And here she was, working in the art department. She took one look at me and said,

– Dad, you look wiped out. What were you doing last night?

I thought for a moment, gave my forehead a loud slap, and said, "Writing and thinking, Liz. Writing and thinking." Peter practically fell out of his tall director's chair, choking back his laughter. That became the slogan for whatever nightly peccadilloes we might engage in: "Writing and Thinking."

In the film, Jack's wish has always been to own the dream brothel: offering fine food, the best wines, a well-run bar, the most beautiful girls in Singapore, superb service. Despite being warned by the Chinese underworld, which controlled prostitution, not to open such a place, Jack does it anyway, and calls it Dunroamin'.

For the brothel, Peter and his set designer found the perfect colonial villa. From the courtyard with its tables beautifully appointed for fancy dining to the lounging area and the rooms upstairs, the colors of the walls, the fabrics chosen to cover the sofas and chairs, and the warm lighting devised by our director of photography, Robby Müller, Jack's brothel would have made even a priest want to take off his collar and stay a while. Liz had worked on decorating it and was very proud of what she'd accomplished.

I wanted the sequences in Dunroamin' to go on and on. It was probably because when we finished shooting there, the plot required that the sets be destroyed by Jack's competition. They would smash the windows, tear up the furniture, and scrawl obscenities on the walls. Nothing would be left whole or standing.

The night came when we were to shoot the scene where Jack arrives to discover his place had been wrecked. The crew was getting ready to go over and destroy the villa and Peter invited me along. When the first window was broken it was like a knife in my stomach. When they tore up the furniture, tears came to my eyes. It was almost as though they were vandalizing my own home. Peter put his arm around my shoulder. It was hurting him, too. We watched in silence as they sprayed Chinese vulgarities on the walls of Jack's dream.

Although Jack was a pimp, he had more honor than most people. Ruining the reputation of an American senator by photographing him in a sexual tryst with a boy prostitute would make him a lot of money, enabling him to return home to the U.S. But Jack can't go through with it. He throws the pictures in the bay. Peter's camera watched as the photographs disappeared, and with them Jack's chance at a new life. That was the thing about Jack that got to me, his sense of honor.

As with *Husbands*, I had trouble saying good-bye to *Saint Jack*. I had become very fond of Peter, especially his grace under pressure. *Saint Jack* was not an easy movie to make. Peter not only rewrote it entirely on the go, so to speak, but he was being second-guessed by the Corman group throughout the shoot. But he stuck to his guns and made the movie his way. I'd worked hard to help him do it. We also discovered common ground in our personal lives. He became the first person I confided in about my marriage, maybe because Peter was having comparable problems of his own. He listened to me with eyes closed and as soon as I'd finished my tale of woe he started spinning a comic version of our sad sagas. We laughed a lot.

The last night of shooting was very tough for me. I didn't want this movie to end. The final scenes to be filmed were set in Jack's apartment. Peter had chosen a place in an old building on the waterfront in Boat

Quay, with a little balcony overlooking the bay. Under a full moon that night we could see the fishing boats heading out to sea. In the early morning, we saw those same boats return with their catch. They could probably hear Louis Armstrong's voice blaring out from Jack's apartment.

It was clear to me that Peter, too, was having a difficult time bringing the film to an end. Absolutely everything had been shot yet nobody said so. Instead, Peter turned to Robby Müller and said, "I think we're gonna need an insert of Ben's hand dialing the phone, don't you?" Robby agreed, and so it was done. That was followed by a shot of the little cockatoos that Jack allows to roam freely in his apartment. Then something else occurred to Peter that he thought "we might need," followed by something else again. George Morfogen turned to me and smiled. We both knew that none of this would be used in the movie. Finally, Peter looked at me and, after a long pause, turned to the crew and said, "That's a wrap, everybody." A happy experience was really over.

CHAPTER 16

AUDREY

WHEN I GOT BACK TO LOS ANGELES, I WAS OFFERED A costarring role opposite Audrey Hepburn in *Bloodline*, a thriller, which was to be directed by Terence Young. He'd also directed the first couple of James Bond movies. I was happy to do the part. I had always admired Audrey's work, having watched her opposite William Holden in *Sabrina*, Cary Grant in *Charade*, Gary Cooper in *Love in the Afternoon*, Fred Astaire in *Funny Face*, Gregory Peck in *Roman Holiday*, Rex Harrison in *My Fair Lady*, and on and on. And now she'd be playing opposite me. The trouble was that I knew that *Bloodline* would never compare to those memorable pictures. Even Gore Vidal, who worked briefly on the script, couldn't bring any life to it. I think all of us knew the film would be just a very good payday.

Our first day of shooting took place in New York's Central Park. Audrey appeared at the door of my trailer as I was trying on some jackets for the scene we were about to shoot. My jaw dropped when I saw her. She seemed to have appeared in close-up. Her large glistening eyes, set in that exquisite one-of-a-kind face, set me back on my heels. I gathered my senses by asking her which jacket she thought I should wear. She chose the same one I'd had in mind.

– You have good taste.

– I have two sons. I like dressing boys.

Audrey gave me a wry look that brought me up short. This was the first time we'd met but something was already happening. I said to myself, *Be careful, Ben.*

Our next location was Sardinia. We were shooting in a spectacular villa overlooking the island's emerald waters. Terence Young was inside the home directing my costars James Mason, Omar Sharif, and Romy Schneider. I waited outside in a canvas-backed chair reading *The World According to Garp*. I looked up and Audrey was standing in front of me, gazing at me with that extraordinary smile she had.

– Do you like the book?

– I'm enjoying it. I couldn't sleep last night and it was good company.

– I have trouble sleeping myself. When it happens to you again, feel free to call me. We'll keep each other company.

She turned and strolled away. I was bowled over. I think I even gulped. I told myself not to get involved, somebody could get hurt. And it might be me.

Paris was our next stop. We stayed there a week, night shooting. The story follows Audrey's character from Sardinia to Paris, where she has a sumptuous home, to Mannheim, Germany, where she is the owner of a very large pharmaceutical company.

Peter Bogdanovich came through Paris on business, so I introduced him to Audrey. He has an almost encyclopedic knowledge of cinema and I was sure he'd tell Audrey things about herself that she'd long forgotten. But he didn't. Peter was polite, approaching her as one might approach a princess. After they exchanged a few friendly words, Peter excused himself and left. The next day at lunch he told me he'd been so starstruck that he was already playing around with an idea for a romantic comedy for me and Audrey. "Terrific," I said knowing full well how hard it was to get a movie off the ground. I considered his proposal a long shot. So many good ideas for films drift away.

One night we shot a scene at the famous Maxim's restaurant, in which Audrey's character becomes jealous of all the attention lavished on me by other women. She walks out of the restaurant, I follow, and catch up to her in front of the Hotel Crillon. I turn her to face me, and ask for her forgiveness. I then kissed Audrey Hepburn for the first time and it was no movie kiss. But we kept it from going any further because night shooting is very tiring and we were billeted in different hotels, so it was not difficult to say, "Goodnight, see you tomorrow." That didn't stop Audrey from coming into my mind more and more often.

Then came Munich. The director and the entire cast were staying in the Munich Hilton. Up until then, when Audrey and I weren't shooting we were always in the company of other people, a situation that kept conversation from getting too personal—it certainly kept flirting between us at a minimum.

It was a Saturday, a day off for the entire company. I was in the hotel dining room having lunch. I smelled a perfume with a familiar scent. I looked up from the book I was reading and Audrey had placed herself across from me.

– Do you mind if I join you? I'm famished.

– Are you kidding? I'd be delighted.

I hoped she didn't see me catch my breath. Her surprise appearance had taken it away.

– What can I get you?

– What are you having?

– Smoked Scottish salmon.

– Smoked salmon. How wonderful! Yes, I'd like that.

From her reaction you'd have thought I'd ordered a truffle-encrusted pheasant under glass.

– Would you like some wine, Audrey? You can't have salmon without a good, chilled white wine.

– I agree.

– Good.

As I ordered, her eyes never left me. When I turned back to her she looked at me with such warmth that I felt as though I were living the beginning of one of those glamorous M-G-M movies I'd seen as a boy. But I wasn't sitting across the table talking to Greta Garbo or Hedy Lamarr or Norma Shearer. Even better, I was with Audrey Hepburn.

– Audrey, you light up a room the way you light up the screen.

She blushed.

– You know, Ben, I've never considered myself a good actress.

– Oh no? Well, I'll tell you what I'll do. I'm gonna get any one of your movies in 35mm, rent a theater, and sit next to you while I point out what you do that other actresses would give their souls to be able to come near to.

She laughed.

– You do know how to make a girl feel better.

– Haven't you been feeling well?

She looked down and after a pause,

– Did you ever have your heart broken, Ben?

– Almost, but I'm still here.

– I'm married to a man who saw fit to fool around. While I worked away from Italy he was playing in our home.

– That's not nice.

– I was so distraught I thought seriously of doing something I'd never imagined I could even contemplate.

– You thought about killing yourself.

– Yes.

– I'm glad you didn't.

She looked at me through those kind, almond eyes and gave me that smile I can still see to this day. My heart melted, as they say.

We shot at the Bavaria Studios, where the brilliant UFA films were made in the 1920s. The material we worked with couldn't be transformed into anything except what it was—an expensive soap opera. Despite it all, everyone did the best they could, particularly Audrey, who was always on time and letter-perfect. She had a relaxed approach to the character, she was in command, and there was never a false note. I don't know if she'd ever studied acting but she sure knew her stuff. She was completely natural, which, with her charmed good looks, made her especially easy to watch. None of us was getting much directorial help but Audrey came in every morning somehow knowing exactly what to do.

One Friday evening, after a dinner hosted by Terence Young, the cast decided to have nightcaps on our hotel's roof, where there was also dancing to a live orchestra. Omar Sharif was there, Romy Schneider, Irene Papas, Kurt Frings (Audrey's agent), and Terence, of course. The drink of choice was champagne. Terence asked Romy to dance. Kurt asked Irene to dance. And I asked Audrey. Omar said he would mind the table.

It was a slow dance and suddenly something happened that I had never before experienced: Audrey started to tremble in my arms. I pulled her toward me in order to steady her. *Are people seeing this?* I wondered. I held her more tightly and finally the trembling stopped. When we got back to the table Omar, who in his day had made many women swoon, had obviously seen what was going on. He looked at me with utter seriousness, bent toward me, and whispered in my ear, "You must."

That night Audrey and I ended up in her suite. Although we'd both had our share of affairs, we undressed in separate rooms like a couple of novices. When I entered the bedroom she was already under the sheets, with the light from two nearby candles flickering across her regal face. She sighed softly as I took her in my arms gently. When we kissed, I was timid; I couldn't believe I was holding Audrey Hepburn. We made love slowly in silence. No promises were made that night. For us it was going to be an "on-location romance."

When Liza Minnelli came through Munich to do a concert, she invited Audrey as well as me, so we went together—our first date. Liza was in great form that night, singing, dancing, and getting a lot of laughs. Audrey and I went backstage to invite Liza to join us for supper in a cozy, candlelit restaurant near the Marienplatz. Audrey was glowing that night and I guess it was easy for Liza to figure out why. She told me she'd never seen Audrey so radiant and proceeded to pay her flattering compliments. Audrey didn't just say "Thank you," she stepped onto her chair and did a sort of joyful jig. I looked up at that dazzling lady, telling myself to be on my guard. It would be very easy to fall in love with her. And then what?

Rome was our last stop on the film. Audrey was still living there with her husband, in sort of an armed truce. The only time we saw each other was on the set where I met her older son, Sean Ferrer. We liked each other immediately. One day he thanked me for taking care of his mother. *Uh-oh*, I thought, *she's told her son. What does that mean?* I'd developed a strong affection for Audrey but I knew, and I thought that *she* knew, that this thing of ours could not go further than the end of shooting.

That day came and, somewhere in between actors hugging and swearing to keep in touch, I found myself alone with Audrey. She handed me her telephone number in Lausanne, Switzerland, where she would be spending Christmas. "Feel free to call," she said. I told her I would but didn't think I should. I was determined not to alter my pattern—end of movie, end of romance.

Time and distance would have ended things, but a month or so after the end of the filming on *Bloodline*, Terence Young decided to play Cupid. It seemed that in a few scenes I had with Audrey certain words were unclear. Street traffic had interfered with the dialogue. He'd decided to dub those sections in Paris. We would all stay at the Crillon. Its charm and elegance made it a perfect place for rekindling a flame. Audrey and I did our work and had a romantic Parisian night—a night filled with far more feeling than any other we'd had together. We were brought together for this brief interlude. Would we see each other again? Should we? Audrey lived in Italy and Switzerland, I in L.A. and New York. However imperfect our marriages, they were still matters of fact. Either we'd have to cross oceans to see each other or one of us would have to alter his or her life completely. Would that be possible?

The next morning as we were saying our farewells in the lobby, Audrey told me that Terence had made her son a production assistant on *Inchon*, his next movie, which would be shot in Korea and in which I would have a starring role. She then smiled and said she might very well find the time to drop in and visit us. Sean would be the perfect beard to cover our romantic reunion. I was pleased, although worried that there might be trouble ahead.

Going back home to Janice was tough. The spirit and expansiveness of strangers were far more soothing than my marriage. I felt no guilt about my escapades and I was sure that Janice was taking good care of her sex life while I was away.

And then there was Audrey. I missed her and so I did what I had told myself not to do—I called her. To me, calling meant promising—and promising meant a future together. I'd been afraid to take that step. She said that I'd been on her mind constantly and I told her that I too thought of her often. When she told me that she was coming to Korea, I felt a mixture of excitement and fear. She was going to fly across two oceans to spend just a short time with me. Where were things heading? We were starting to move into dangerous territory. "I can't wait to see you," I said.

I hadn't been in L.A. long when Peter Bogdanovich called with the news that he had finished the first draft of *They All Laughed*, and had sent a copy to Audrey's agent. Would I like to read it? Of course I would. As it turned out, I liked it a lot. If Audrey agreed to do it, we'd be able to play out our romance on the screen. What would that be like?

Peter didn't have to wait long to hear back from Audrey. She thought the screenplay was charming so Kurt Frings and producer David Susskind, who was now with Time Life Films, made the deal for Audrey's involvement. I now had a film to come back to after Korea. And there'd be Audrey, too.

—Chapter 17—

FALLING IN LOVE

In June 1979, I flew from New York to Seoul to make *Inchon*. It was intended to be the ultimate film about the Korean War, the masterly plan General Douglas MacArthur came up with to roll back the Chinese from the Korean peninsula. Laurence Olivier played MacArthur and I played the heroic romantic lead.

Upon landing, I was met by a film crew awaiting my arrival. I saw a sign that said, "Beng Azara." *How charming*, I thought. But then why should a Korean know how to spell my name?

At the hotel, I found a note from Terence Young saying that if I was not too tired I should come out to the set and have lunch. I showered, shaved, made a few phone calls to the States, and was then driven to the location. Everyone—actors and crew—were seated under an enormous tent, being served a four-course lunch. On a Terence Young picture, everybody lived well. He asked me to join his table. Jacqueline Bisset, David Janssen, and Rex Reed were there. Olivier and Toshiro Mifune had not yet arrived. *I hope this movie turns out to be as good as the people involved*, I thought.

As I was greeted by my fellow actors, I turned to my left to see at the end of the table a stunning woman. She had soft blue eyes, silky smooth skin, high cheekbones, and a long, elegant neck. A knockout. Terence introduced us.

– Ben, this is Elke.

She nodded politely and, in a charming accent I couldn't quite place, told me she was very sorry that she wasn't able to be with her crew at the airport; she was the producer of the documentary on the making of *Inchon*. She'd had a terrible night, she said, swollen tonsils. George Roberts, a good friend of Terence and the executive producer of the movie Elke was producing, sat nearby. I turned to Elke and said,

– How do you spell my name?

– Oh, was it not correct?

– Almost, but not quite.

– I'm so sorry.

"Should I fire her, Ben?" asked George. He could see that I was taken by this woman. She didn't know who I was but I didn't care. She looked splendid. She was wearing a mustard-colored outfit with a zipper running the length of it, topped by a straw hat. I was wearing a red T-shirt with Manila Polo Club written on it. (I'd made a film in the Philippines a few years before.) She became interested and asked me if I was a polo player. I said yes, even though all I'd played was water polo. She asked what my handicap was. I didn't know what that meant, so I figured the lower the number, the better you are. I said three. She seemed to buy that—of course it was believable that an actor would be a three because ten is the top. I was thoroughly charmed by Elke and danger signs ran through my head. I could run away with this woman, I thought.

There'd been a lot of political unrest in Korea so a curfew was enforced. Some of the Italian members of the crew, with whom I had worked on *Bloodline*, created in our hotel what they called the Spaghetti Room. Everyone would congregate there after eleven. I found myself seated across from Elke. I gave her my whole repertoire of sexy looks, the "deeply interested" look, the gloweringly hot "I want you" look. I demonstrated a quick wit, I poured on the charm, but still I could not get her to come back to my room.

I let about a week go by before I made my next move: I invited her to dinner. She accepted. I'd been told about a particularly good Chinese restaurant so I booked a table there. About halfway through the meal I asked Elke what a beautiful woman like her was doing on her own in that part of the world. She told me that she was not alone, that she had her eleven-year-old daughter Danja with her, who was helping on the movie. She said she herself had come to Korea because of a facelift.

Elke had been a model and traveled extensively. Recently she and her daughter had been living in Brazil, where her work had taken her—just in time, she said. Her native Germany had become a sad place for her. She wouldn't tell me why but she and Danja enjoyed Brazil so much that they stayed much longer than had been planned. She put Danja in a school there. She made new friends and was given work whenever she liked. The situation was perfect.

Ivo Pitanguy, the celebrated Brazilian plastic surgeon, was a friend of hers. Terence Young came to Brazil to see his girlfriend, who was having some work done on her face prior to appearing in *Inchon*. They were having lunch on Ivo's island near Rio de Janeiro and the girlfriend told Terence that she would love Elke, whom she was very fond of, to come along to Korea. "But of course," said Terence. He said he would create an interesting job for her and even put her daughter to work. Elke thought it might be a novel experience.

As a matter of fact, she had been in that part of the world only two years earlier, when she was invited to organize and direct a group of models to represent German fashion in Taiwan. She met Chiang Kai-shek, who took a fatherly liking to her. She dined with him, his son, and other officials several times—always the only woman at the table. Chiang loved speaking German; as a young man he had studied in Heidelberg, and he knew a great many German songs and insisted that Elke sing along with him.

She asked me whether I'd ever heard a Chinese man sing in German. She stood up and proceeded to do an imitation that gave Sid Caesar, the master of dialect humor, a run for his money.

– You're a funny lady. Have you always been that way?

– I had to remake myself. I didn't have a very good time as a child so I found ways to amuse myself. My three brothers thought that I was funny. They always asked me to do imitations because I made them laugh.

She smiled and said,

– Now, let me tell you a joke. A friend of mine went to Bonn. When he got back to New York, he was at a party where someone from the German embassy asked him how he'd liked it there. "It was so-so," he said. "But once, at two o'clock in the morning, we were in a nightclub, the door opens, and guess who walks in? Mozart!" And the man from the embassy said, "That can't be true. No nightclub in Bonn is open at two o'clock in the morning."

She burst out laughing. I didn't think it was that funny, but I enjoyed watching her enjoying the joke. I couldn't stop looking at her. She brought cheer to the room. Imagine, I thought, what she could bring to my life. *Amazing*, I thought. I was falling in love with Elke and I hadn't even kissed her.

Our next few dinner dates were shared with other people involved in the making of the movie. When the time came for us to be alone, we made love. I was sure that I'd met the woman I'd been waiting for. No one had ever touched me so profoundly.

The next evening, I called Elke's room.

– How are you feeling? I've been thinking of you all day.

– Who is this? Please don't call here again.

She hung up and I thought that maybe I'd missed something. The woman might very well be disturbed. *Well, fuck her*, I said to myself. *I'm not going to talk to her anymore. I'm not about to make myself vulnerable. She's gonna have to get down on her knees before I talk to her.*

We saw each other every day on the set and I simply ignored her. She didn't seem to mind. I felt used. I had given her the best of myself. It was enough to make a guy very insecure. Maybe she thought I had been a bad lover; maybe she was disappointed. Two weeks went by and, I must admit, I suffered.

One day I had a love scene with Jackie Bisset, who played my wife. Jackie wasn't feeling well and had gone home early, so Terence calls out,

– Elke, dear girl, would you come in here and be Ben's eyeline? Be Jackie for a moment?

She stepped in and as soon as I delivered my lines, she crossed her eyes and stuck out her tongue. It was adorable. I was suddenly defenseless. *All right, I'll give her one more chance.*

There was a big battle scene to do that day. There were five hundred tanks, two thousand Korean soldiers, the smoke was going like crazy— we were the Americans waiting for the North Korean tanks to come closer before we opened fire. Everybody was ready to start the scene. Terence was sitting high up on an enormous crane and suddenly he yelled,

– Stop everything! Take me down, boys.

On the way down, he called out,

– Elke, would you book a table for twelve at Giovanni's tonight? You come too, wear something beautiful. Ben, you're invited also. Take me up, boys.

Terence's dinners sometimes seemed more important to him than the film.

I asked Elke if I could escort her that night. She said yes. We agreed to meet in my suite for a glass of champagne. I heard chimes coming from the hall. Then she appeared, wearing a gorgeous pink outfit and a belt with bells on it. *This woman is trying to drive me crazy*, I thought, *I'm gonna tell her straight out to stop playing games.*

– Listen, may I ask you something? Why were you so strange on the phone that day?

– Me? Strange? You never phoned me. It was you who stopped talking to me.

– I phoned you the next day, when you came back from work that evening.

– What room did you phone?

– 1901.

– No, in the morning they changed my room. I'm now in 1064 with my daughter.

I had gotten the wrong woman! Maybe another German. Misunderstandings like that can have tragic outcomes, but it was all resolved in an instant, and our romance took off. Elke was the first woman I'd ever known who woke up smiling. She was the perfect antidote to my melancholy side. She made me laugh all the time. It was a relief to be with a woman who played no games. With Elke, you got what you saw.

One morning, during breakfast, I looked down onto the hotel garden where there was an Olympic-sized pool and saw a man swimming back and forth—at least twenty laps. I was impressed. Later in the day I learned that the swimmer had been Laurence Olivier. Terence said Olivier was ill and this was certain to be his last picture. (It wasn't.) The next morning, there he was in the pool again. Elke and I watched him come out of the water, put a towel around his waist, slowly take his bathing suit off from under it, and walk into an area full of flowers to wring it out. When he'd finished and turned to walk back into the hotel, he stopped, leaned down, and smelled a rose.

That's when my phone rang. It was Peter Bogdanovich calling from Venice. *Saint Jack* had been given the Critics' Prize at the Venice Film Festival as the best movie of 1979. I told Peter that even though it was seven-thirty in the morning in Seoul, I was going to order a bottle of Dom Perignon and drink to us and to our movie. And that's what I did. Elke had a sip or two but I imbibed a glass or three. That day I serenaded Elke during the entire fifty-mile trip to the location. My work was rewarded and I had met the woman who I realized was the love of my life. I was on top of the world.

Olivier phoned me that evening and said,

– My boy, I always like to have dinner with my leading man.

– I'd be delighted.

And I was.

He started dinner with three scotches-and-soda. It was then that he told me that he would not appear onstage again. He described himself as an old wine that must be drunk slowly. Sitting there with him, I was disappointed more than ever that I didn't have a major scene with this actor; all our scenes were in passing—a line here, two lines there. *Jesus Christ*, I thought, *here's the man who's considered one of the greatest actors who ever lived and I won't be able to go toe to toe with him.* During dinner there was not one word about acting. We talked about England, about Italy, about women. It was then that I told him,

– I think I'm in love, Larry.

– Dear Ben, I've lost my umbrella so many times.

That made me laugh. Larry had obviously stopped being sentimental about love. Should I be less optimistic, too?

We finished off a bottle of wine, he had two cognacs, and the next morning at six I saw him in the pool going up and down and down and up. *If that man is dying,* I thought, *my hat's off to him. I hope I have his courage when I reach his point in life.*

A month into the filming of *Inchon*, rumors about Moonies started flying around. Word had it that the picture was being financed by a religious group known primarily for brainwashing its young constituents. It seemed that the North Korean Reverend Sun Myung Moon, a powerful businessman who had formed that sect, was a big admirer of General MacArthur. Some people therefore saw the movie as a homage to him and to the war against Communist North Korea. One could argue that, in effect, we were making a propaganda film.

At first there were denials from everyone in production, including Terence. But one night Tung Sung Park came to visit the set. Park was a lobbyist noted for a huge Washington scandal that led to long congressional hearings. He was charged with corrupting congressmen in order to obtain favors for his government. I came to see why a politician would choose to be in his company. Park threw me a lavish birthday party and invited the entire film company. The food, the drink, the service were of a quality reserved for royalty.

Elke met T, as his friends called him, before I did. Park was very fond of her. Once while the three of us were on the set chatting, T's attention wandered. Looking at someone in the distance, he asked,

– What's Ishii doing here?

Elke told him that Mitsuhari Ishii was one of the producers, that every so often he went to Japan and came back with bags full of money.

– Of course he does, that's where his boss, Reverend Moon, has his headquarters.

Something about the situation made T nervous. He excused himself and left our film location. The cat was out of the bag.

When David Janssen heard the news he shouted gleefully, "We're shooting for the moon." Everything was now clear to everyone. When a hundred extras would have been enough, we had two hundred. When a hundred armored tanks and cars were needed, we had five hundred. When three hundred soldiers would suffice, we had a thousand. Moonie power! It was never more evident than on the day when all the principals were to appear in a scene together. Seoul was about to be occupied by the North Koreans and our forces were pulling back. I have never seen more extras and vehicles on a set—anywhere.

We waited as Terence choreographed the movement of these masses. Rex Reed and David Janssen played newspaper reporters who find themselves in Korea when all hell breaks lose. They were waiting for Olivier to be made up. Larry had been the most splendid Shakespearean actor of his day. His films *Hamlet, Richard III*, and *Henry V*, as well as his great interpretations in the theater, proved that he was enormously gifted. When he finally appeared he had a new, false nose and chin that looked obviously artificial. His vocal equipment had always been extraordinary but now, when he spoke, some sort of strange sound issued forth—an American accent I'd never heard before. But what the hell, he was Olivier, so nobody, not even Terence, said anything.

That day I had a scene with Jackie Bisset—a bittersweet good-bye moment. Richard Roundtree was also there telling me that we had to vamoose in a hurry. All this while there are explosions in the distance and mayhem on the streets.

And that was when I saw at least three people collapse. They'd been standing or running in the hot sun for hours and there was no water for them. Not a drop. No provision had been made for it. After all, they were Moonies, ready to suffer for the reverend and his church. As a matter of fact, when we shot the scene, a tank rolled over one of these wide-eyed young church members and killed him. The filming didn't stop. There was no mourning, nothing. The boy would be rewarded in the afterlife, wouldn't he? But a lot of people were being rewarded in the here and now. *Inchon* cost forty-five million dollars and all that money was not on the screen. Where did it go?

One night I played a scene with Toshiro Mifune, who had starred in some of Kurosawa's greatest films, *Rashomon* and *The Seven Samurai*, among others. We had to swim to a North Korean ship in order to place a bomb under it. The water was ice cold; to keep us warm we were wearing wet suits under our costumes. A dinghy picked us up between takes. We climbed on board the boat, where we'd wait to jump into the water all over again. Mifune spoke no English and no Italian—only Japanese. His interpreter was not in the water with us so we were compelled to invent a kind of universal sign language. We got along very well.

When we finished this scene, Sean Ferrer told me his mother would arrive in two weeks to visit him. He had seen what was going on between Elke and me, and he was asking me, in effect, how to handle Audrey. I took the coward's way out and suggested he tell her that it would be best if she did not come. And if he thought it prudent, I added, he should tell his mother that I had begun to see Elke. She didn't come.

Things moved quickly between Elke and me. Our affair went from an on-location romance to a full-fledged relationship. I was in love and I felt twenty years younger. But I was still married, even though I had successfully pushed that to the back of my mind. My home life would have to be dealt with soon.

Elke decided to join me during the last three weeks of shooting in Rome. Once her work on *Inchon* was done, she had gone to Düsseldorf to put Danja in school, making sure she would be comfortable for the time she was gone.

On the flight from New York to Rome, I told David Janssen about my new love. He said,

– Go home, Ben. Go home. It's gonna cause a lot of trouble, a lot of problems.

He was warning me that it was going to be a very tough challenge—to get rid of all those years of old baggage was easier said than done.

That was the first talk I ever had with David. We had never been friends and, up until *Inchon*, not even acquaintances. He was not a happy man. For one thing, he drank much too much. I had heard that the reason for this was his deep disappointment at never becoming a movie star. His television stardom and the worldwide notoriety he earned from his very successful series, *The Fugitive*, were not enough for him. He wanted something more. But there was something else. His personal life gave him no pleasure. Maybe he should *not* have gone home.

Despite all this, David and I talked nonstop during our flight. We were getting along well and found each other amusing. At one point he opened an expensive-looking attaché case. What I saw inside made everything clear to me: vial after vial of pill after pill in every color of anybody's rainbow. I then knew how David could drink and not appear drunk, drink and avoid punishing hangovers. The answer was right there in that lovely case.

One night in Seoul, David had fallen asleep with a cigarette in his hand and had set the bed on fire. He got away with mild burns on his arm and neck. But things would get worse. After he finished in Rome and was back in his house in Malibu, David was walking through his gourmet kitchen when he opened the refrigerator and collapsed. He was reaching for a carton of milk. He thought he had heartburn. He didn't. David died.

CHAPTER 18

CHANGES

WHEN ELKE ARRIVED AT THE AIRPORT IN ROME, MY HEART jumped. She was even more stunning than I remembered. I had arranged a beautiful suite in the Hotel de la Ville near the Spanish Steps. Elke was unpacking in the bedroom when the phone rang in the sitting room; it was Audrey.

– I want to see you.

I didn't know what to say, but I had to be honest. I told her that I was with someone. Silence. I didn't hear the phone touch its cradle. It was the loudest hang-up I never heard.

Elke said she hadn't slept at all the night before. "Too excited, I guess," she said. I suggested she take a nap so she'd be in shape for the fantastic day of sightseeing I'd planned for her. While she slept, I tried to avoid thinking about Audrey. *Should I call her? Or maybe meet her somewhere before Elke woke up?* I owed Audrey an explanation. After struggling with that idea for some time, I reached for the phone and dialed her number in Rome. She answered, but I said nothing. A very long time passed with neither of us saying a word. She didn't say my name. She simply whispered "Good-bye."

* * *

The view of Rome from our terrace was spectacular. We took many of our meals there, enraptured by Rome's golden panorama. It was during one particularly romantic dinner on the terrace that I asked Elke to marry me.

—You are married.

– I'll take care of that.

– Ben, you know I love you and I don't want to make trouble for you.

– My marriage has been over for a long time.

– I don't want you to feel obligated.

I *did* feel obligated. I wanted to tell her that she'd saved my life. That I'd thought I could never fall in love again.

We shot the interior scenes for *Inchon* at the famous Cinecittà studios. The streets were tree-lined and the soundstages painted in warm, burnt-umber colors. Things seemed less hurried there than on an American lot. The work got done, but nobody seemed rushed. Our soundstage was second in size only to the one that Federico Fellini was then using for *City of Women*, which starred Marcello Mastroianni. I was wandering on the lot one afternoon when I heard someone say "Ben Gazzara?" It was Mastroianni. He introduced himself and said that he went to very few movies but a lady friend forced him to see *The Killing of a Chinese Bookie*. He thought it was splendid. I now had the chance to tell him how much I loved his work, how much I envied his long collaboration with Fellini. "Would you like to meet him?" he asked. I told him I'd be honored.

I followed him into an enormous soundstage with its walls painted black. Fellini was standing alone in the center of the dark space, holding a long red silk handkerchief and directing a special effect—the magical appearance of a coach without horses. It would come bursting through a wall. I sat far to the side with Marcello, watching this great director as he rehearsed the sequence over and over. I wondered if he took the same time and care with actors. Finally, he said "*Va bene*" but didn't seem entirely convinced.

Fellini walked toward us and Marcello introduced me. Fellini did something that no one had ever done to me before: he took my face in his hands and said "*Che bella faccia.*" He liked my face. In response I wanted to say, "*Che bel cervello*"—what a beautiful brain—and tell him that his work always thrilled me. I wanted to ask what it felt like to explore your dreams and your fantasies on film, to answer to no one but yourself. Instead I simply said, *"Grazie, Maestro."*

When my work on *Inchon* was done, I accompanied Elke back to Germany. It was a way to deepen my commitment to her, to make it impossible to extricate myself. Like Audrey, she lived in Europe, but she was free. What would happen when I left for the States? Would she change her mind and decide to stay in Germany without me?

The Düsseldorf airport was shut down because of fog and rain. We landed in Cologne and drove the eighty or so kilometers to Elke's home. It was night, with a heavy downpour. I could see very little of the city that she'd told me was so charming. It rained for three days and so we played house in her beautiful terraced apartment overlooking the Rhine.

One morning, as I walked through her warm and cozy living room, filled with silver-framed photos placed here and there on every side table, I stopped in front of the largest one in the room. It was a black-and-white photo of a handsome fellow leaning against the neck of a very pretty horse. Elke appeared and said, almost to herself,

– That's Mandy. Some years ago, I met and fell in love with him. He was young and healthy. He played polo, flew his own plane, could even water-ski on bare feet. But he became ill. Cancer. We went to the best clinic in Düsseldorf, where they tried every treatment possible. I stayed with him day and night, slept in the hospital. He fought so hard to stay alive but the cancer wouldn't let him.

– So you left Germany and went to live in Brazil.

– Yes.

– I like his face.

Her eyes filled with tears and I took her in my arms. *Is all life an accident?* I wondered. If that young man hadn't died, if I hadn't gone to Korea, would my life be changing? Was I sorry that she'd lost him or was I happy that I found her?

* * *

When the weather cleared, she showed me her town. And indeed it was a sort of "Little Paris," with cobblestone streets leading to larger avenues such as the Königsalle, a paradise for shoppers. She took me to a local family bar where I tasted German *altbeer* for the first time. I became a convert on the spot. We went to the Zum Schiffchen restaurant, where Napoleon had eaten, and had *eisbein* and sauerkraut. After visiting a couple of museums, we took a boat trip up the Rhine to the beautiful Moselle wine country. She wined and dined me and wouldn't let me pick up a check. The girl had style.

After a week, I left Elke to return to the States. I wanted to prepare things for her arrival. I was determined not to lose her.

I landed at JFK Airport and was pleasantly surprised to see Peter Bog-danovich outside customs. I'd told him my arrival time, but never expected he'd be there to meet me. I had already apprised him of my situation—that I had no intention of living in the New York apartment I kept with Janice even though she was three thousand miles away in California—so he'd booked a room for me at the Pierre, where he was residing. After the hugs and the arrival of my bags, we walked out of the terminal to where a stretch limousine was waiting. Peter always went first class and was generous to a fault. I sensed, though, that something was amiss. There was mainly small talk until we hit the FDR Drive and then Peter said,

– Audrey doesn't want to do the picture. She says it would be too difficult for her. You know that David Susskind and Time Life Films will probably slip out of the deal if she walks.

– Peter, I'm sorry I've created this problem, but this ain't no fling. I'm in love and I'm going to marry the girl.

It was a classic situation. A middle-aged man falls in love with a beautiful young woman who gives him the kind of affection and care he got only from his mother. In Korea I'd broken through a dam of emotions and out rushed the love and the passion that had been bottled up inside me for too many years. I'd been able to tap into it, to feel it in my work, but until now I had been unable to reach those feelings in my personal life. Suddenly, I felt as if I was twenty-eight years old instead of forty-eight, I was better looking, sexier, more considerate, and definitely luckier. I'd found the woman I wanted to spend the rest of my life with.

– Look, Ben, I've got an idea. Audrey will be passing through New York on her way to L.A. She'll be staying at the Pierre for a few days. If I could set up a meeting between the two of you, would you be amenable?

– I'll certainly meet with her. I don't know what I'll say, but I'll think of something. I'll play it moment by moment.

When I knocked on Audrey's door, I felt those butterflies in my stomach that always come before my first entrance in a play. I hadn't prepared a speech. I was scared. Her son must have told her about Elke. How badly had I hurt her?

The door opened and there she was, lovely as ever. She was dressed simply in a beige turtleneck sweater and a beautifully cut brown skirt, no jewelry, and very little makeup. She greeted me warmly but we didn't touch. She led me to an armchair while she sat on the bed, looking down at me. It was a single room—not a suite, which had been the norm.

She smiled that smile only she possessed and her eyes seemed to say that she understood the position I was in. She must've known I didn't mean to hurt her. We trusted each other. At least I knew that much. She would make it easy on me. I think she knew our relationship could not have gone on much longer, so she never spoke of it. She rose from the bed and walked to a sort of desk. She picked up the *New York Times*, handed it to me, and said,

– Look at this, Ben. Did you see the ad they're taking out for *Bloodline*? You can't even tell who's in it. What did they hire us for?

I knew what she was doing. She wouldn't allow me to embarrass myself by apologizing. I looked down at the ad. It was an enormous full-page photo of a rather pretty girl with a red ribbon tied around her neck. In the film, the murderer used a red ribbon to kill several women. The names of the actors were bunched up, one after another, near the margin of the page. The author of the book on which the film was based, Sidney Sheldon, got bigger billing than all the actors combined. Someone must have figured that the title *Bloodline* was all they needed to sell the picture. Audrey wasn't happy about it and she had every right not to be.

We talked about that and we talked about Terence Young, Omar Sharif, and then *They All Laughed*—anything but our thing. She never asked one question about Elke. Audrey was a class act. We walked in silence to the door. I turned to her and said, "Audrey, I'm so sorry. I didn't want to hurt you. I'll never forget the time we had together." She nodded, as if to put the subject to rest. I stood there staring at her when she closed the door, slowly and softly. Then I remembered why Peter wanted me to have the meeting. I was supposed to get Audrey to do the picture. I hadn't done that. I hadn't done much of anything.

Audrey left for Europe without committing to the movie. Everyone was nervous. So when Kurt Frings called about two days later to say that she was in, we were elated.

We had two weeks before shooting would begin. That gave me time to fly to L.A. and ask Janice for a divorce. Jay Julien had advised me to remain in New York, get Janice to visit, and slap her with a subpoena. I'd certainly get a better deal in a New York divorce than in L.A. But I couldn't do it. Not after all our years together, even as contentious as they were. I was sure that we could settle amicably.

Luckily, Peter had business in Los Angeles, so we flew together. "You can stay at my house, Ben. We'll return in three or four days." I was hesitant. I wasn't looking forward to facing Janice. *She* might have been ready for a confrontation but I was never good at them. I thought about picking up the phone and just saying "Janice, it's over." But I couldn't let myself off the hook that easily. I had to show some courage.

When we drove through the gate of Peter's Bel Air home, he said,

– Ben, you don't have to get out. I'll have someone unload our luggage, then the driver will take you to your place and wait for you.

– Thanks. I'd better get right over there.

– I don't envy you. Good luck.

During that short drive, I said to myself over and over, *Keep calm, Ben. Try to make it as painless as possible.* As we approached the house, I saw Janice standing in the doorway. I walked up to her, took her by the hand, led her through the living room, in silence, into the den, where we sat. The house was strangely unfamiliar to me. It was as though I'd pushed all memory of it out of my mind. Hoping to get through the moment as fast as possible, I dove right in.

– I found someone else, Janice.

– It's Audrey, isn't it?

Where the hell did that come from? I thought.

– No, Janice, it's us. We left each other a long time ago.

Everything moved more quickly than I'd expected. There were no tears, no pleas, no recriminations. It was as though she was expecting it to happen and wanted out of our marriage as much as I did. She might have been relieved. When she walked me to the door all she said was,

– We'll have to tell the children.

– I know, I'll call them.

When I got back to Peter's house, Frank Sinatra's voice could be heard singing a track from what I thought was Sinatra's best album, *Only the Lonely.* Some months before, I'd bought it for Peter. That day suddenly felt like a lifetime ago. Well, I wasn't ready for what happened next. As I sat down next to Peter and listened to the music, I started to cry. No sound came out of me but there were an awful lot of tears. He put his arm around me. He'd been through the same kind of scenario with his wife, and he knew the feeling.

The next morning, the telephone in my bedroom rang insistently. I was lying in the bed where Orson Welles had slept so often when he had lived in Peter's home. At last I picked up the phone and it was Janice. She was crying, pleading with me to come over right away. There was much to discuss, she said. We needed to meet and talk about how we could make things as painless as possible. No lawyers, she added. I told her I'd be down in an hour.

I felt relieved that the divorce would be handled in a civilized manner. I drove quietly up the circular driveway, got out of the car, and rang the doorbell. The door was thrown open and *Whap!* a summons was slapped into my left hand by a very fat and sweaty process server. "Sorry!" he said, and disappeared quickly. Janice burst into tears, saying she had to do it, that she was so afraid, to please forgive her. Here was the professional actress at work. Her tears were produced not by grief, but by the story they were intended to tell. Disappointed, I told her that I understood, and I walked away. I'd been ingenuous, if not stupid. But when I got back to Peter's house, I did as Janice suggested. I called the girls, Kate first in L.A., whom I hadn't spoken with much over the past few years.

– Your mother and I have separated.

– I know.

– If it's anybody's fault, it's mine.

– Don't be too hard on yourself.

– Take care of her.

– Take care of *yourself.*

Then Liz in New York.

– Liz, your mother and I are splitting.

– Who left who?

– I think I left her.

– What took you so long?

– You're funny.

– I'm going to work on *They All Laughed*, Dad.

– Nobody tells me anything.

– Peter called me yesterday and said that, among other things, I have to look after you.

– I'll be all right.

– I love you, Dad.

– Love you, too.

On the plane trip back east with Peter I was tongue-tied, unable to speak much. Peter left me to my thoughts. He didn't push conversation. I knew I'd be deadly company anyway so I pretended to sleep.

We arrived about five days before principal photography was to begin. By the time the first day of shooting rolled around, I was in bad shape. I hadn't slept at all the night before. At six A.M. I started calling people to tell them I couldn't make it to the set, that I wasn't well. Peter had to rearrange that day's entire schedule around me. I had begun to make things difficult for a man I respected and was very fond of. Guilt was piling on top of guilt.

Elke arrived in New York to stay with me but she lasted only a week. She tried in every way possible to get me to tell her what I was feeling, but I didn't know how to express what was tearing me apart. I wanted Elke with all of my heart but I'd been glued to a marriage for almost eighteen years. Despite the fact that love had disappeared long ago, the setup was safe for me. I was like a junkie who knows the stuff is killing him but can't kick the habit. I'd been with Janice so long that I felt obligated to remain. My sense of fairness told me that I shouldn't leave a woman who'd given our marriage so many years of her life.

Elke realized that I was struggling to make a decision. She decided to get out of the way and return to Germany, giving me the time to think my life through. I let her go even though I knew I'd be lost without her. And of course that made things even worse. It added to an all-embracing despair.

Somehow or other, some night or other, I found myself in Elaine's, the famous restaurant-saloon where you rub elbows with writers, actors, directors, music people, and journalists, the lucky and the not so lucky. Elaine Kaufman treats the place like her living room. I don't remember who I was with or how I got there. Nor do I know what I was doing when somebody took me by the shoulder and said, "Let's take a walk, Ben." It was Gay Talese. We were not friends, but I liked him and I knew he liked me. The fact that we were both sons of immigrants from the south of Italy may have had something to do with it. We'd talked to each other on occasion, mostly small talk, and I had read his books about the *New York Times* and the Bonanno crime family. I always liked Gay because he looked a lot like my cousin Joe Messina, who I was very fond of—and I was impressed by the stylish way he always dressed.

Gay took me to his place, poured some good wine, and tried to persuade me to talk about whatever it was that was causing the pain that must have been evident to everyone. I told him the story, but only the shell of it. I didn't yet know the reasons for these feelings that were driving me crazy. I was ashamed. One of the greatest investigative reporters ever in the game was asking me questions and I was sure I was boring him badly.

I made a gesture that sent my glass tumbling to the floor, red wine spilling onto the spotless white rug. But Gay didn't flinch. He carried on as if nothing had happened. *A classy guy*, I thought. I continued to struggle to find a compelling reason for my bleak condition, but I was certain that everything I said was trite. Why would anyone—much less a guy whom I barely knew—care? I knew that Gay and others were concerned but I couldn't return their kindness no matter how hard I tried. When I made the effort to express myself, the words simply wouldn't come out.

John Scanlon, who'd been my friend for years, and his wife, Julienne, invited me to their loft to watch the Academy Awards. John had the perfect Irish kisser—fair skin, curly red hair, a full red beard, and a body that clearly showed he enjoyed the good things in life. When we first met, I liked him immediately. He not only quoted Yeats, he sang the poems to you. I told John I couldn't make it, but Pete Hamill, whom I'd known longer than I'd known John, insisted I go.

Pete and I first became friends when he was working at the *New York Post*, writing a daily column I'd always enjoyed. Pete was the only New Yorker I knew who drove a car in the city. He saw the shape I was in, so maybe that was why he invited me and Elke to go down to Little Italy and have lunch with him. As this was the first time Pete and Elke met, probably he wanted to take a look at the woman who was altering my life. I don't remember saying one word for the three hours we spent together. I was a zombie.

After Elke returned to Germany, Pete knew I'd need a friend. He took me to an East Side club called Dangerfield's to see Rodney Dangerfield perform. He's a comic who always made me laugh but that night I didn't break a smile. Pete didn't give up. He said he'd pick me up and take me down to the Scanlons' loft to watch the Academy Awards.

When he arrived to collect me on Oscar night, I saw there was a woman sitting in the car next to him. She turned and smiled—it was Jackie Kennedy. I got into the backseat and she made a comment about how lucky I was to live in a building with such a beautiful façade. I managed to respond politely but I don't remember what I said.

Scanlon's building had been an old Tribeca factory, and we rode up to his loft in a large, old elevator that had an iron gate but no door. Even through my fog I appreciated the fact that Jackie was a good sport. I wanted to throw a funny compliment her way but instead I remained there mute.

The loft was crowded with a lot of people I knew. I stepped back at the Scanlon's door and let Pete and Jackie join a group of friends. I wasn't about to put a damper on their evening. I drifted from one group to another, pretending to listen to conversations, even nodding in agreement to what I wasn't hearing. Jackie and Pete had moved to the part of the loft where people were sitting on a big bed watching the awards. I peeked at the TV set but saw nothing. I couldn't focus, couldn't care. I was having trouble breathing. I didn't want anyone to see how bad things were with me, so I slowly backed out of the place. I knew Pete would understand. I hopped a cab and went to my empty apartment, where no one would be able to see me.

I was a mess. In quick succession, I'd wounded Audrey, I'd left my wife, and I'd brought Elke to America, where she'd found a stranger. To make matters worse, my work was badly affected, I was losing Peter's trust and friendship. Worse, I couldn't find my way out of it. I thought Elke would never come back.

My daughter Liz was again working as a production assistant. Her job was to see that I didn't wander off the set and never come back. I saw the sadness in my daughter's eyes as she attempted to do her work responsibly. She noticed that I was always looking for a phone, trying to contact Elke, who was never home. Where was she? Had she pushed me out of her mind? I felt overwhelmed by fear and guilt. I knew the trouble I was creating for Peter but I couldn't stop myself.

Many of the scenes in the picture were filmed in the Plaza Hotel. One was shot in the lobby. I'd just finished a scene and Liz told me it would be some time before I was needed again. She took me to a holding room, set aside for me to relax in. She said she would come back when I was needed on the set.

– Dad, they won't be ready for you for at least an hour. Why don't you try to call Elke? Who knows? She might finally be there.

– Thank you, sweetheart, maybe I will.

And when Liz left, that's what I did. Still no answer. I dialed at least ten more times and finally there was a voice, so quiet, so sad.

– Elke?

– Ben?

– Elke, please come back.

– No, Ben, I couldn't take it.

– I can't live without you.

– Oh yes, you can.

– I want you to be my wife.

– How are you? Are you well?

– I'm fine now. I've missed you.

– How could it come to this, Ben?

– Because I was a fool.

– Yes, you were.

– But it's over. You're my one and only woman. I never loved anyone the way I love you.

There was a pause.

– I'll have to think hard about it, Ben. Call me in a few days.

After that call I felt part of myself revive for the first time in weeks. She'd said I could call her. I was sure I'd be able to convince her to return. When I got back to the set, the gloom was less heavy. I was hopeful. I was able to focus. I was anxious to go to work.

* * *

Peter was getting delightful performances from Audrey and from John Ritter as well as from nonprofessionals like Patti Hansen and the beautiful Dorothy Stratten. While working very hard on the picture, Peter's life was changing. He'd fallen in love, too, but the situation was complicated. Dorothy was married. There we stood—me with my problems, Peter with his, and both of us with a romantic comedy to make. Audrey showed a lot of courage. No one would've guessed that we'd ever been close. It must have been much harder for her than for me. My mind was someplace else. In a way, I was glad that Audrey saw me in this sad state. I wanted her to feel relieved to be rid of me.

During that unhappy period I started seeing a psychiatrist—I needed one to pull me out of my deep hole. I saw him every day I could, either early morning or late at night. I had an appointment with him at eight P.M. on the day I shot a bedroom scene with Audrey. We were lying under the covers, supposedly naked after having made love. I'd been anxious about playing that scene with Audrey—skin touching skin for the first time since our affair, but she made it easy for me. She was tender without being sentimental.

It was seven o'clock, and Peter had already printed a few takes, but I knew he was going to want more, and the way things were going, I wouldn't be able to make my shrink appointment. I wrote down the number of Dr. Marcus and asked Liz to call him.

– Tell him I'm running late, Liz, and ask him to please wait for me.

Of course everyone heard this, including Audrey and Peter. I was desperate but I could have passed for a normal guy who was just melancholy: a very difficult job of acting on my part. I wanted to seem as normal as possible so that no one would suspect how troubled I really was.

At last the lights were set, the camera crew was ready, and Peter said, "Roll 'em!" I played that love scene thinking only of whether I'd be able to see Dr. Marcus that night or not. What came across on film was that I was keeping some sort of secret from the character Audrey played. She, of course, had plenty of her own private thoughts, so the scene as we played it was never nailed down. It stayed off-center, just the way I like it.

CHAPTER 19

THE WEDDING

ELKE RETURNED TO NEW YORK AND TO ME. MY FOG WAS lifting and my luck seemed to be changing, too. On the day she arrived, Frank and Barbara Sinatra invited us to Frank's concert at Carnegie Hall and dinner afterward at the 21 Club.

I'd only dined with Sinatra once before, during the making of *They All Laughed*, also at 21. Frank had invited Peter Bogdanovich, Al Pacino, and me, along with our wives and girlfriends, of course. Elke had just returned to Germany. Meanwhile Janice must have had a spy or two in New York, because she lost no time in flying in to "say hello" to me. Peter had thought the dinner would do me good, get my mind off everything. Frank was in New York filming *The Detective* and he'd told Peter he'd like to meet me. So I went. That is, Janice and I went. At any other time, I would have been anxious and flattered to dine with Sinatra. But in those unhappy days you could have added Our Holy Father the Pope to the guest list and it would not have excited me. Even booze tasted bad, so I couldn't get drunk. Then Frank turned to me.

– Hey, actor. You and I shared a full page in *Life* magazine once.

– 1956, Frank.

– You were on top, I was on the bottom.

– Sorry about that, Frank.

This was when he'd made the movie *The Man with the Golden Arm*, based on a terrific book by Nelson Algren and directed by Otto Preminger. I was on Broadway, in *A Hatful of Rain*. We both played drug addicts, which was a subject that hadn't been dealt with much, if at all, onstage or in film.

That night at 21 was not one of my best. Peter noticed that I was tongue-tied during the meal and did a masterful job of keeping the evening going. Barbara Sinatra, who'd seated me to her left, kept turning to me, trying to draw me out. I gave her my best shot, but could not have been good company. If Barbara was aware of a problem, she never let on. She and Frank were gracious throughout the evening. I was told later that Frank had heard about what I was going through, but to his credit, he behaved as though nothing out of the ordinary was going on at that table.

Sinatra knew a thing or two about heartache. His personal troubles were legendary. In the early fifties he lost his voice over Ava Gardner. When she left him, his vocal strength was diminished suddenly, as if she took his voice with her. He was a wreck. I know this because I was told a firsthand account of that time in Frank's life.

During the late eighties Burt Lancaster and I made a movie in Rome, entitled *The Day Before*. One day on the set I told Burt how much I enjoyed *From Here to Eternity*, in which he'd starred with Frank. Burt didn't go into too much detail, but he talked about director Fred Zinnemann and about Frank, who played a flashy supporting role. He said that Frank was always on the phone, drinking too much, trying in vain to reach Ava in Madrid, where she was having a torrid affair with one of the leading bullfighters. She must have had very special material to offer. I know of three guys who made love to her and they all went crazy when she left them. She always left them.

From Here to Eternity proved to be Frank's turnaround. He won an Academy Award, he regained his voice, and he went on to make some records that today are classics—the music charged with the kind of hurt that can come only from love. I think it was at that moment, when he was again at his best, doing what he loved most, that Frank acquired the strength to let Ava go.

* * *

At Frank's Carnegie Hall concert, Elke and I were seated in a box with Barbara and Bob Marx, Barbara's son from her former marriage to Zeppo Marx. I asked Bob if he'd ever heard of Martin Block, the man who was responsible for my hearing Frank sing for the first time.

I recalled the big RCA Victor radio we had in the living room on Twenty-ninth Street. It wasn't one that you put on a table or sat on a shelf. No, this was the kind that stood on the floor like a piece of furniture. The show I'd listened to almost every afternoon while growing up was Martin Block's "Make-Believe Ballroom." In particular, I loved the "Battle of the Baritones," a segment so popular that there were bets on the street as to who was going to win. The contest went on a long, long time, and listeners cast votes. I never phoned in to vote, but I was rooting like hell at home. Along with Sinatra, there were baritones like Buddy Clark, Dick Haymes, Perry Como, Andy Russell, and Bing Crosby, who'd long been considered the king of the crooners. But the first time I heard Sinatra sing "All or Nothing at All," I was hooked. I'd never heard the story of a song presented in such a simple and tender way. The voice had a sweetness that was unsentimental yet moving. The man was a major talent—and on top of that, he was Italian.

Frank was my baritone of choice throughout my youth, and here I was, thirty-six years later, wearing a tuxedo, sitting in a box in jam-packed Carnegie Hall as his guest, and looking down at the man onstage who I thought was the best. He may have lost his top notes by that point in his career, but he hadn't lost his heart. His singing still had clarity and real feeling—what we actors are always struggling to attain.

Frank's performance that night was colored by the news, heard an hour before the show began, that Grace Kelly had been killed in an auto accident. He was very fond of her and her death clearly affected him. During his performance there were very few funny asides. He concentrated only on his music.

After dinner at 21, Teddy Kollek, the mayor of Jerusalem, talked about how Frank helped get guns and food to Israel during its wars. My old producer friend Sam Spiegel introduced Frank, who made a few touching remarks about how, being an only child, he felt those of us in the room were his family. Later, we gathered around Frank while Sergio Mendez and his group played and Frank offered me a drink. I said, "No thanks." He offered me a Cohiba Cuban cigar. Again I said, "No, thank you." Then he said, with that dazzling smile,

– What do I have here, an altar boy?

I laughed and said,

– Okay, Frank. I'll have a scotch on the rocks.

– Attaboy.

– Frank, you were terrific tonight.

He looked over toward Elke, who was talking to Barbara, and said,

– Is that the broad you were torching about?

– I'm afraid so.

– You hit a home run, actor.

We were staying at the Wyndham Hotel. When we arrived back at our suite, I kissed Elke. We embraced for a long time. I enjoyed her warmth and the movement of her heart beating against my chest. Standing in the dark, I thought about the pain I'd caused her. I was afraid I'd ruined our chance at a happy life together.

—I'm so sorry.

– Ben, I don't want you to be sorry, I want you to be happy.

– I was a fool.

– It's the past, Ben.

– I was crazy.

– I know.

I looked into the eyes of this patient, loving woman.

– What a jerk I've been. I almost lost you.

– But you didn't, Ben. We're together. It's time to live. Life is all we have.

On a beautiful Friday in the summer of 1981, we were invited by John and Julienne Scanlon to spend a weekend at their home in Sag Harbor, on the south fork of Long Island. Elke liked them both, she loved their house, and she fell in love with Sag Harbor. Its main street is the length of one city block, made up of low wooden buildings lined with boutiques, antique shops, restaurants, and a movie house. Just before you get to the picturesque marina, there's the American Hotel with its fine dining and an exceptional wine cellar.

Elke asked John if anything was for sale in the vicinity. We were told there just happened to be a place nearby. He drove us to a little house perched on a knoll, surrounded by trees and lush greenery. My divorce from Janice was a contentious one, so I had been advised by my attorney not to buy anything. It would only complicate matters. But when I saw the joy in Elke's face as she walked through that house I knew I had to make an offer. We bought that house before my divorce was final.

As luck would not have it, I'd gotten myself a hanging judge for my divorce proceedings. He was merciless toward me. But fortunately a job came along to soften the financial blow. I was offered an on-camera commercial for Purolator Courier. They perform a service not unlike Federal Express. I turned down their first offer of $100,000, even though I really needed the money. Coming from the generation of actors that thought doing such a thing was a surefire career killer, I was adamantly opposed to doing a commercial of any kind, ever. They offered $200,000. I still said no. Then three. Again, I declined. It seems that a top man in the ad agency was a big fan of mine. Well, the offer went all the way up to $500,000. I was about to say they should no longer bother, that I was never going to do it, when Elke said, "Hold it now, Ben, you just went through a divorce that cost you a lot of money. This offer has come from heaven to help make up for some of what was lost." Jay Julien was handling the matter for me, and he, too, had advised me against the commercial, but when I repeated what Elke had said, he gave me his wife's reaction, "You guys are crazy even to think of *not* doing it." So it was the dispassionate logic of two women that convinced me to go ahead.

In order to appear in top physical form on television I'd have to lose at least seven or eight pounds. There wasn't much time. The commercial was to be shot in four days, which left me only three days to lose the weight. Elke had heard a lot about a weight-loss miracle worker by the name of Stuart Berger. He had written a couple of best sellers on the subject.

Dr. Berger had a very expensive-looking office on Fifth Avenue. He was tall, thin, affable, and he talked faster than he thought. The words sort of machine-gunned out of his mouth. I told him what I needed. He asked about my eating habits, drinking habits, bowel movements, and whether or not I exercised. He then told me to take a good look at him.

– Would you ever imagine, Ben, that I was once a very fat man?

– No, I wouldn't.

– Well, I was. I weighed exactly one hundred pounds more than I do today. I took that weight off five years ago and haven't put back an ounce since.

– Congratulations.

– This is just to tell you that it's not just a matter of calories, it's a question of mind-set.

– That makes sense.

– We'll get into that at another time. Let's begin with the here and now.

He then put me through a long and tedious allergy test. Elke had never been tested so he gave her one, too. Through it all, he remained jovial, making the experience a fun one. We liked him.

Immediately he put me on a liquid diet and guaranteed that I would lose at least six to eight pounds in time for my TV spot. The product he prescribed was loaded with vitamins and minerals but tasted like rancid soup. I was to drink one can three times a day for a total of eight hundred calories. I held my nose and drank the stuff. After two days of this, my eyeballs hurt and my fingernails were splitting but I weighed myself and was indeed getting the results he promised so I stayed the course.

The morning I was to shoot the commercial, I looked hard at myself in the mirror and saw a thinner but haggard-looking guy. I got on a scale to discover I had lost nine pounds. Stuart Berger had delivered. I wore makeup for that assignment, something I never did. My face had more definition but I still looked pale and tired.

Everyone was thrilled by how well the shoot went. They were certain they had the makings of a campaign that would please the client. The commercial consisted of me looking into the camera and saying how fast and reliable this Purolator Courier is, or me walking through an endless warehouse full of cardboard cartons, saying how fast and reliable Puro-lator Courier is. For all the money they had given me, I was required to be available for about one half-day, two or three more times during the next twelve months for the shooting of new commercials. When the commercial finally aired, it dropped dead. Purolator thought it was awful. The ads went nowhere and the man who hired me, and advised the client to pay me all that money, was fired.

Noel Behn had been my friend for a long time. He had gone from off-Broadway producer to author in one fell swoop when he wrote the best-selling novel *The Kremlin Letter*. Now, he had written a second book and there was to be a party at Elaine's restaurant. Elke and I were told that we could bring a guest or two. We invited Stuart Berger. We thought that Berger, being a writer himself, might find it interesting to hobnob with the literary set. After dinner I showed him my fingernails, most especially my right thumb where the nail had split halfway down the center after being on the diet he had put me on. "Not to worry," said Stuart, "within a week or two your nails will be like new."

He excused himself and walked toward the lavatory. A few moments later, Elke went to the ladies' room. I was alone but Elaine sat and kept me company. She has been fighting to lose weight most of her life, so I recommended Berger to her. She listened but I could see she wasn't con-vinced. Elke came back to the table and appeared agitated.

– Ben, Elaine knows that the wall of the ladies' room is also the wall of the men's room. Well, do you know what I heard through that wall? Terrible sounds. It was Dr. Berger throwing up his food.

Elaine nodded her head,

– Of course, that's how the moron stays so thin, he vomits. There's a name for it.

And the three of us raised our voices in unison:

– Bulimia!

– Bulimia!

– Bulimia!

Not too long after that, Dr. Berger died. My thumbnail is still cracked.

Elke and I were married on a warm day in February. You saw very few overcoats that month. I remember that detail because I was acting in a TV movie in New York, and had finished shooting the day before the wedding. It was called *A Question of Honor*, and was produced by Sonny Grosso, one of the real-life detectives who busted the famous "French Connection," and was also involved in the making of the movie of the same title. *A Question of Honor* was especially dear to Sonny because it dealt with a friend of his—a detective who was charged with taking bribes and would be exonerated only if he informed on his fellow officers. He chooses suicide instead. I liked Sonny and I realized how much this movie meant to him. He had been very close to his friend. I was determined to do the best I could to bring him alive.

We were filming downtown near the prison known as "the Tombs" when I decided to drop in on my brother Tony. He worked nearby with a criminal lawyer, entering pleas, taking depositions, even writing briefs. All that, despite the fact that he wasn't a lawyer. He was good at his job, so the headman put him to work a lot. It was hard for me to believe. I'd always thought that Tony would end up teaching Romance languages at some small midwestern college.

He took me to lunch at a nearby restaurant. As we entered I heard "Hi, Tony" at least twenty times. The bar was packed with a mixture of plainclothes cops and criminal types. They were having fun with each other, laughing and drinking, and it seemed they all knew my brother. I was proud he was so well liked.

I told him I was getting married in a week and I wanted him there. He looked at me and smiled, "Get it right this time, brother of mine. She's a very nice woman." Although Tony was in his midfifties, he had not yet come out as gay. I wanted to ask my brother about his life, but personal conversations had been taboo for so long that I stayed away from it. We talked about our work instead.

My friends John and Suzanne Mados, the owners of the Wyndham Hotel in midtown Manhattan, hosted our wedding reception there. We were married by a judge in the hotel penthouse. My brother came to the wedding and so did Sonny Grasso. John Cassavetes and Gena Rowlands flew in from L.A. They knew about all the dramatics in my life leading up to this wedding day. When John heard about it he said,

—That's not depression. It's grand opera.

Peter Falk and his new wife, Shera, came too, and they stayed at the hotel with us. Liz was put up there, as well. She was now a grown woman, working as a film editor on interesting low-budget movies.

John showed up for the ceremony with purple hair. Peter Falk was running late because he was dying his hair, too. John came in giggling his sweet giggle, because he knew the hair was purple—he'd used the wrong color dye. Then Peter came in and the three of us smiled knowingly at each other because we knew that we all colored our hair. It had been ten years or so since we'd made *Husbands* and I loved them even more. None of us ever imagined that we'd create a myth of friendship that would last so long. How often I'd get into a taxi and the cabbie would ask, "How are your two buddies?" They felt we belonged together. How did they come to see us that way?

Jessica Tandy and Hume Cronyn joined the party. Hume had had one eye removed due to cancer. Peter, of course, had lost an eye when he was a child.

A lady had been calling me for months asking me who did Peter Falk's prosthesis. She even phoned me in Capri. In fact, she phoned me everywhere,

– My daughter has this problem and I have to find her a prosthesis. Who did Peter Falk's?

So I told Peter that I had this woman calling. He said,

– Have her call me. I'll try to help her.

– Peter, I've gotta tell you the truth, I think Hume's eye is better than yours.

– What are you talking about? Let me take a look at that.

And he weaved his way through the crowded room to where Hume was standing, stared at his eye, and said,

– You think your eye is better than my eye?

Hume looked carefully at Peter's eye.

– Quite frankly, yes.

– Well, I don't think so.

And Hume, who was holding his pipe in his hand said,

– Can you do this?

And with the end of the pipe, he hit his eye—bap bap bap bap bap bap bap bap. And Peter took a glass, a whiskey glass. And hit *his* eye with it—bang bang bang bang bang. Peter's very competitive.

The music played, I asked Elke to dance. John danced with Gena, Peter danced with the judge's wife. There were at least a hundred people at that wedding reception and they stayed later than expected—the sign of a good time. For me it was as though shades had been lifted and the sun I'd been screening out came pouring in. A new day had begun.

CHAPTER 20

EUROPEAN MOVIES

IT WAS DURING THE 1980S THAT MY WORK STARTED TAKING me to Europe, to Italy in particular. In 1982 Marco Ferreri, a sometimes outrageous artist, asked me to play the writer-boozer Charles Bukowski in *Tales of Ordinary Madness*. Marco had already made that truly scatological black comedy *La Grande Bouffe*, in which four or five male friends eat themselves to death, and *The Last Woman*, in which a man cuts off his penis with an electric bread knife. So it was no surprise that he'd be attracted to the dark and bizarre works of Bukowski.

Although there was no screenplay, I agreed to do the picture. I'd been so impressed by Ferreri's work that I based my decision on that, as well as on reading and enjoying the six Bukowski short stories from which the movie would be adapted. Another deciding factor was that the movie would be shot in English in direct sound. Jay Julien was in Rome to close the deal with Ferreri. Jay, Vittorio Squillante, my Italian agent, and I were having a drink at the bar in the Hotel de la Ville when I was called to the phone. It was Elke.

– Ben, you can't do this picture.

– Why not?

– Let me read you something. "I took it out"—meaning your penis, Ben—"and she examined it closely and said, 'My, it's so bent and purple. How did it get that way?'"

– Elke, my love, it's all tongue-in-cheek. It's satire. It's not meant to be pornographic.

– Are they going to ask you to take all your clothes off? Do they intend to put makeup on your *pisellino* to make it look bent and purple?

– I never thought about it, but I know what to do. I'll just put a clause in the contract, "No Nudity."

And that's what I did. There was no problem. Ferreri never intended to bend me or color me purple.

I'd seen strange things during my years of making movies but Marco supplied the most peculiar of them all. The first day of shooting took place on a beach in Savannah, Georgia. I played my first scene, in which Bukowski is drunk, with the character played by the lovely Ornella Muti. Ferreri was smiling when he said, "Cut. Print it." To save money Marco shot very little film; he printed no more than one take per setup. Like John Ford, he did his editing "in the camera," so to speak. That's risky business and he knew it and that may be why I saw him do what he did.

When he was some distance from us, he began to punch himself in the face. I mean, he landed some Muhammad Ali–like blows to his chin, his cheekbones, and his temples. He was really pummeling himself. At first I was taken aback, but the more I thought about it, I was more and more impressed. I decided that this was his unique way of reminding himself not to settle for less—to make sure that things were always the best they could be. It wasn't the only time it happened. He did it often. I was afraid he'd send himself to the hospital. But we finished the picture and it was very good. Maybe Marco with his self-flagellation was on to something.

During our filming of the Roman locations Elke and I decided to drive down to Positano for the weekend. It was the off-season and there would be very few tourists. I was standing at the newspaper kiosk in the *piazzetta* and I saw it: a large photo of Dorothy Stratten on the front pages of all of the Italian newspapers. She had been brutally murdered by her jealous husband. She returned to the home they'd shared in order to talk to him about ending their marriage. He had other things on his mind. He locked her in the house with no hope of escape and then, after abusing her, he killed her and himself.

Images of that lovely young girl came to me in a rush. How frightened she must have been. How defenseless. How fragile. I winced when I thought of how much he'd made her suffer. *How will Peter cope with all that?* I thought. *Is there anyone around him who will help him?* Our friendship hadn't yet been repaired. We'd become estranged during the filming of *They All Laughed,* so I didn't feel that I could call him. I didn't know what to do, so I did nothing. I felt bad about that.

Elke and I attended the opening of *Tales of Ordinary Madness* in Paris. It was shown in four theaters in the original English-language version, so audiences would be hearing my voice and not that of an actor dubbing my lines in French while my mouth moved in English. We stayed at the Hotel George V, where Marco and Ornella Muti were also staying. Although we didn't attend any of the screenings, we lurked around one or two theaters to listen to the audience reactions. We were not prepared for the raves that followed from the public and critics alike. The next day there were long lines at all four theaters. The movie was a smash. While Bukowski was not prized in the States, in Europe he was a star.

For a time, Ferreri had trouble finding an American distributor, and even after he did, it was clear that little money would be spent on prints and advertising. Unless the picture scored immediately, it would not get the support necessary to build an audience. As I feared, the movie was disliked in the States. It dealt with a man who wanted only to drink and write. He's interested in nothing else except an occasional woman. The picture had no easily accessible storyline and the leading character was often disagreeable. That's tough for American audiences, where everyone wants to root for a hero. I, on the other hand, have always been drawn to playing difficult people. The success that *Ordinary Madness* had in Europe brought me a lot of offers, so Elke and I decided to stay in Italy a while.

Her daughter, Danja, had come to live with us in America. It didn't take me long to see that there was absolutely no contact between her and her father. I offered to adopt her. I hoped it would give Danja a feeling of belonging and give me another family. After a lot of paperwork and agreement on her father's part, it was done. Now it was time to bring her to Italy and she was excited about that. She arrived knowing exactly where she wanted to go to school. Like my Liz, she'd chosen Florence.

Living in Italy is like having someone pour delightful drops of beauty into your soul. You have breakfast, you see a Raffaello. You have lunch, you see a Bernini. You have a cocktail, you see a Michelangelo. Rome is a living museum. It's almost at the center of the country. In one day, we could drive north to Mont Blanc in the French Alps or south to Reggio Calabria at the tip of the peninsula. We'd drive up to Florence to visit with Danja, and continue on to Verona or even Venice. When we headed south, we always stopped at one of the most beautiful hotels in the world—the San Pietro in Positano. It's built into the side of a mountain and can be seen only when you approach it by sea—and then only when you get very close. Frank Lloyd Wright would have approved.

Our apartment in Rome was near the Spanish Steps, and from it we could see the charming cobblestone streets and the palazzos painted in warm, Roman colors. But our place lacked double-paned windows. If the daytime traffic was annoying, the noise at night was unbearable. There was a homeless lady who lived on the steps of the church across from us, but she never slept because all night she would speak to someone who wasn't there. She screamed, "Monica, Monica, Monica, you are a *troia*, a *puttana*" (a tramp, a whore).

I was preparing for a movie and wasn't getting much sleep. The lady's shouting always happened late at night and when I would leave for work in the morning, she was gone. But one day I had a particularly early call. I had to be out of the house by five-thirty so that I could be driven to the location, which was a little over an hour away. As my driver, Attilio, opened the car door for me, I saw her. I walked toward her and, as I got closer, I saw that this lady, seated between large bags filled with God knows what, was one of the most attractive women I'd ever seen.

She was about fifty years old. Her face was clean and she had aquiline features, big gray eyes, and porcelain skin in which the green veins of her temples were especially prominent. She had made a home for herself—a kind of cardboard shed—in the corner of the main entrance to the church. The three steps leading to it were covered with cigarette butts. She had one in her mouth when she said,

– Do you have a cigarette?

– I only smoke cigars.

– Too bad.

We spoke Italian, of course.

– You're Ben Gazzara. I saw you many times. *Lei è molto bravo.*

She spoke a beautiful Italian, from Tuscany, I surmised. And her movements were graceful, almost noble. How did she end up here? I wondered.

– Do you go to the cinema?

– I used to, I used to do a lot of things.

– This Monica, this woman you talk to at night, was she a relative of yours?

– She was a friend and she took my husband and my daughter away from me. May she rot in hell.

– Is she dead?

– Who knows? They all went to live in South America. She took everything I had, including the love that was in my heart.

Can it be, I thought, that a woman in calm possession of herself in daylight can become an enraged animal at night?

People are seldom all they seem. I don't know of anyone who would have cast this woman as a bag lady. To me she looked like a countess who was down on her luck. It was another proof that in creating a character, finding the opposite is paramount—to find calm where there is turmoil, kindness where there is cruelty, sweetness where there is bitterness, humor where there is pain.

The movie I was making was entitled *Il Camorrista*. The offers from the States weren't coming as often as they once had, and the parts themselves were not as good as those I got in Italy. One day a young director brought me a book that dealt with the man who headed all the organized crime in the province of Campania, of which Naples is the center. The *camorra* is the Neapolitan version of the Sicilian Mafia. I asked the young man to tell me his story, which he did with exceptional visual detail. I signed on to his film there and then. The young director was Giuseppe Tornatore. This would be his first film. *Cinema Paradiso* would be his second.

When I arrived at the studio for my fittings, I drove the costume designer insane. I insisted on changing almost everything we had agreed upon. The clothes now seemed to me too stereotypical of a gangster type. Instead I wanted my character to dress in suits by Brioni and shirts by Albertelli. I wanted him to look as though he would fit comfortably in any upper-crust salon. I huddled with Tornatore and told him that I wanted to play this man like a kind and considerate professor, and to let the evil he does speak for itself. To Tornatore's credit, he agreed.

At home that night there was no shouting from the lady. I looked down from my window and saw no cardboard shelter on the church steps. They told me the police had moved her on. Where did she go? How would she survive? I'd been touched by that woman.

During the first day of shooting *Il Camorrista* I felt uncomfortable with my handling of the part. I wanted my character to seem authentically southern Italian but I was having trouble doing so while speaking English. I decided to try playing a scene in Italian. With that switch, everything became easier and more relaxed. The character's gestures, his walk, elements that had seemed difficult until then, now came easily. They dub almost everything in Italy and all the other actors were speaking Italian, so I dove right in. I tried to do the entire film in the best Italian I could conjure up. There is no doubt that the language a person speaks dictates his or her body language, and I think my decision actually enriched the picture.

With Tornatore's first setup, it was clear that he had a good sense of placement. I wondered though how this first-time director would be with the actors. He dove right in like a pro. He had strong opinions, but he never told you how to act. I've never liked working with a director who spelled things out anyway.

* * *

Early one Saturday morning Elke and I drove to Calabria. It was there that I met Renato Guttuso. He and I were honored along with Gianni Versace. Guttuso was recognized for his work as one of Italy's leading painters. Versace was honored for fashion, of course, and I for acting. I liked Guttuso right away. He was of medium height and had a full head of soft, white hair above a handsome face with a warm smile. His easy manner made me feel as if I'd known him for years. Perhaps that was because he, like my parents, was born in Sicily. He had the same soft voice my father had.

He greeted us with affection and generosity that is typical of many Sicilians. His wife, Mimise, took an immediate liking to Elke. She had been born a countess in Milan and as a child had had a German nanny. She spoke German perfectly and enjoyed practicing it with Elke.

In Rome we saw each other quite often. On occasion we would dine at the Guttusos' home, which was in one of Rome's most beautiful palazzos. Renato's studio was always filled with interesting types—painters, writers, politicians, and an occasional cleric. The talk was invariably lively, full of insightful comments. I was made to feel at home.

Renato was a quiet, elegant man who produced an acclaimed body of work. Unlike actors, who have to wait for a director or producer to involve us in a project (hopefully with a script that will permit us to create something special), Guttoso woke up every morning, walked into his studio, and began to paint—good or bad, complex or trivial, surprising or banal, he painted. I could only envy such a life in art.

The Guttusos invited us to their home in Palermo for the Christmas holidays and there too Renato had an enormous studio where he would paint every day. He allowed me to join him there and I would keep him company for hours, which flew by like minutes. There were a number of paintings leaning here and there against the walls of the studio. I couldn't take my eyes off one of them—a vivid and colorful study of the famous Vucciria, Palermo's central marketplace. The work was so vivid I could smell the fresh fruit, the vegetables, and the many exotic spices. I hadn't been to Vucciria yet, but I felt that if I could walk into that painting I'd be back on Twenty-ninth Street, strolling through that very same market, taken to New York by Sicilian immigrants a century before.

Guttoso enjoyed listening to me trying to speak in the Sicilian dialect. While I struggled to remember the words, he coached me and was pleased with my pronunciation. Moments like these were my happiest while in Italy. I was in Sicily where my parents were born, sitting in a splendid Baroque palazzo, speaking the language I'd spoken as a child.

A man with a beautiful name, Pasquale Festa Campanile, called me in Palermo and said he wanted me to costar in his new movie with Ornella Muti. Not unlike many beautiful young women, Ornella had been cast in her first movie without training of any kind. When I first worked with her in *Tales of Ordinary Madness* she was still learning her craft on the go, so to speak. She was only in her twenties, and she'd become a good actress in a short amount of time. *Ordinary Madness* had been a critical and financial success in Italy, so the producers thought that our pairing would do business again. I agreed to do the picture.

Pasquale said the male lead was a very exciting role, made to order for me. The movie, to be called *The Girl from Trieste*, was adapted from one of his own novels and would be shot in Trieste, that lovely but melancholy city where James Joyce taught English and wrote *Ulysses*. One of the pleasures of working on a movie with Pasquale was that he chose such beautiful locations—Venice, Verona, Rome, Paris.

A few days after we finished shooting, we were dining with Pasquale in one of his favorite Roman restaurants when we noticed Marcello Mastroianni seated nearby with a group of friends. He came over to our table and said in Italian, "I've come to say hello to your beautiful wife." Pasquale invited him to join us. He returned to his table, grabbed a half-full bottle of grappa, brought it back, and sat down.

Marcello was considered a champion at handling that firewater. I was almost a contender; Elke was a newcomer. But Pasquale could give him a real battle for the crown. He could handle any type of booze and in large quantities. He drank a lot and took mood elevators to give him the energy to make films by day and write books at night. But the time was coming when Pasquale's body would no longer take the battering. Much too soon I'd lose this new friend.

Marcello was my kind of guy. Nobody worked harder, but when he left the set he knew how to relax. Elke asked him why he wasn't in L.A. that day to attend the Academy Awards. (He'd been nominated for his performance in *Dark Eyes*.) He told her that it would have been torture to fly all the way to California and sit for hours in a crowded auditorium, only to lose to someone else. On top of that, sitting next to all of those American actors with their big muscles would make him feel inadequate. He was smart not to go. He didn't win.

Not long afterward, Pasquale and I made another movie together. Pasquale was a man of action, not one of those guys who take a year or two to dream up a movie. In *A Proper Scandal*, I played an amnesiac for the second time in my career. My character is claimed by a very wealthy woman from Turin, although she knows full well that he is not her husband. Based on a historical incident, this case became the talk—and the scandal—of Italy in the late 1800s. Even today they still argue in Verona: was he or wasn't he? Like a number of the films I made abroad, the picture was of very high quality. I believe that if some of the other movies I'd made in Italy had been shot in English, in direct sound, they would have found an American audience.

Shortly before *A Proper Scandal* opened in the theaters, Elke and I had dinner at the Guttusos with the French painter Balthus, who had been living in Italy for decades with his young Japanese wife. Balthus had just come from the Venice Film Festival, where he'd been a member of the jury and had seen all the films. Renato asked if he'd seen *A Proper Scandal*. Balthus said, "I didn't care for the film, but I liked the actor very much." Renato said, "Well, he's here, sitting right next to you." That tall, elegant man, who up till then had been rather cold to me, put on his glasses and examined my face for a very long time. Then he said, "My compliments, very good." It was nice to be appreciated, even if my film was not.

* * *

Italy had become my second home. Like they say, go where you're loved. In the 1980s the Italians obviously had a crush on me. In my next picture, *Don Bosco*, I'd be playing my first saint: a priest who formed the Salesian Society, devoted to the care and nurturing of homeless boys. I had just shot a scene with some of the young boys and was in my dressing room, feet up on the table, when the phone rang. It was Tom Korman, my agent, telling me that Gena Rowlands was going to star in a new Woody Allen movie called *Another Woman*, and that Woody would like me to play one of the important men in her life. Tom had been told that there were three or four good scenes, and they would take about a week to shoot.

– Could the Italians arrange to shoot without you for that long?

– I don't know, Tom. I'm in almost every scene.

– Well, see what you can do.

– In the meantime, why don't you have them Fed Ex the script to me.

– Woody Allen doesn't send a script to anyone. But he'll call you tonight and tell you everything you want to know.

I'd never met Woody. Whether he wanted me because he liked my work or the fact that Gena and I had worked so well together, I'll never know. But we had a pleasant conversation that night. He filled me in on the character and told me the dates that I would be needed in New York City. I'd never committed to a project without having read the material. I told myself that if I did this movie, it would be entirely by virtue of Woody's strong reputation as well as my affection for Gena. John probably would be with her in New York, so we'd get to spend some time together, too.

I told Woody I didn't know if it was possible to get time away from Italy, but said I'd try. He replied that I should do what I could on my end, while he would do the same on his. The Italians were gracious and generous; they rearranged the entire schedule to make it possible that I give Woody the week of shooting he needed.

I landed in New York on a Saturday and went immediately into a jet-lagged wardrobe fitting. Elke remained in Rome, because it was going to be a very short gig in New York. I didn't sleep much that night and the next day I was picked up at six-thirty in the morning and driven to a location somewhere in New Jersey. A production assistant showed me to my trailer and asked if I wanted breakfast. "Just coffee," I said. My wardrobe was hanging there so I changed into it, and as I never wear makeup I was ready to go. Time passed; too much time.

I read the *New York Times* front to back. When it was ten o'clock, I lay down on the sofa and closed my eyes. There was an insistent banging on my door—another production assistant asking me if I wanted lunch. I declined and told him to call me when it was time to go to work. He never did. It was late afternoon when a bona-fide assistant director came to tell me that Woody didn't like the clear skies for the scene we were to shoot. He wanted lots of clouds. I understood and respected that so I went back to New York. I was staying at the Wyndham Hotel, where I knew Gena was staying. I'd hoped that John was with her but they told me he hadn't come east yet. I couldn't think of anyone else I wanted to see on such short notice so I went to bed.

The next morning, there was not a cloud in the sky. This time, they had me wait only a few hours before they surrendered and said, "See you tomorrow." On Wednesday the weather was still too lovely to shoot the sequence. We were in trouble. I called for the first assistant director and told him that I'd done some investigating and there was not one cloud east of Colorado. Did Woody forget that I had to be on a plane on Saturday? He asked if I could possibly get more time from the Italians. I said that they'd waited as long as they could and that I had given them my word I'd be on the set the following Monday morning.

That's how it went for the rest of the week. Thursday and Friday were beautiful days and on Saturday I was on a plane, flying back to Italy and to Elke. Woody never said hello and he never said farewell. Somebody said it was because he's shy. As it turned out, I didn't miss much. Even the gifted Gene Hackman, who ended up in my role, couldn't do much to make the part very interesting.

Don Bosco was a success but Elke and I couldn't celebrate. Money—the loss of it—had become a big concern. We had invested heavily in a stock that was a "sure thing." But, whaddya know, it wasn't, and now we had to prepare for the future.

CHAPTER 21

BALCAZAR

IN THE NICK OF TIME, I WAS OFFERED A LOT OF MONEY TO do a movie to be shot in the most beautiful parts of Spain. It was about love, bulls, and bravery. I would play a man who raised fighting bulls. He has just taken a beautiful young wife and never been happier. And then, we have betrayal. His son sleeps with his wife. Although the plot was rather clichéd, I thought I could bring a new slant to the scenario. Besides, I needed the money.

On our way to Marbella to start the movie we flew to Barcelona to meet the producer. His name was Balcazar, and though he was in his late fifties, the lock of hair that fell over his forehead and his wide-open, sunny smile made him appear much younger. He and a couple of his investors took Elke and me to an elaborate lunch. There were oysters and other crustaceans, served with champagne, followed by striped bass so tender it melted when it touched your tongue. There were superb wines and rich, delicious desserts. *This producer's really a sport*, I thought. We chatted about Spain, about bullfighting, but very little about the picture. We were going to stay the night before continuing on to the south of Spain. Balcazar insisted on accompanying us to our hotel, to the door of the splendid suite he had chosen for us. When he left, I turned to Elke and said,

– This Balcazar is a very generous man.

– And so nice.

The man couldn't do enough for me. When I suggested bringing Anthony Foutz, a writer I'd been collaborating with, down to Marbella to work on the script, he agreed right away. When we arrived in Marbella there was no Balcazar, but the first-class treatment continued. He had sent his personal driver to see to our needs. His name was Andreas and he was always there for us. He became so fond of us that he'd pop in to see how things were even if we'd not called him.

Four weeks of shooting went by smoothly. It was now time for the crew, the actors, writer, and director to move to Jerez de la Frontiera, where we would shoot on a ranch that raised the most highly prized fighting bulls in all of Spain. It would take an entire day to transport everyone and so the filming would start the following day. The trip was tiring, but when Elke and I arrived at the hotel, we were pleasantly surprised by the comfortable-looking sofas in the cozy lobby. I ordered dry sherry for both of us. The drinks had no sooner arrived than my name was announced. There was a telephone call for me.

I never like surprise calls so I approached the phone more slowly than usual. It was Vittorio, my Italian agent, saying that I was not to go to work the next day, that no money had been paid. I was shocked. I could not believe that the man I met in Barcelona would ever double-cross me. There must be some explanation, I thought, and I was sure Balcazar would be in touch. I waited but never heard from him.

I was in virtually every scene in the movie so that when I made it clear the next morning that I would not be working until the money appeared, phones started ringing. People started scurrying. The French coproducer was running around the hotel swimming pool, whispering instructions to his staff. Finally, he came to me with a proposition. Balcazar would be arriving the following day with a certified check. Everyone was waiting on location—the crew, the extras, the actors. If I went to work, it could do me no harm. The film could never be released with only the material they had shot so far. I liked this Frenchman—felt somehow that I could trust him—so I said yes.

That day I had to fight a bull. It was a female bull, but a bull is a bull, and I'm a New Yorker, not a matador. Elke usually never comes on the set but when she heard I was to face a bull, she insisted on being there. On the way to the set I noticed something quite remarkable. The ranch must have covered thousands of acres but there wasn't a single telephone pole to be seen. This was before the era of cell phones, so how did they communicate? Did they bury all the wires? I never found out. I asked Andreas to stop so I could get a better look. It was as though the land had remained unchanged for centuries.

Elke was at my side when I heard what I thought was thunder, but there wasn't a cloud in the sky. The sound grew closer and became more insistent. I looked over to a nearby hill and out of the early morning mist came a lone horseman followed by hundreds of jet-black fighting bulls on a furious gallop to their pastures below. Elke and I still talk about the simple power and beauty of that moment.

There were a hundred or so extras seated around the bull ring. They were playing friends who watched as I tested the female bulls for their courage. Only the truly courageous are allowed to mate with a superb fighting bull, therefore producing even more brave bulls.

My character has chosen this occasion to humiliate his son, to show him what courage is. I had already taken lessons from a real *torero*. We were standing in the center of the ring, the director, the *torero*, and me. The director was talking into my left ear, telling me where his cameras would be, asking me to lead the bull in this or that direction. *Lead her*, I thought. *Are you crazy? I'll be lucky if she doesn't kill me.* His only concern was getting the shot they'd need in a single take.

The *torero* was whispering in my right ear assurances that nothing would go wrong and that if it did he would be right there—behind a barrier. Then the director gave a signal and ran like hell. So did the bull-fighter. Members of the crew fled in fear, hiding behind other barriers as the bull appeared. She trotted into the ring, then stopped dead when she saw me, as if to say, "What the hell are *you* doing here?" What *was* I doing there? I was an actor who hadn't been paid, risking his life for a picture that might never be seen. And then above the noise of the crowd I heard a voice that echoed my thoughts.

– Ben, you're crazy. Get out of there. Look, everyone else is hiding.

It was Elke. She was behind me so I couldn't look at her. I wasn't to take my eyes off the bull. That was lesson number one. I raised my arm to let her know that I was going ahead. I couldn't walk away now; it was *my* courage that was being tested. I stared into the sad-looking eyes of the confused animal and called her: "Haa, toro!" She didn't move. "Haa, toro!" Nothing. And then I remembered. If she doesn't move, wiggle the cape. So I did. "Haa, toro!" And she came. I did a pretty good veronica and got my first "Olé."

The sun bore down on me, but I was too scared to be bothered by the heat. I walked over to a barrier, never taking my eyes off the bull, and exchanged the long pink cape for the shorter red *muleta*. I held the cloth by the slim stick that gave it its spread and approached, ever so carefully, my opponent.

She watched every move I made. I was beginning to feel in control. "Haa, toro!" And she came—this time, much closer. I felt the side of her left horn slide across my body. "Olé." said the extras. *Olé yourselves*, I thought. I should have stopped it there but I told myself I'd let the bull do one more pass and then call in the real *torero*. I would retire at the top of my game. My mistake. The bull must have been tired of missing. This time, when I said, "Haa, toro!" she didn't go for the *muleta*, she came right at me, horns at the ready, aiming for my entrails. *Holy Christ*, I thought, *I'm gonna get gored like the great Manolete, and die in a bullring in Spain. At least he was a bullfighter; this is not even my line of work.*

I heard someone yell "Cut." The real bullfighter appeared with his cape just in time to lead my charging opponent away. The French producer had tears in his eyes when he said, *"Magnifique."* I was a hero.

We shot a lot of other stuff that day, including a great many close-ups of me during my valiant performance. When it was over, I was exhausted. Andreas later gave me my biggest compliment of the day. "Hombre," he said, and then he put two thumbs up. Elke said, "I am proud of you, but you must promise never to volunteer for anything like that again." I've since had no trouble keeping that promise.

The day after was *it*, the moment of truth. If I wasn't paid, I wasn't going to stick around. I was having coffee in the lobby when through the glass doors I saw Balcazar getting out of a white Rolls-Royce. He was followed by a man in a tightly tailored suit with dyed black hair and a goatee of the same color. Balcazar approached me with a big, open smile. His arms were outstretched to embrace me. I got up and let him do it. The man with the bad dye job was an American. He introduced himself and suggested we go to the bar, where we could talk. As soon as we entered, he ordered a bottle of champagne,

– We've got to celebrate. Sorry for the mix-up. My banker retired and the new guy just screwed things up.

He opened an attaché case and produced a check for the full amount owed, plus a week. Balcazar looked directly into my eyes.

– Ben, I would never cheat any man, most especially you. I love you.

And so I sent the check by overnight courier to my agent in Rome. The next day I went back to work. I thought the movie might have something special so I threw myself into the part with even greater energy, trying to make every moment as good as it possibly could be.

Before we left Jerez to return to Marbella, Elke and I asked Andreas to take us to Gibraltar before we went back to the hotel. When we got to the passport gate, the guards on the Spanish side asked Andreas a lot of questions, all in Spanish. We knew immediately that something was wrong. They told him to park the car on the side of the road and to come with them. That's when Elke went to work.

– Leave this man alone. He's a hardworking man. Why are you doing this?

I told Elke to stop interfering, that this was a Guardia Civil. They'd throw her in jail, too. Then Andreas indicated that we should go into the town while he straightened everything out. Well, needless to say, our stay was not enjoyable. We hurried through lunch and walked back to the Spanish checkpoint, but Andreas was missing. When we asked about him, a guard showed us to a steel door. He searched for the key among what could have been a hundred others, opened it, and there was Andreas, sitting in the corner of a barren cell, looking like a lost child. Neither he nor the police would tell us what he had been charged with.

Andreas gave us a number to call for another car, and we told him we'd find someone who could get him out of there. He looked at us and said it again: "Hombre, *gracias.*"

When we got back to our hotel in Marbella we went straight to work and made sure that the proper person was going to handle Andreas's case. It was then that Elke and I were told our kind and gentle Andreas was wanted for murder. It seems that he'd killed one of his brothers-in-law in a barroom fight in Madrid. He'd hired a lawyer who guaranteed him that, for the proper fee, the case would be handled and promptly closed. The lawyer disappeared and so did the fee. That story made me even more tired than I already was. All I wanted was a cold shower.

I was singing and scrubbing when Elke's face appeared from behind the curtain to say Vittorio was on the phone.

– So, Vittorio, did you get the check?

– Yes, I got it. It's no good.

– Well, I'll be a sonofabitch. What do you think I should do?

– Come home.

And that's what we did. From that moment on, whenever I've been deceived or taken advantage of, I don't say I've been screwed, I say I've been "Balcazared."

—CHAPTER 22—

LOSING JOHN

ELKE AND I HAD BOUGHT A NEW YORK APARTMENT BEFORE
settling in Rome and it had been sitting empty ever since. Now we
were looking forward to spending a good deal of time back in the U.S.
in the city we both loved. It was good to be home. We were looking forward to seeing friends and family, and catching up with plays and
movies. But simply walking through the city—just being in New
York—was enough for us.

A few days went by when I got a call from John Cassavetes. He was
at the Wyndham Hotel. He told me that Meade Roberts had written a
play, *Thornhill*, and he thought it might be fun if we got together the
next day for a reading of it. I had known Meade since my early days in
theater. He'd managed to get his work produced both in the theater and
in film, but the past few years had been a struggle for him. At his height,
Meade had written screen adaptations of *Summer and Smoke* and Tennessee Williams's *Orpheus Descending*, the latter (retitled *The Fugitive
Kind*) coauthored with the playwright himself. He was now living in Los
Angeles, where John gave him office space free of charge. John never lost
faith in anyone, especially if he saw that the artist was still trying.

When I arrived at the fourteenth floor of the Wyndham, I heard
loud laughter. The door to John's suite was open and as I entered, I saw
a good bunch of actors—Carol Kane, Patti LuPone, Murray Hamilton,

and John Pankow—seated at a couple of tables that had been pushed together. Of course, John was there and so was Meade, who was wearing a floor-length brown-and-white Moroccan caftan, which acted as a kind of camouflage; his stomach had become quite large. John assigned the parts and the reading began.

I read the part of Thornhill, the leading character; Patti LuPone played my most recent wife; Carol Kane, my girlfriend; Murray Hamilton, the role of my father; and John Pankow, my son. When we finished reading the first act, which to me had felt very long and uneventful, I saw that John was moved. He rose from his chair, walked to the window, and turned his back to us so that we wouldn't see the tears. *I must be missing something*, I thought, but I was starting to see where the play was headed.

In *Thornhill* we were dealing with a writer much like Eugene O'Neill, for whom writing is the paramount thing in his life. He lays waste to wives, sons, fathers, and lovers in the quest for his place in the pantheon of great artists. The second act was better, but even longer than the first. *Good actors can perform miracles*, I thought, *we're almost making this work.* The third act was shorter, but not short enough. *Who's gonna care anyway? A play about an artist is always a difficult sell.* That's how I saw it. John signaled to me that he had something to tell me. I followed him into the bedroom.

– You like the play?

– Yes and no.

– Well, I think it can be terrific. So this is what we'll do. Barry and Fran Weisler wanna do it but they want to see a workshop of it before they come up with the big bucks for a Broadway production. They think it's too long.

– I agree with them. If you put it on as is, it will run as long as *Strange Interlude*. You'll have to have a dinner break.

– We'll find out what's too long and what isn't. Anyway, let's talk turkey. Everybody out there wants to be part of it. Gena and I will start making *Love Streams* in a couple of weeks but I'm gonna bring it back and cut it right here in the Wyndham. So I figure we can start rehearsals for the play in about three months.

– I just don't have the time and energy, John.

I had plenty of energy, but I knew that Cassavetes would never take only four weeks to put on a play. It would be more like twelve. I'd be putting in that kind of time on something I didn't think had a chance in hell of succeeding. If it were a film, he'd be able to bend and twist it into a story he wanted to tell. But here, he'd be obligated to work only with the text he had. I didn't have it in me to work that hard, knowing the production would end with disappointment. And that's how John left it. He didn't try to convince me to do the play. In fact, he didn't pressure me at all. It was over. I wasn't going to do *Thornhill.*

A couple of days later, John's mother died. John was crazy about her. She wasn't an actress, but she appeared in four or five of his movies—and she was good, too. John always gave her interesting parts to play. Elke liked John's mother a lot and so did I. I'd known her for almost twenty years. She didn't trust people easily, but we hit it off right away. She was a great deal like my own mother. She'd always try to get me to tell John to save his money, to think of the future. Fat chance.

The funeral took place in Port Washington. John's mother was buried next to his brother and his father, who had died some eight years earlier. It was the same cemetery where John, Peter, and I had buried our friend at the beginning of *Husbands.*

John was devastated by her death. When we got back to Manhattan, a group of us had lunch at the La Scala restaurant. I was seated next to John with Elke to my left. He looked more tired than I'd ever seen him. Maybe there was more going on in his life than I was aware of. After the antipasto, he turned to me and said,

– So you're really not going to do the play?

Elke joined in.

– You must do the play, Ben. You haven't worked with John in a long time. It will be good for you.

Beware of Greeks bearing grief. I was surrounded. He knew I couldn't say no. How could I say no? He was my friend and his mother just died. I said yes.

* * *

My mother used to say, "When you need money nobody will give it to you." In this instance, she was proven wrong. Someone must've told John that I was hurting for money. On one of those gray, gloomy, New York mornings a Federal Express envelope arrived at our apartment and in it was a check for $50,000 with a note from John saying, "Another fifty will be there next week. Have dinner on me." I was astounded. I picked up the phone.

– John, I can't take this money.

– You're gonna have a lot of work to do on *Thornhill*. I don't want you to be worried or distracted.

– It's too much.

– Give me back what you don't spend.

– But we stop here, John. No more.

– The rest is there if you need it.

Within twelve weeks John was back at the Wyndham with his editor and all the footage he'd shot on *Love Streams*. They took over a good part of the fourteenth floor. I thought I'd stop in and see him, but I didn't like what I saw. His skin was pale and he'd lost a lot of weight. Although he looked lean, his stomach had swelled. I was concerned.

– John, have you been to a doctor?

– What for?

– Your stomach, John. That's what for.

– I know what it is.

– What is it?

– A hernia. I was horsing around with Nick, I picked him up, and something tore.

John's son Nick was six foot four and weighed about two hundred and thirty pounds. So I sort of bought the story even though I had my doubts.

A few days later we started rehearsals and predictably I started liking the play. The other actors were putting flesh and blood around the words, giving them a life that hadn't been evident when I read them. Patti

LuPone, who John had seen and loved in *Evita*, gave a dignity to her character that I hadn't realized was there. Carol Kane didn't use her unique voice and actor's savvy just to get laughs. Instead, she dug deep and was adorable and touching. Murray Hamilton, who was very good in *Anatomy of a Murder* but even better in *The Graduate*, played my father with intelligence and passion. And John Pankow, who I didn't know, surprised me with his stage presence and his emotional range.

I wandered around for some time, trying to get a handle on my character. To tell the truth we were all wandering in our parts. John was not so much staging but allowing the scenes and our impulses to dictate our movements. That worked well in his movies but I wasn't sure we'd get away with it onstage.

Sunday was a day off and John and I were in Chuck Barris's suite at the Wyndham watching a basketball game. The New York Knicks were playing the Chicago Bulls. For a time Chuck had been the king of the game shows. *The Dating Game* and *The Gong Show*, among others, were his creations, offbeat and goofy—a lot like Chuck himself. He had sold his TV company and was now writing books that were getting published. His novel, *You and Me, Babe*, had been a hit. *Confessions of a Dangerous Mind* was a better book but, being a memoir, a harder sell.

Chuck's back was out so his doctor wanted to put him in the hospital, where they would try traction. He said no way. He connected a machine to his big hotel bed that had all these pulleys and weights, and he controlled his traction sessions himself. Chuck was pissed off about being bedridden. He loved going to the gym and he liked playing sports. We'd become friends five years earlier while playing a game of racquetball at the Century West Club in Los Angeles. I must admit he beat me that day.

When the three of us got together it was great fun. We laughed a lot. The talk was mostly about sports, rarely about movies. We might discuss a book, but that didn't happen too often.

John was sitting on the bed to Chuck's left and I was in a wicker chair to his right. We had made some bets against each other in order to liven up our interest in the game. While the machine grabbed, yanked, and stretched Chuck's spinal column, we watched TV. As I remember, it was an action-packed contest. But, sometime during the first quarter, John fell asleep. I remember saying to Chuck that in all the years I'd known him, I'd never seen John Cassavetes close his eyes. He slept through the entire game. That worried me.

During the first week of rehearsals for *Thornhill*, Elke and I took John to dinner. Gena had gone back to the Coast for a few days; he was alone that night. We took him to Nanni il Valletto, where we'd always enjoyed ourselves. John didn't drink much that night, but I noticed that his speech became a bit slurry. I'd been with him when he'd had far more to drink but that had never happened.

After dinner, we strolled along Park Avenue. I pointed out the Delmonico apartments where Robert Altman lived.

– Let's go up and see him.

– John, it's one A.M.

– He's still up.

Elke was concerned.

– I don't think so.

"Come on," he says, and walks right up to the concierge. He asks to see Mr. Altman. I saw the guy was nervous about disturbing a tenant at that hour but he did anyway. Bob invited us up.

John and Altman had not spoken since the midsixties, when they both had offices in the Screen Gems Building. They'd been hired to come up with television and movie ideas for that company and saw each other daily. Bob had a secretary named Lynn Carlin, whom John got to know and like. But Lynn was more troubled than either John or Bob suspected, and one day she tried to kill herself. Later, for some reason or other, Bob fired her. John stopped talking to him on the spot.

This was around the time John was preparing to shoot *Faces*. He had not yet found his leading lady and became intrigued by the idea of using Lynn Carlin, despite the fact that she'd never acted much. John saw in her the sweetness and vulnerability he felt the role needed. John's hunch paid off. He was able to get a performance out of Lynn that was honest and touching. What's more, she was nominated for an Academy Award as Best Supporting Actress.

The door opened and there was Bob dressed in a short silk Japanese robe that ended halfway down his thighs. He clutched the robe at the crotch area. Obviously he was naked underneath and didn't want it to fly open. There was a lady present, and Bob was a gent. He poured scotch for the three of us—Elke drank water—and after some hesitant conversation, John told him that he'd enjoyed *Nashville* very much. That picture was released in 1975 and this was 1983. Altman had made at least ten pictures since *Nashville*. Did John know that? I had to bite my tongue to keep from laughing.

John then proceeded to tell Bob the story of a movie he was going to make starring Gena and me. It would be a love story between a catatonic (me) and a manic-depressive (Gena). John sat on the floor, with his back against the couch, and began to tell a story that I'm sure he was creating as he went along. The beginning was very good—funny and touching. Then, something happened. John took a detour and couldn't seem to return to the plot. That's when Altman said,

– John, I don't like your movies.

I was offended. After all, I'd been in three of those movies. I thought John would be pissed off too, but if he heard it you'd never have known. He was drunk but he found his way back and finished telling the story of the movie he would never make.

When we were on the street again, I asked John,

– Are you really going to make that picture?

– Sooner than you think.

– Couldn't you make the man a manic-depressive and the woman a catatonic?

– It wouldn't work.

– What the hell am I going to do with that part? Stare into space? Look down at my shoes while Gena gets all the laughs?

– I'm going to give you a lot more close-ups.

That guy knew how to get to me.

We'd been rehearsing *Thornhill* for four weeks and it was time to show the Weislers our results. John's willingness to allow us to find our own staging worked very well. The actors were interacting in surprising ways and all of us were enjoying ourselves. But would the Weislers be pleased? In spite of the play's excessive length, John hadn't cut a line. He liked the play as it was. He thought that when the Weislers saw what we'd done they'd be happy. Boy, was he wrong!

After the first act, Barry and Fran said that rehearsals would be suspended, that there would be no workshop, that they were out. John of course put up his own money, stepped in, and paid the costs for the rest of the way. It was announced that *Thornhill* would be performed for three nights. Well, word must have gotten out that John Cassavetes, that remarkable movie director, was putting on a play in downtown Manhattan because when I arrived for the first performance there was a line snaking its way down the block and around the corner. That night the loft was packed. People were standing against the walls and sitting on the floor. Some people told us they liked it, some said they hadn't, but nobody walked out. Not everyone thought it was too long. Many said that for them it could have gone on longer. But to go to Broadway, the play would have to have been cut in half. There was also the matter of money. We didn't go.

Elke and I went back to Europe, where I made more pictures and some good money. In the summer of 1988, I shot one of those movies in Umbria, a gorgeous region of Italy between Rome and Tuscany. We enjoyed our time there so much that we decided to buy property. It would be our home away from home. We found land that looked out upon a high, lush, rolling expanse of trees that showed every possible shade of green, with the blue, snowcapped Apennine Mountains off in the distance. On a hill close by, a large medieval castle almost seemed to be floating on air.

We made an offer on the land and a ruin of an old farmhouse that came with it, and it was accepted. I had to go back to Los Angeles but I wouldn't be away for long, so Elke decided to remain in Italy. While I was gone she worked on lining up an architect and a construction team.

I was excited about the project I'd come to film in Los Angeles. *An Early Frost* was the first TV movie dealing with the pain and horror of AIDS. Aidan Quinn, a fine actor, played a young man with AIDS. Sylvia Sidney, an actress I'd so enjoyed in my early youth, played his grandmother. Gena Rowlands played his mother and I played the father who at first is more disturbed by his son being gay than by his impending death from AIDS. The story becomes particularly moving when the father finally breaks down to show his love for his son.

Like many people at the time, I'd read the headlines and heard stories about AIDS but actually knew very little about it. Nevertheless, our director, John Erman, cared deeply about the material, as he had lost friends to AIDS, and this movie was especially personal for him. As for me, I felt it was important that *An Early Frost* helped open eyes about a subject some people were terrified about. We were afraid there'd be no audience for it, but it was a big success and drew a large number of viewers.

On the first day of shooting I asked Gena how John was doing. I'd heard through friends that his cirrhosis had become grave. She looked at me and said,

– John knows you love him, Ben.

Before I got the chance to phone him, John called to invite me up to his house for a reading. I found him standing at his kitchen stove watching over a huge pot of steaming water, filled with giant-sized artichokes. He was jabbing at them, making sure they were cooked to the right texture. Other guests had been invited, too, so I arrived earlier than the rest because I wanted to spend some time alone with him. I hadn't seen him for a year but I wasn't prepared for what had happened. His thin, lean body had been massacred. His stomach was distended, blown up, ballooned. His shoulders had become bony. I could see that beneath his clothes, his arms and legs were much too thin. But his face, though gaunt and having suffered, was more handsome than I'd ever seen it.

– Would you like an artichoke? They're supposed to be good for your liver. Its probably too late for mine but maybe it'll do yours some good.

– Sure, I like artichoke. What do you have to dip them in?

– Oil and vinegar. Simple.

It was there, in that kitchen, eating artichoke, that I realized just how much John meant to me. I'd been floundering in my life and work and he'd given me the chance to have an adventure I'd never forget. He did that again and once again. He brought more laughter into my life than anyone else ever had before, and he seemed to be able to read my mind. I thought I was good at hiding my feelings but he always knew when I was down. It was always at the right time that he'd tell me how good he thought I was. That meant a lot to me.

– John, you do know that there've been quite a few successful liver transplants done in this country.

– Not for me. No, thanks.

– I'll make a deal with you. I haven't had a complete physical in years. They say that the Mayo Clinic is the best. Why don't we check in there for a week? While they see if anything is wrong with me, they might come up with a way to help you.

– All they could do for me is to tap my stomach and drain the water out so that I might be able to get into my pants again. But that's only cosmetic. This cirrhosis is gonna reverse itself or it's gonna kill me.

– Nobody's gonna die, John.

– It could be worse. At least there's a body of work out there. Some people might enjoy it.

There was murmuring and laughter of guests. John rose and peeked into the entryway to see who'd come in. I reached into my pocket, pulled out a cashier's check made out for fifty thousand dollars, and placed it near his dish. He came back to the table, looked down, and smiled.

– My widow thanks you.

– The interest'll be paid in love.

The others had arrived. We sat around and read a new play, *Begin the Beguine*, that John had written. Peter Falk and I read the parts of two men who rent an apartment in Santa Monica, overlooking the ocean: a splendid view. When they enter, the first thing they do is pull down the shades, go to the phone, and call some hookers. There would be a series of them visiting that apartment. These young ladies would act as a sounding board for our theories on life, love, sex, friendship, death, you name it—pure Cassavetes, finding the humor in the pain. The material was so funny that Peter and I often cracked up and had a hard time continuing. And the people who had been invited to listen really enjoyed it.

The actor Sean Penn was among the guests. He sat quite close to Peter and me as we read. I looked at his face and saw his father, Leo, who I'd known in my early days at the Actors Studio. He was a good actor and had been my understudy in *Cat on a Hot Tin Roof*. Later in his life, Leo Penn gave up the struggles and disappointments of an actor's career and turned to directing. As a matter of fact, he directed two or three segments of my TV series *Run for Your Life*.

When I got back to my hotel, I found a message from Tony Foutz telling me that our Bali picture was in place. Tony and I had been working on *Beyond the Ocean* over a period of three years. We were getting the chance to make a movie in a place we both loved. I was tickled pink.

I called Elke in Rome and gave her the good news. I told her there'd be an awful lot of flying in our future. In a few days I'd be through filming *An Early Frost* and would fly to Rome. I would have a month to work on preparations for *Beyond the Ocean* before we turned around and came back to L.A. to work, so that we'd have a comfortable cushion for the year or more I would have to devote to my Bali picture.

Road House would pay for that. It would be a big studio picture produced by Joel Silver of *Die Hard* fame and would star Patrick Swayze. He would play Dalton, an enforcer in big and rowdy bars, the top bouncer who gives the orders wherever he goes. He takes a job in an infamous road house that has gotten too rough, and his attempts to clean things up put him in conflict with Brad Wesley, the richest person in town and a guy with a mean reputation. That's who I'd play, and I thought it was the most colorful part in the picture.

I'd have five weeks before starting, so I went back to Italy to work on *Beyond the Ocean*. I had a lot of work ahead: haggling over the budget, meetings with the director of photography and the producer, Augusto Caminito. And Tony Foutz and I would have to make a trip to Indonesia, this time with Gianni Saragò, our production manager, and Franco Di Giacomo, the director of photography, who'd done such a splendid job for Nikita Mikhalkov on his movie *Dark Eyes*. We were going to take another look at the locations we had in mind and agree to rent them if they were indeed what we wanted.

I was both starring and directing, so I needed as much assistance and support as I could get. Franco would be a big help and so would Tony, who I thought of as my third eye. Within two weeks we'd taken care of business in Bali, and I had to get back to Rome, where I'd only be able to spend one day with Elke before we flew to Los Angeles together.

When I got to our apartment in Rome I found our dining room table strewn with large rolls and sheets of blue and white paper, and a man I'd never seen before seated next to Elke. She introduced me to our architect. I joined them at the table and saw that this fellow and Elke had come up with some terrific plans. After two or three hours of give and take and take-away, we gave him the green light. It was the beginning of November 1988. The architect told us that by October 1989 we'd be able to move into our new home. That was perfect timing because my Bali movie wouldn't wrap until the end of July. Editing and postproduction in Rome would take another couple of months, and at the beginning of October we'd be able to see our new house.

Elke and I made our way back to Hollywood. She accompanied me this time because shooting would take weeks. The flight from Europe to L.A. was exhausting. We checked into the Sunset Marquis Hotel, which was sort of our home when we were out on the Coast, and went right to bed. She was up in three or four hours but I slept until morning, and was picked up to be driven to the location in order to start shooting.

I would have to shift gears, move my mind away *Beyond the Ocean* and try to focus solely on the character I would play in *Road House*. The director, Rowdy Harrington, and my fellow actors made the experience a lot of fun for me. The first week of shooting went very smoothly. Playing a bad guy is where I came in. The script had funny dialogue. It felt good to be back in a big Hollywood movie. I'll bet that the money paid to feed the cast and crew on the set of *Road House* was more than was spent on the making of *Husbands* or *Saint Jack*.

As we had weekends off, I found myself on my first Saturday in Hollywood in John Cassavetes's garage with Peter Falk, reading *Begin the Beguine*. We weren't far into it when John picked up an 8mm camera with a zoom and started filming the two of us in action. I knew, right away, that he was already thinking of turning it into a movie. But how? A movie takes far more energy than a play and even holding that small camera for a short length of time seemed to tire him. On the other hand, I knew never to underestimate John.

During my remaining time in L.A., I tried to see him as often as possible. On my last day of shooting *Road House*, I could have taken the red-eye home to New York but I felt I had to see John once more before I left. We made a date to have dinner that night. The shooting finished later than I'd expected, so my good-byes to the cast and crew were quick, perhaps abrupt. I didn't want to keep John waiting.

I walked into the restaurant to see that he had company. There must have been three or four people at the table, but I only remember John and Peter Falk. John looked up at me and sort of nodded to himself. He was glad I'd made it.

My character in *Road House* sings a few songs in the picture so I decided to sing one of them for John. I thought I was terrific but Peter stared at me in wonder. John said,

– It's a good thing you can act.

Then the conversation turned to sports, which had been a big part of all our lives and could still generate a lot of passionate discussion.

When we were in the parking lot, I embraced John and told him to take care of himself, "Keep battling," I said. He replied,

– I'm not worried, Ben, I know you'll come to my funeral.

– John, if you die, I ain't gonna speak to you again.

– Okay then. I won't.

He climbed into his car and drove away. I watched him head north on La Cienega Boulevard and disappear into the night traffic. I prayed.

I didn't enjoy the two days Elke and I spent in New York. I was anxious, agitated, and short-tempered. The one play we saw was hard for me to sit through. I couldn't concentrate. During the intermission, Elke touched my cheek lightly and said,

– You're thinking about John, aren't you?

– Yes, I am. I wonder if I'll ever see him again.

Then I was back in Rome. Tony and I were finally going to make the picture we had worked on for so long. A couple of days before we were to fly to Indonesia to start principal photography, a phone call came. It was NBC asking me what I thought about the death of John Cassavetes. I couldn't speak. "Phone me back," I said. When they called back, I tried to talk about John as a friend and artist but could say very little.

It was hard to sit still that evening. I paced up and down the whole night. Elke and I booked a flight from Rome to Los Angeles for the next day. Packing without sleep, we just made it to the plane. During that very long flight, how often I thought, "Yes, John, I'm coming to your funeral."

John was laid to rest at Woodlawn Cemetery, a small, green place. I didn't even seek out Gena as soon as I arrived. During the ceremony I had to step away. I couldn't stand still. I paced and I cried.

Peter Falk was wearing the same navy-blue coat he'd worn in the opening scene of *Husbands*, so many years before. That picture opened with John, Peter, and me going to the funeral of our best friend—and here it was, the real thing.

—— CHAPTER 23 ——

BACK TO WORK

IN 1989 ELKE AND I GOT OURSELVES OUR SPLENDID NEW
house in Italy, I went to Bali to make the picture I dreamed of making,
John Cassavetes died, I sunk into a deep depression, and my daughter
got married. Some year.

Only a few days after Liz's wedding, Chuck Barris showed up at my
apartment and insisted we take a walk. He was one of the few people Elke
had confided in about my condition. She knew he'd be there for me and
that I'd enjoy his company. He appeared regularly, unannounced, and
saw to it that I got out of the house. We'd walk and he'd talk.

This time we strolled north on Madison Avenue. There was a good
Jewish delicatessen on Eighty-sixth Street and it was nearing the lunch
hour so Chuck suggested we go in and have something to eat.

– I'm not hungry.

– Well, I am. You're just gonna have to keep me company.

We sat in a roomy, circular booth. I picked up a menu and pretended
to be interested. Chuck ordered.

– I'll have a bagel and cream cheese. Ben?

– Cup of coffee, please.

– I'm kinda hungry. Why don't you also bring me a corned beef on rye?

The food arrived. Chuck started on his bagel and something happened. Smelling the corned beef, seeing the kosher pickles, began to get

261

to me. I reached over, picked up half the sandwich, put some mustard on it, and bit into it. It was good. In no time at all the half was gone, and soon the second half followed. I was like a child who's taken his first steps. Chuck was beaming.

– Would you like some dessert?

I was excited. My appetite was back. Just like that, I was back.

– I'll have some ice cream. A scoop of vanilla and a scoop of chocolate.

Chuck didn't join me but he watched with pleasure, smiling and nodding his head in approval. It was that day, that lunch, that convinced me I was ready to get back to work, that it was time to get back to Rome to recut my picture.

I'd been thinking a great deal about *Beyond the Ocean* and felt I knew a way to make it work. But when I got back into the cutting room, it was clear that the editor wasn't pleased to see me. I'd sent word that I intended to recut the picture, which pleased him even less. I suggested I work with his assistant, a pleasant woman and a good worker, and that's what happened. I reshaped and realigned many of the scenes, making the movie less linear and more surprising. We put in very long hours and within three weeks I was able to finish my cut.

I showed what I'd done to a small group of people who'd worked on the movie. Our producer, Augusto Caminito, was there, and so were Franco Di Giacomo and his camera operator. Elke and I sat in the last row, where I'd be able to pick up signs of restlessness or, even worse, boredom. When the screening ended and the lights came up there was applause. Everyone was excited. But I knew the film still wasn't good enough. I hadn't been able to shape the material as I imagined it should be. As Caminito was telling me how pleased he was, I told him I'd like a couple more weeks in the cutting room to make things even better. He was amenable.

When we got home, Elke convinced me that I should stop, that I had to let it go. She was afraid it might drive me crazier than I'd already been. She suggested that we lick our wounds back in the States, and I took her advice. I walked into Caminito's office, told him I'd done as much as I could, and held out my hand. He jumped up from his chair, came around his desk, and embraced me. "*Grazie di tutto*, Ben," he said. He was thanking me for everything despite the fact that I'd given him a lot of anxious moments. I gave him a hug and told him to take care of himself and our movie.

Before we left Italy, Elke suggested we drive up to Umbria and take a look at our house. I'd really lost interest, but Elke's spirit and enthusiasm made me put on a happy face. I wasn't ready for what I saw. I was bowled over by what she'd accomplished. While I was trying to make a movie, she created a paradise.

She decided to call our house Casa Bali; it would be, in effect, a Mediterranean house with an entirely Balinese interior. She'd found beautifully made furniture, superbly crafted artifacts, and even tracked down two of the leading Balinese artists and bought many of their unique and colorful paintings.

I don't know if it was the beauty of the place or that my dark journey had finally ended, but at that precise moment I finally forgave myself. Suddenly, I was able to separate what I'd done as an artist from what I felt I should have done. I could stand back and think, *Not bad at all, Ben*. I was able to look at my beautiful wife and enjoy the sight of her as much as when I'd first laid eyes on her, some ten years before and half a world away. When *Beyond the Ocean* opened in Italy to mixed reviews—and received no financial backing or push from the distributor—I should have felt depressed. But I didn't. Instead, a strange calm came over me. Perhaps because I'd expected this outcome.

It wasn't too long before Alexander Cohen, the noted Broadway producer, contacted me to say that he was running a theater in Stamford, Connecticut, and that Al Pacino wanted to perform a play called *Chinese Coffee* there. It would be a short run of about three weeks with two weeks' rehearsal. He told me the play ran one hour and a half and would be played without intermission. Pacino had done the play a couple of times before but would now alternate it with Oscar Wilde's *Salome*. I would be needed only in *Chinese Coffee*. Cohen said that both plays were terrific, would I be interested? I was. He sent the script over, I read it the same day, and laughed out loud so often I was convinced that Pacino and I would knock them dead. The part in *Chinese Coffee* was delicious. I could taste it. I felt I had to do it. I called Alex Cohen and told him that I was in. I couldn't wait.

I hadn't seen Al since that dinner at 21 with Frank Sinatra and Peter Bogdanovich. When we met he told me that because he was doing *Salome* he wouldn't be available for much rehearsal for *Chinese Coffee*. I figured that with a good stand-in for him and our director Arvin Brown overseeing things I'd be able to handle it. Brown had already mounted a production of the play at the Long Wharf Theatre. That made me rest easy.

There's that famous saying "Be careful what you wish for, you might just get it." Well, I sure did. I had no idea when Al told me we might not have a lot of rehearsal time together that he really meant next to none. We had only one rehearsal with Arvin Brown, and I never saw him again. He was busy running the Long Wharf. I expected someone else to take over but that didn't happen. On two or three occasions Pacino showed up but there was no one out front to guide us in any way. So we sort of created our own staging.

The rest of my preparation was with an aspiring young actor who substituted for Pacino and read his lines, badly, while I struggled to find my character. Attending all these rehearsals was the author, Ira Lewis. He was always present. The play was his entire life and his nerves got on my nerves. My part was highly verbal and the dialogue was intricate, but I'd always found that if I could look into the eyes of the actor I was speaking to and interact with him, remembering lines was a piece of cake. I wasn't used to sitting alone and staring at printed pages of dialogue, repeating the lines again and again to myself. I was being asked to learn lines before I knew what I was doing. Far from the creative environment I'd expected. This was like upscale summer stock.

The action of the play takes place at night. My character is a photographer without many clients. There's a knock on the door of his seedy
apartment and Al Pacino's character appears. He's down on his luck and
has come to collect the money I owe him. After many very amusing pas-
sages about life and love, the play turns. It seems that the man Pacino
plays has written a book using my character's life as its source, which my
character does not like at all. He considers it a horrible violation of his
privacy and of their friendship. But the thing that really hurts is that the
book is good. He never imagined that his friend had such talent. "You
stole my life," he shouts at Pacino.

We were getting close to opening night when Pacino finally dragged
himself away from *Salome* to rehearse with me. There was no one out front
to guide us. But there was Ira Lewis. At a certain point I stumbled on a
word, mistook it for another, and heard an angry voice shout a correction
from the audience. It was Lewis. I never felt more insulted in my life. I
wanted to dive into the audience and strangle the man. I waited for Al to
tell Lewis he was out of line but he didn't. He simply lowered his head and
said nothing. Lewis was his friend. Al owned the rights to the play and had
been mounting it here and there for the last couple of years. He chose to
do nothing and so did I. To avoid a confrontation with a virtual stranger I
pretended that I didn't hear. But my inside temperature rose. I was angry.

Expletives roiled in my brain. *Fuck these two pricks*, I thought. *I'm just
going to walk out of this theater and never come back.* But then I remembered what a very wise man once said, *Don't get mad. Get even.* No one
had ever made me take a backward step on the stage and it wouldn't
happen here, either.

I got through opening night and that was my first victory. The audience ate it up. The next night was even better, but on the third night the
lack of preparation reared its ugly head. Halfway through the performance I went blank for the first time *ever* in my career. I sat in silence
waiting for Pacino to say his line, but nothing. Then I realized it was my
turn, but for the life of me I couldn't remember what to say. Al knew the
play so well he found a way to bring it around, and that pause was so
interesting the audience thought it was part of the play.

Only by the end of the first week was I free enough to explore the humanity of my character. I was starting to enjoy myself onstage, starting to find things that were new and revealing. When it came time to close the show I was just warming up.

CHAPTER 24

THE DESIGNATED HITTER

ELKE AND I WERE IN OUR HOUSE IN SAG HARBOR. A couple of friends had come over for lunch. We were sitting on our deck, drinking and laughing when the phone rang. I excused myself, stepped into the house, and answered.

It was David Mamet. He was to direct a movie, *The Spanish Prisoner*, which he had written, and he wanted me to act in. When I read the script I liked it but I wasn't the lead—and I didn't like *that*. Was it over for me? When you're too old to get the girl are you too old to get the part? Who knew if and when a leading role would come my way again? I had to make peace with the fact that I was now a character actor. But you're not an actor if you're not acting, so I said yes.

I learned that Campbell Scott would play the protagonist. *Amazing*, I thought. I worked with his father, George C. Scott, in *Anatomy of a Murder*, which was his first film and my second. I had met Campbell years before when I did *Who's Afraid of Virginia Woolf?* with his mother, Colleen Dewhurst. So there it was—father, mother, and their talented son, who made himself available to go over lines with me even when I didn't ask. He worked hard.

Our first location was Key West, Florida. We worked and lived a stone's throw from the ocean. During the day there was always a cool sun, and at night a warm, caressing breeze. If you're going to have a romance, that was the ideal place for it.

My very first conversation with Steve Martin, who was also in the movie, was about just that: romance, or rather the end of it. I don't remember whether it was a marriage that had ended for him, or an affair, or both, but he was obviously still perplexed by it. He asked me if I had ever had a major heartbreak in my past. I'd been married to Elke for sixteen years and had to dig back a bit. I thought hard about it and even if I hadn't, I would've made one up in order to keep him company. And then it came back to me with all its pain and sadness: the night I'd discovered Janice in the arms of someone else. But I said, "I guess I've been lucky, Steve. I've managed to avoid it."

Mamet was keenly interested in physical detail—the fit of a suit, the color of a tie. He always made sure that mine was centered properly. He spent more time talking to the cameraman than to his actors. That was all right with me. This was not Chekhov, after all. The film was a whodunit and, of course, David's focus was largely technical. There was no talk about character or intention. That was good for me; I always worked well with directors who left me alone but knew how to give a creative suggestion if I was stuck.

From the warm breezes of Key West I wound up in the chilly winds of Buffalo, New York, making a sort of autobiographical movie that was written and would be directed by Vincent Gallo. It was called *Buffalo '66*. Vincent would also star in it. I'd play his father, with whom he'd had a complicated and troubled relationship. Anjelica Huston played his mother, who devoted more attention to professional football than to him. Vincent did an outstanding job both as actor and director. I hit the ball pretty hard myself. My scenes with Anjelica and Vincent were lively and very funny.

I got a series of offers from leading independent filmmakers. John Turturro invited me to take part in *Illuminata*, his ode to love and the theater. Next, Spike Lee asked me to play a Mafia don in his exciting *Summer of Sam*. I also enjoyed working in the Coen brothers' *The Big Lebowski*, in which I was a sort of king of the porno flicks who has fun tormenting the hero of the piece, who was played by Jeff Bridges. Following that I joined the cast of Todd Solondz's *Happiness*, a screenplay I found remarkable. The main character is a psychiatrist who just happens to have a fetish for young boys, including his son's best friend. I wouldn't be playing that part; I'd play the father of neurotic girls. Solondz invited me for lunch at Balthazar's in the SoHo district. We each ordered a dozen oysters; he ate his with vinegar, I ate mine with lemon. As he dipped and I squeezed I told him that *Happiness* was a risky picture to make, but I thought he'd get away with it because it was very funny. He said,

– I hope it's more moving than funny.

I liked that observation and I liked Todd. So I signed on. I was honored that such a talented artist wanted me in his movie.

I enjoyed working in those films, but lately I was a hired gun, riding into town, doing my job, and riding out again. I felt like the designated hitter in baseball. He doesn't play the full nine innings. He makes an appearance, has his moment, and sits and waits for a chance at another turn at bat. I had to make peace with the fact that I might never have a full and collaborative experience with a director again. That might have its advantages, though. There's a lot less stress when you're less involved.

Then along came a leading role in a terrific story to be filmed in a beautiful location. *Nella tera di nessuno* (*No-Man's-Land*) had it all.

The movie would be shot on Pianosa, a tiny island near the much larger island of Elba. It had once been a maximum-security prison, the Devil's Island of Italy, and had been closed down only recently. It was decided that the island was too beautiful to be used for punishment, that it should be used, instead, for pleasure. Plans were afoot to build luxury hotels and even a gambling casino.

When we got there, nothing was left on Pianosa except an unused prison, an empty village, an all but abandoned port surrounded by clean, clear waters. It had a serene and savage beauty. Living quarters had been constructed for the cast and crew, designed to protect us against the millions of mosquitoes that had made Pianosa their safe haven. We were to shoot for two weeks and then move on to Rome. Because there were no amenities at all, it was decided that Elke remain on Elba while I commuted to and from the location, forty minutes away by motor launch.

I was having a good time making that picture. The director, Gianfranco Giagni, had suggested I do the entire film in Italian and it was going very well. I felt completely at home and the language gave colors to the character that I couldn't have achieved if I'd performed in English. I played an attorney who finds himself defending a young terrorist who has been placed in the toughest prison in all of Italy. The film follows me, step by step, as I discover the diabolical cruelty of the prison and its chief administrator. I was having a good time with that character.

The cast and crew would eat in the old prison mess hall. We had cooks and caterers from Rome and the food wasn't bad at all. On about the third night, while I dined with Gianfranco and a few of my fellow actors, I had the feeling that someone had lit a match under the tip of my tongue. It was hot and it was burning. This was strange because the meal had hardly begun and I had eaten only a simple green salad. I drank some cold water and it passed. But a few nights later I made the mistake of eating a spicy pasta dish; it was as though a flamethrower had been let loose into my mouth. It was murder. I asked for ice and packed three or four ice cubes on top of and under my tongue. Gianfranco and the boys got a kick out of my predicament. I started laughing, too, and the ice cubes cascaded onto my plate. After a while the burning abated. The next day there was no trace of it.

Visiting Elke on Elba was a game of chance. If the sea became rough and I couldn't get back to the set on Pianosa our shooting schedule would be screwed up. On one occasion that's exactly what happened. I was stranded on Elba, so Gianfranco had to shoot material that didn't involve my character. On the plus side, this gave me a chance to enjoy Elba. I walked the beach with Elke and Maxi, our pretty miniature dachshund. The sea was not rough near the shore so Elke and I swam while our honey of a hound watched. She never took her eyes off us. After lunch we rested and read on our flower-filled terrace overlooking the emerald sea. Dinner was a leisurely event with delicious food and excellent wines. A perfect day to be stranded.

That night, as I lay in bed, I yawned and felt a slight discomfort in the back of my mouth. It passed immediately. I kissed Elke, turned off my reading lamp, and wished her happy dreams.

The next day I was back on Pianosa. Everything went smoothly there, and soon we were in Rome at the Hotel de la Ville, in the same suite Elke and I had shared when we were first together in Italy. We had a splendid view of the Eternal City and an enormous terrace where Maxi could run and cavort with her ball.

I finished the movie in Rome. I had been there for three weeks when I felt the burning sensation. I thought it had disappeared forever. Elke suggested that I dissolve an all-purpose seltzer powder she had into some warm water and gargle. The burning passed but not for long. It returned the next night. I still figured it would run its course and go away again. I would just have to live with it for a while longer.

The movie was going well. Elke and I walked the streets of Rome, dined with friends, visited churches and museums. We were still very strongly attached to that beautiful city.

It was during one of those crisp October days that Anthony Vitale, who'd directed a picture called *Kiss Me, Guido*, which had received some attention from the critics, offered me a very funny movie to be shot in Los Angeles. It was entitled *Very Mean Men*. He faxed me the script, I liked it, and I said yes. I was looking forward to doing it, but I had a scary surprise waiting for me.

Chapter 25

BAD NEWS

THE PROBLEM WITH MY TONGUE CONTINUED ON AND OFF for the entire shoot of *Very Mean Men*. I decided at last that something had to be done. A cast member mentioned a Beverly Hills dentist who had dealt with the symptoms I described. The next day I was in his chair and he was pulling, turning, and yanking my tongue. He stopped, and looked at me for an uncomfortably long time.

—Mr. Gazzara, I don't know what's causing the burning tongue but I'm glad it brought you to me. There's something in the back in your mouth that must be biopsied.

– Is it bad?

– Let's hope not, but we have to make sure.

I liked Dr. Gerald Berke right away. He was the top man of the head and neck department, which occupied an entire floor at the UCLA Medical Center. He ushered me into the examination room and asked me all those questions about smoking and drinking. It was now 1999. I had quit cigarettes in the sixties and I'd been off cigars for five years. The drinking I'd done in my life is what I call Actors' Drinking—not too moderate and sometimes too heavy.

– Okay, Mr. Gazzara, let's take a look. Open please.

And with a wooden tongue depressor, he gently moved my tongue aside. He then pressed a gloved finger along the lesion. It hurt a lot. He looked at me and said that it did not look like cancer, it looked more like a papilloma, a benign tumor. My heart jumped happily. I seemed to levitate from my chair.

– But let's take a biopsy and by the day after tomorrow, we'll know everything.

Removing the sample for the biopsy from my mouth didn't take more than a few minutes. I rushed back to my hotel to call Elke. Before I picked up the phone, doubts came. Was Dr. Berke just being kind? Did he say those things to allow me a few nights of peace? I told myself to give my wife only good news, to be optimistic. She'd been through this before with another man who had died and I didn't want her to worry. My gut feeling told me that I had cancer, no doubt about it, but I was going to do a little acting for Elke. I dialed New York.

– Guess what? You know that burning tongue I've been bothered by?

– Did you go to a doctor?

– I went to a dentist and he sent me to a doctor.

– So, what is it?

– Nothing. A papilloma. A benign tumor in the back of my mouth.

– So, what does that mean?

– In a couple of days, when I finish the picture, they'll take it out.

– I'm getting on the first plane I can possibly get. I'll be there tonight.

– No, Elke. You get a good night's sleep. You can catch a plane in the morning.

– I'll call you back and tell you when I'll be landing.

– You don't have to do that. It's nothing. Everything will be fine. It's a piece of cake.

– I don't care what it is. I'm coming.

I picked her up at the airport. I don't usually tell jokes, but on the way to the hotel I came up with a couple. I love her face when she laughs.

I was on the set the next morning having breakfast with Charles Durning, Matthew Modine, Burt Young, and Martin Landau. Charlie was telling one of his many jokes. A cell phone was handed to me by a production assistant.

– Mr. Gazzara, this is Harriet. Dr. Berke would like you to come in anytime today.

– Good or bad news?

– Just a moment, Dr. Berke would like to talk to you.

– The biopsy was positive, Mr. Gazzara, but the cancer has not entered the lymph nodes—that will make it much easier. I would like you to come in so we can talk about the options.

Tom Korman, my agent, offered to drive Elke and me, and that was good because my mind was racing. Tom showed himself a good friend through the entire ordeal.

We arrived at four and I was introduced to the surgical team. It was Monday; my filming ended on Wednesday; the operation would be on Friday. I preferred to know as little as possible about the procedure. It was enough just knowing that it was complicated.

I was admitted into a large and sunny, almost cheerful hospital room a few days later. Elke quickly went about charming the nurses. She wanted to make sure that I was well taken care of. Having sneaked Maxi into the hospital for a visit, she had let her out of her carrying case to frolic on my bed. There was a soft knock and Dr. Berke entered. He immediately started to pet and to play with the dog. A nice guy. He told me that the surgery would take place at eight A.M. He was certain that all would go well. I advised him to go home and get some sleep. I wanted him well rested. He smiled, nodded, and took his leave.

I got out of my hospital bed, opened my arms, and Elke walked into them. I took her face in my hands.

– You know why I refuse to die, don't you? Because then I would never see you again.

– Oh, Ben, we'll be looking at each other for a long time to come. Wherever you go, I'll be going with you. So you'd better choose some happy and exciting places.

I kissed her long and tenderly and assured her that we would beat this thing. I walked her out to the elevator. It was hard to let her go. I returned to my room, sat on the bed. What would they do to me? What if the cancer had spread to the vocal chords? Would I wind up like Jack

Hawkins, an actor without a voice, without a career, without a life? What if the cancer had entered my jawbone? Would my face be disfigured? How could this damn thing be happening now? This had been one of the most exciting years that Elke and I had spent together. It was a raw deal, a rotten break.

I lay down, turned off the light, and dozed off. My mother and father were suddenly standing over me, telling me to not be afraid, that everything was going to be all right. They beckoned me to come with them. I reached up and took both of them by the hand. I was their child again. "Am I dead, Mama?" I asked. "Ssshhh, you're not to worry," she said. We arrived at a place with palm trees and blue lagoons. The beach seemed to go on forever. The sea sparkled as if it were filled with jewels. "Papa, am I going to stay with you forever?" He placed his hand softly on my head. My mother crouched down, kissed my cheek, and pointed to something in the distance. It was Elke. She was calling to me. But I couldn't hear her, I ran toward her but I had trouble reaching her. With every stride I took, she seemed to be farther away. I was frightened.

The door opened with a loud bang. A gurney was rolled into the room. Doctors and interns, dressed in green and white, circled my bed. I was injected with something, rolled into the operating room. Dr. Berke was out of focus when he greeted me. I attempted a smile and went to sleep.

As if no time had passed, I felt a cool hand on my forehead and someone whispering in my ear. It was Elke's voice. I could feel her lips and her warm breath.

– It's over, Ben. They got it all out. You're going to be all right.

I looked into Elke's face. She was leaning over me and saying something but I couldn't hear her above the noise. I'd always thought an intensive care unit was where everyone walked on their toes and spoke in whispers. Not this one. Nurses were shouting instructions to each other, and firmly and loudly dealing with uncooperative patients. *Nobody could die here*, I thought. *It's too noisy.*

Dr. Berke was pleased with the results. The cancer had not touched the throat or the jaw, which was a great relief to me. He had not expected there to be difficulty in those areas but still, the cancer was more aggressive than he'd anticipated. It had entered four of my lymph nodes after all. He'd removed thirty-five of them for safety's sake. The doctor then told me that the operation had taken fourteen hours—seven to remove the cancer and seven for reconstruction. "Mr. Gazzara, you can now safely say that you've been run over by a Mack truck."

Past an open trachea, through a raw and swollen throat, I gurgled something about time—I wanted the facts. He told me that my cancer was the Stage Three type and that the survival rate in the first year was twenty to fifty percent. "Not very good odds," I croaked, trying to remain upbeat, "but I've always liked the underdog." He said he was betting that I would make it. He wanted me to remain in intensive care for two weeks and then he would move me to a private room for three or four days. He realized that it would be difficult for us to stay in California for an added six weeks of radiation but he insisted I remain close for another month after I left the hospital so that he could oversee my recuperation.

If there were ever a time to cry, this was the moment. But I didn't shed a tear. And if ever a man with my history had a good reason to be depressed it was *then*, but that didn't happen either. Like a horse with blinkers on, somehow I never looked left or right. My focus was straight ahead on my survival; concentrating on helping my doctors as they worked to make and keep me healthy. There was little room left for sad or somber thoughts.

When it was finally time to go, some five weeks later, we took the red-eye to New York. As our car crossed the Triborough Bridge and approached Manhattan, my heart began pounding. This is where it all began for me and I thanked God that it had not ended before I saw its glowing majesty again. Elke squeezed my hand. I rested my head on her shoulder and told her how happy I was to be home and how lucky I was to have her.

– As soon as you're strong and healthy, we're going to our house in Italy. Would you like that?

Nothing she could've offered would have made me happier. I had these damn six weeks of radiation to look forward to and she was helping me to hope and to dream. She was promising me better days to come.

If I thought the surgery was tough, radiation and its side effects was a living hell. I know now why doctors don't tell cancer victims what's really in store for them. They're afraid that some of us might opt for death. Elke, who had been acting as head nurse, put her foot down. She said that there would be no Italy until I put on at least half of the forty pounds I had lost during the surgery and the recovery period that followed.

Weeks passed. My mouth was an abomination, as dry as a bone. Everything was swollen, my throat included. There were blisters on my tongue, my speech was slurred. I felt myself losing more and more strength, and there were still two more weeks of radiation to look forward to.

One day I was in our kitchen, trying to drink a large glass of a high vitamin and protein substance, but it wouldn't stay down. Before I could get to the sink I threw up all over the floor, the cabinets, the stove, and the dishwasher. I fell to the floor and I heard Maxi let out an alarmed bark. She ran to call my wife, who was about to step out for a moment. Maxi caught her at the door and brought her to me. Maxi saved the day. She's in my will.

Elke said,

– That's it. We are putting you in a hospital, where they will feed you through a tube. It should have been done from the beginning.

And that's what they did. I wound up in Beth Israel Hospital and as they were getting me ready to insert what they call a peg into my stomach, my mind drifted to that play by Pirandello, *The Man with the Flower in His Mouth*. Would I be able to make time stand still as the man does in that play?

After the insertion of the rubber tube into my stomach, through which the food would flow, I felt a lot of discomfort. They had prescribed liquid morphine to be administered as needed. On or about my fourth day in hospital, those little white cups filled with that painkiller must have gotten to me: I saw two monkeys standing on Elke's shoulders!

On one of her shoulders was one dressed in short pants made of a brilliant orange material, held up by suspenders over a bright green shirt; on the other stood the second monkey, wearing nothing at all. Later, when Elke told me about it, she did a right-on-the-nose imitation of me telling her to get the monkey dressed because we had to shoot in fifteen minutes and I didn't like naked monkeys. It seems I also shouted to someone across the room,

– You don't know your lines so you can go home. I'm not going to waste precious film on you. So come back tomorrow when you're prepared. That's a wrap everybody, have a good day.

And then I saw Federico Fellini sitting impatiently in a hospital chair; he was very angry. I said to Elke,

– Did you greet the maestro?

She didn't understand.

– Don't you see him? Say hello to him.

But Fellini got up and left.

– You see, you hurt his feelings.

Then I turned my attention to what I saw as two very pleasant men. They were producers from Cuba. They wore orange-colored plaid suits with extra-wide lapels, two-toned shoes, Panama hats, and chocolate-brown shirts with ties depicting the sun, the sea, and palm trees. They offered me a big Monte Cristo No. 1 cigar—I took it but I did not light it. "I'll smoke it after dinner," I said. These guys wanted me to take my "four-ring circus," the first of its kind, to Cuba. It would be a national event, they said, and money would be no object. They had taps on their shoes and when they made what they thought was an important point, one or both of them would stand and do a short tap routine. They were good. I remember telling them that I had to clear everything with Fellini because he was my partner with anything to do with the circus. Elke tells me that the hallucination was on and off for at least two days. I guess I was enjoying it too much to let it go.

Then the nurses started feeding me through a tube like a force-fed

Strasbourg goose. *They* would see to it that I was fattened up. I had no choice in the matter. Beth Israel Hospital was where I was receiving radiation therapy so at least I didn't have to travel back and forth every day. Mine was a good-sized room; Elke had them make up another bed for her. She intended to stay with me and, in no time at all, she took over my care and feeding. There would be no mistakes this time. And I was pleased to see her in action. I was proud to be treated to the kind of love and devotion I'd received as a child.

I was released almost two weeks later. Elke continued my feeding at home. I was also able to take some food by mouth. Finally, I gained back the weight. It was time to go and soon there I was in bell'Italia.

CHAPTER 26

BOAR AND BARCELONA

LUNCH, ALWAYS A LONG AND LANGUID HAPPENING IN ITALY, was served on the patio, where we looked out on the beautiful Umbrian countryside. The pasta was waiting for us at the table. Hot steam rose from the homemade tagliatelle topped with a generous amount of truffle sauce. The elegant aroma would have made any normal person salivate. But not this one: my salivary glands were asleep, maybe dead. I would have to sip water with every mouthful. I also had to thin my wine with water, as my father did for me when I was a child. Even its low alcohol content made my mouth burn a hell of a lot. On top of that, my taste buds were not operating at full capacity.

After Franca, our housekeeper, served us and returned to the kitchen, Elke followed my every move. She knew I would often give up before I'd eaten what she thought was enough. The peg was still in me so when I became frustrated it was almost a relief to resort to my trusty feeding tube. But on that day I was giving it my best effort.

– Did you see what's happened around the pool, Ben? The *wild-schweine*, the wild boar, have torn up the grass.

– To keep them out we'd have to fence in the entire property. You know what that'd cost?

– Well, we've got to do something because those big boar are really bad.

– Why don't we kill them?

– No, no, no, there'll be no killing.

– Too bad, their meat is very tasty. A wild boar has no fat at all. That's because they take walks. And the way they cook it here in Umbria is so delicious.

– I'm glad you feel that way. Franca made some for our main course.

And indeed, when the platter arrived, it smelled so good and looked so inviting that I was sure I'd be able to eat and enjoy it. The meat was in bite-sized pieces, bathed in a light, spicy, tomato sauce. I tasted a few pieces but that was all I could eat. I proceeded to pick at it, pushing it with my fork from one side of my plate to the other. It would take more time before I'd be able to enjoy food again. But I was proud of myself for being able to keep the banter light, even amusing, while inside I was as sad as I'd ever been. I was afraid that my mouth would never right itself enough for me to return to the thing I loved most. Acting was where I was able to show the best part of myself—so what would life be without it?

Coffee was served in the den. As soon as I sat in my chair, Maxi jumped onto my lap. Elke appeared carrying a large chocolate cake topped by one golden candle. She'd remembered my sixty-ninth birthday, which I'd forgotten. I looked at this woman who was a lot younger than I was when we married and now seemed younger still. She just wouldn't catch up. As she walked toward me singing "Happy Birthday," Maxi made some very high-pitched coyotelike sounds. I made a wish and blew out the candle. Elke bent over and kissed me and said,

– I'm so proud of you, Ben. You've been so brave.

– Just acting, Elke.

Franca entered, saying that a Mr. Sanchez was calling from Rome. José Maria Sanchez is a very talented director who I'd worked with a few years before. We'd shot a movie in Tunis and I was impressed by his work.

– Ben, this is José. Do you still love me?

– More than ever.

– Good. We'll have our honeymoon in Barcelona.

– When?

– Almost right away. I have a story I think you'll like very much. It's a comedy.

Holy Christ, I thought, *will I be able to work?* My mouth still had virtually no saliva. I might dry up in the middle of a scene. What would I do? And that wasn't the only problem. My voice tired easily. Could I go on for a full day? I had to try.

– I'd love to do a comedy, José.

– The comedian Lino Banfi, who's loved here in Italy, will be in it.

– Send the script to me. I'll read it right away.

– You play the ex-husband. I think you'll love the part.

– Good, I'm crazy about Barcelona.

Elke had found a Swiss food product that ran smoothly through my peg. We have a very good friend who lives in Switzerland, so when we entered our suite at the Ritz in Barcelona, there they were—cartons full of the stuff.

I was still unable to take in enough calories through eating the normal way so I still needed four cans of that high-calorie, high-mineral, high-vitamin liquid three times a day to keep my weight steady and, with luck, even increase it.

On my first day of shooting *Piovuto dal cielo* (*It Rained from the Sky*) I was very nervous. Luckily my character wore a raincoat, so I was able to keep a bottle of water in my pocket. I sipped whenever I could. No one seemed to notice anything out of the ordinary. There were many comments about how much weight I'd lost and how much younger I looked. Funny, but that was good to hear.

My voice was another thing entirely. At times it was truly my old, authentic voice, but often it would get hoarse and raspy: I had no control over it. On top of it all, I was playing the part in Italian.

I told José that I'd had oral surgery performed and that things would return to normal soon. And I'll be a son of a bitch if he didn't say that he loved my new voice, not to change a thing.

Elke and I would have lunch in my trailer. She would appear about a half-hour or so before the break, to make sure that I ate. She placed the feeding bag on a clothes hanger that she would suspend from the top of an open closet door. One day, early in the shoot, as she was arranging my tasteless dinner, there was a knock on the door and José entered. Feeling as if he were intruding, he politely turned to leave. I called to him,

– José, you should try some of this food. It's made especially for me by the greatest chef in all of Europe.

José poked his head into the trailer,

– Ben, I knew it. You don't have to tell me what it was. I can guess.

Elke pulled José into the trailer. She poured him a glass of wine,

– José, this is the biggest gift you could have given my husband. He was so worried that he might never work again.

– He will work even more. He's wonderful.

Those words were the gift that started me on my way back. I began to feel I could lick the damned thing that had almost killed me.

The Ritz in Barcelona is a splendid place. When I was there shooting *Voyage of the Damned* I was alone. Now I could share it with Elke. The spacious, high-ceilinged rooms and the gracious service are unbeatable. Its location is ideal—only a few blocks from the Ramblas, the lively thoroughfare full of flower kiosks, restaurants, and performance artists. The Ramblas takes you to the foot of the beautiful Mediterranean.

On a gorgeous, sunny Sunday, Elke and I were at an outdoor café, having coffee and croissants, admiring the statue of Christopher Columbus as he looks out to sea, standing high up on top of a tall column. A woman came up and asked for my autograph. I was pleased. Some minutes went by and another woman stopped and she, too, asked for my autograph. It didn't end there. While we sat, while we strolled, it happened again and again. I was pleased that this was happening in Spain, a land completely foreign to me. It was the right time in my life to be appreciated, to be receiving that attention.

We walked and talked our way to the splendid Antoni Gaudí Cathedral of the Sacred Family. The first time I saw its spires years ago they bowled me over. But now they took my breath away. The only way a man could have created something so playful and yet so sacred, so universal and yet so personal, is if God himself had put his hands on the blueprints. When we entered the never-completed cathedral, Elke headed for the candles. It was time to make a wish. *What the hell*, I thought, *I'll make one too.*

We walked the length of that fantastical place, but found no candles. We were about to turn back when I looked to my left and in a dark corner, almost hidden, was a stand holding rows of them. Elke slipped some coins in the slot for the offerings, took a rather long, tapered candle, placed the wick against a lit one, bowed her head, and made a wish. I followed suit. My wish didn't take me long. I'd already made it quite a few times. More time is what I wanted.

CHAPTER 27

HERE'S TO LOVE

SUMMER WAS NEARLY OVER WHEN WE RETURNED TO OUR home in Italy. We spent one joyous week there before the time came to close up the house for the season. Maxi knew it was time to leave. She was in the driveway, positioned near the luggage. I was talking to the plumber and our handyman. We were trying to determine if there was a leak in our system. Elke came out of the house,

– Ben, is Maxi outside? I'm going to lock the doors.

I looked to the driveway where I'd seen her last, but she was gone. I called her name. Nothing. Elke went back into the house to search for her. I walked across the terrace, calling, but she didn't come. I headed toward the field, now yelling her name. I walked through the vineyard but she wasn't there, either. I became frightened. I raced to the pool, afraid she'd fallen in. No. Elke was now in the guest house calling, "Maxi." She was beside herself.

The iron entry gate had been left open for the workers. What if she'd walked onto the road? What if she'd been killed by a car? I wouldn't be able to take it. Elke would be crushed. As I got to the gate our friends arrived to drive us to the airport in Rome. When they saw my face, they knew there was a problem. When I explained it, Michele backed up his car and headed down the road looking for Maxi.

Elke then called to me,

– Ben, she may have jumped into the plumber's car. Maxi loves cars.

Maybe so, I thought. Luckily I had his cell phone number. When I called and he answered, I asked if my dog was in his truck. There was a pause and then he said, in Italian:

– No, the dog is not here. The last time I saw the little animal was when we were checking the meter outside the wall.

– Hold on, I'm walking that way now. Hold on. I'm opening the door.

When I opened it to the other side of the wall, my heart sank. Maxi wasn't there. I called her once, twice, then again and again. And finally, from up at the far end of the narrow, country road, Maxi's little face appeared. Her gleaming brown-and-black eyes seemed to be saying, "I've been waiting for you. Where have you been?"

– Maxi, come here, you beautiful little girl.

She raced toward me. I opened my arms wide, she leapt into them and began licking my entire face. I heard the plumber's voice; he was still on the line,

– Signor Gazzara, Signor Gazzara, did you find the dog?

– Yes, thank you, I found her.

Elke came and took Maxi out of my arms, hugging and kissing her and getting kissed in return. I looked at my wife and said,

– Imagine what would happen if I lost *you*.

The morning after we arrived in New York, I picked up the phone and dialed Liz. When she answered, I said,

– I love you.

– Dad?

– I love you, Liz.

– Dad, are you all right? Is Elke with you?

– I'd like to take you to lunch tomorrow.

– You're on. Where do I meet you?

– There's a place downtown I like, the Union Square . . .

– The Union Square Café. Good choice. What time?

– How's half past one?

– That's perfect. Welcome home, by the way.

– I love you, Liz.

– Are you sure you're all right, Dad?

– On top of the world. I'll see you tomorrow.

Elke appeared from the bedroom.

– Should I put the coffee on?

– Please.

– Your brother will be here at ten.

– Yeah, that's right.

– If I didn't have this toothache, I'd go with you.

After breakfast I dressed, kissed Elke, told her I'd see her later, and headed for the street. I walked through the lobby and was greeted by Scotty, our friendly and spirited concierge.

– Welcome home, Mr. G. You're back in time for the World Series.

– Who you betting on, Scotty?

– The Yankees, of course.

I stepped out onto the sidewalk and stood under the awning, waiting for Tony. We were going to Queens to visit our parents' grave. I never wanted to go there. I felt no need to look at a tombstone in order to remember them. They were never far out of my mind.

My brother drove up. He was accompanied by his companion, Akram, who was born and brought up in a Palestinian refugee camp. He knew a lot about suffering, but I never saw him without a sunny smile. I liked the man; he made my brother happy. As I climbed into the front seat and was saying my hellos, Elke appeared. She said she had a present for the two of them. It seems that some four years before, without telling me, she had bought a space for herself and for me in our quiet little cemetery in Sag Harbor. I'd told her many years earlier about the family plot in Calvary Cemetery having room for me and my brother and she'd remembered. Like my mother, Elke was thinking about *her* family and was planning ahead. She'd made sure we'd be together. So my brother now had a vacancy to fill.

The news made everybody laugh. Akram sprang up out of the back

seat and said, "Tony, I've never been happier. We're gonna be together."
"Welcome," my brother said. I turned to Elke and said, "Looks like I'll
never get rid of you." There were a lot of jokes about what Elke had done,
but the fact is that we were all at peace, now that we knew where we
would *rest* in peace.

Calvary Cemetery was not as foreboding as I'd feared. The sun was
shining down from a cloudless sky that day. The place is enormous, with
endless rows of tombstones. We had to search a while for the grave.

"This is it," my brother said. The name GAZZARA was written large
on a simple but elegant tombstone. Below it was my father's name and
dates, Antonio 1880–1947. And my mother's, Angela 1885–1963. The
last time I'd stood there was in 1963 and before that in 1947. And, as we
often say, it seemed like only yesterday.

Akram moved to the side as Tony and I placed a wreath in front of
the tombstone and looked down on the short green grass that covered our
parents' grave. I saw their faces, remembered their words, and felt their
love. I kissed the tombstone and told them I'd be back soon. Oh, how I
wanted to take them with me. How they would have enjoyed our house
in Italy. I'd walk under the olive trees with my father. He'd tell me how
to take care of them so that their olives would make the best oil in all of
Italy. He'd become master of the vineyard and there'd be no better wine
in the entire region. My mother would stroll with Elke through our land,
enjoying the flowers. She'd gather vegetables from our garden and prepare
unforgettable meals. She'd finally find the sun she always looked for in
that dark New York apartment.

The following morning I told Elke I wanted her to take a drive with me,
there was something I wanted to show her. I hired a town car and told
the driver to take us to Twenty-ninth Street and Second Avenue. I wanted
to walk that street again, to see what was still there. After only a few steps,
I saw that there was no street life—a few pedestrians, that was all. The
street seemed deserted and sad.

I looked to my left and there was the Boys Club where I had learned to hope. They were tearing it down. But for me it would always remain whole. It seemed that everything had been demolished and replaced by cement blocks, cloned by committee; there was no warmth, no feeling. These new dwellings certainly could not have been built with people in mind. The stoops, where neighbors could stand or sit, talk, laugh, and gossip were no more. And so it was with the grocery store, the butcher shop, the produce markets.

— It's all gone, Elke.

— No, it's not. It's still part of you and part of many other people.

I looked up to where our apartment would have been and I saw my mother, leaning on her pillow, taking in the activity on the block. She could look down and see my father talking to other fathers while he puffed away on his strong, twisted Toscano cigar. She could also see me and my buddies playing our childhood games: boxball, stoopball, ring-a-livio, Johnny on the Pony. Her main fear had been that I would get hit by a car. There was a deep dread of automobiles in those days, though they seldom came up our street.

When I was older, stickball became the game. We played on Sunday mornings against teams from other neighborhoods. The games would end just in time for the big midday meal. Even if I had just eaten two of the chocolate-covered donuts they baked in the factory across from my house, and washed them down with a cold Mission Cream soda, eating was never a problem. As I climbed the stairs to our third-floor apartment, the sublime scents of sauces simmering and roasts baking in the ovens of almost every apartment were guaranteed to arouse any-body's appetite.

We walked east toward the corner of First Avenue. I was sure that my church would still be there but it, too, was gone. A French restaurant and a couple of upscale boutiques stood in its place.

We headed to the river. The wooden docks were no longer there but there was a lot of cement—cement walkways, cement railings, and cement benches. We sat in silence. I took Elke's hand and looked out at the river. I thought about my friend Iggy, who got lost in its dark water. Was he able to find his way into Paradise? Did he happen to run into my parents on that white, endless, heavenly beach during one of their early-morning walks? Did they stop and talk to him? Do they know how often I think of them? My eyes followed the tide that had carried so many of my childhood dreams to the open sea.

We walked back to Second Avenue and as I waved to our driver I thought I heard what sounded like suppressed laughter. When it became louder I knew whose it was. I didn't have to look up to hear his words. "You see, you're still thinking about me, Ben." And I'm still talking about you, too, John. You and a lot of other people. That's what I said to him. As we left the corner of Twenty-ninth Street and headed uptown, I closed my eyes, leaned back, and remembered.

I was in rehearsal for *Thornhill*. John and I were discussing how to attack a particular scene between Thornhill and his dead father. The writer I played was having to face his ghosts, the people he'd loved and the people he'd hated. At that time in my life, 1983, it all seemed like a neat literary conceit. Not now. I don't know if I was being haunted but I was certainly being visited. They came to me in montage, floating slowly through each other, the faces of those who made up my existence. Most especially the people I'd loved, those who were still in my life and those I'd allowed to drift away. Those who were living and those who were dead. I thought of them, I missed them, even the ones who'd disappointed me. I think acting taught me more about forgiveness than any book I'd ever read. I'd always tried to find the good in the bad or the bad in the good. And I'm sure it's acting that'll help me beat this damn thing that came to kill my bliss. It ain't gonna happen. There's going to be no despair or fear—no, sirree. There's going to be only joy and laughter.

The phone was ringing when we entered our apartment. It was Tom Korman.

—Let me read you this letter, Ben. "Dear Mr. Gazzara, I have been a fan of your remarkable work for some time. The films you made with

John Cassavetes were an inspiration for me. I would be honored to have you in my film, *Dogville*, which will shoot in Sweden this winter. Nicole Kidman will play Grace. I hope you will play Jack McKay. Looking forward to your response, I am, respectfully, Lars von Trier."

— The man's a very talented director, Tom.

— The script is on its way to you. I think you'll like it.

— My voice ain't what it used to be.

— It will be.

— From your mouth to God's ears.

— The movie won't make us rich, but I think you should do it.

— How's the part?

— You have a couple of very good scenes.

— Okay, I'll read it.

I looked for Elke and I knew where I'd find her. She was in her walk-in closet, unpacking, arranging and putting her things in order. I sneaked up behind her and drew her to me.

— I have only one thing to tell you.

— What?

— I love you.

— And I love you, Ben.

— That's good enough for me.

I kissed her, returned to the living room, and walked on into the kitchen, where I reached into the refrigerator. I brought out a bottle of champagne, filled two glasses, and headed back toward Elke. I wanted to celebrate. I felt good. I felt strong. I'd beaten the devil. There'd be more time.

ACKNOWLEDGMENTS

My thanks to Albert D'Annibale and Jerome Rudes for their early enthusiasm toward my book. Also many thanks to Jane Kramer, Brooke Allen, and Pete Hamill for their encouragement. I'm grateful to Don Weise, my editor, for his keen eye and wise counsel, and to my agent, Jennifer Lyons, for helping to get my story published. Much appreciation is extended to Douglas Ladnier and Jane Gruchy for their computer saavy and support. And additional thanks to Linda Kosarin, Lorie Pagnozzi, and Maria Torres for designing my book and to Carroll & Graf publisher Will Balliett for his support too.

FILMOGRAPHY

THEATER

End as a Man (1953)
Cat on a Hot Tin Roof (1955)
A Hatful of Rain (1956)
Strange Interlude (1963)
Traveler Without Luggage (1964)
Hughie/Duet (1975)
Who's Afraid of Virginia Woolf? (1976)
Dance of Death (1977)
Shimada (1992)
Chinese Coffee (1993)
Nobody Don't Like Yogi (2003)

FILM

The Strange One (1957)
Anatomy of a Murder (1959)
The Young Doctors (1961)
The Passionate Thief (1962)
Convicts Four (1962)
A Rage to Live (1964)
The Bridge at Remagen (1969)
Husbands (1970)
High Velocity (1973)

The Neptune Factor (1973)
The Sicilian Connection (1974)
The Killing of a Chinese Bookie (1976)
Voyage of the Damned (1976)
Capone (1977)
Opening Night (1977)
Bloodline (1979)
Saint Jack (1979)
A Question of Honor (1980)
They All Laughed (1981)
Tales of Ordinary Madness (1983)
The Girl from Trieste (1984)
A Proper Scandal (1985)
The Camorrista (1986)
Control (1987)
Don Bosco (1988)
Secret Obsession (1988)
Quicker Than the Eye (1989)
Road House (1989)
Beyond the Ocean (1990)
My Son, Infinitely Dear (1992)
The Day Before (1993)
The Shadow Conspiracy (1996)
Farmer & Chase (1997)
Stag (1997)
Too Tired to Die (1997)
The Big Lebowski (1998)
Buffalo '66 (1998)
Happiness (1998)
Shark In a Bottle (1998)
The Spanish Prisoner (1998)
Illuminata (1999)
Summer of Sam (1999)

Believe (2000)
Blue Moon (2000)
No Man's Land (2000)
Hysterical Blindness (2003)
Dogville (2004)
Broadway: The Golden Age (2004)

Television

Danger (1952)
Playhouse 90 (1959)
Arrest and Trial (1963)
Run for Your Life (1965 – 1968)
Pursuit (1972)
Fireball Forward (1972)
QB VII (1974)
Richie (1977)
The Trial of Lee Harvey Oswald (1977)
An Early Frost (1985)
A Kiss Before Dying (1985)
Lies Before Kisses (1992)
Parallel Lives (1994)
Convict Cowboy (1995)
The Dogfighters (1996)
Lady Killer (1997)
The List (1999)

INDEX

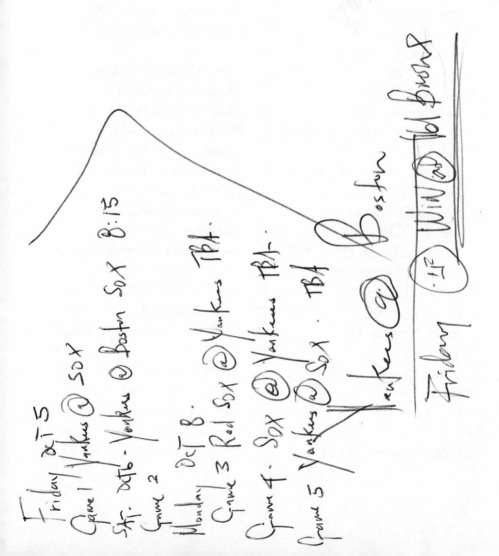